5/93

D0515093

SEXUAL Harassment ON THE JOB

By Attorneys William Petrocelli and Barbara Kate Repa

Nolo Press Berkeley

Your Responsibility When Using a Self-help Law Book

We've done our best to give you useful and accurate information in this book. But laws and procedures change frequently and are subject to differing interpretations. If you want legal advice backed by a guarantee, see a lawyer. If you use this book, it's your responsibility to make sure that the facts and general advice contained in it are applicable to your situation.

Keeping Up To Date

To keep its books up to date, Nolo Press issues new printings and new editions periodically. New printings reflect minor legal changes and technical corrections. New editions contain major legal changes, major text additions or major reorganizations. To find out if a later printing or edition of any Nolo book is available, call Nolo Press at (510) 549-1976 or check the catalog in the *Nolo News*, our quarterly newspaper.

To stay current, follow the "Update" service in the *Nolo News*. You can get a two-year subscription to the paper free by sending us the registration card in the back of the book. In another effort to help you use Nolo's latest materials, we offer a 25% discount off the purchase of any new Nolo book if you turn in any earlier printing or edition. (See the "Recycle Offer" in the back of the book.)

FIRST EDITION	
First Printing	MARCH 1992
Editors	RALPH WARNER
	MARCIA STEWART
Book Design	JACKIE MANCUSO
Cover Design	SUSAN WIGHT
Index	JENNY JONES
Proofreading	ELY NEWMAN
Printing	DELTA LITHOGRAPH

Petrocelli, William.
    Sexual harassment on the job / by William Petrocelli and Barbara Kate Repa : editors. Ralph Warner & Marcia Stewart. -- 1st national ed.
      p. cm.
    Includes index.
    ISBN 0-87337-177-1 : $14.95
    1. Sexual harassment of women--Law and legislation--United States--Popular works. 2. Sex discrimination in employment--Law and legislation--United States--Popular works. I. Repa, Barbara Kate.
II. Warner Ralph E. III. Stewart, Marcia. IV. Title.
KF3467.Z9P47 1992
344.73'014133--dc20
[347.30414133]

92-9076
CIP

Acknowledgments

Many people worked hard and fast to help make this book possible. We owe special thanks to:

Lisa Guerin, for her unflinching and good-humored assistance in research and writing,

Our editors, Jake Warner and Marcia Stewart, whose ever-ready pens, ever-probing minds and energy kept us going, and

Jackie Mancuso for her high-speed and highly elegant book design.

And our thanks to the many others who contributed their time and special expertise, including:

Beth Behner of the Anchorage Equal Rights Commission, Trisha Brinkman of Brinkman & Associates, Attorney John Erickson, Psychotherapist Elizabeth Evans, Ron Glover of Digital Equipment Corporation, Barbara Jerich of Honeywell, Inc., Sharon Kinsella of 9to5, Attorney John McGuinn, Attorney Margaret Murray, Susan Nelson of Women Employed Institute, Attorney Wayne Outten, Sandy Pope of the Coalition of Labor Union Women, Attorney Kenneth Pratt, Vera Repa, Rita Risser of Employment Law Specialists, Jane Walstedt of the Women's Bureau of the U.S. Department of Labor, Brian L.P. Zevnik of the Alexander Hamilton Institute, Inc.

Contents

CHAPTER 1

Background, Causes and Effects

A. Defining Sexual Harassment 1/2

B. The Causes of Sexual Harassment 1/7

C. The Effects of Sexual Harassment.. 1/10

D. Sexual Harassment Laws: A Checkered History..................................... 1/19

E. Ending Sexual Harassment: The Alternatives.. 1/25

CHAPTER 2

The Legal View

A. Conduct of a Sexual Nature 2/4

B. Conduct That Is Unreasonable... 2/15

C. Conduct That Is Severe or Pervasive.. 2/18

D. Conduct That Is Unwelcome 2/21

CHAPTER 3

First Steps To Stopping Harassment

A. Have You Been Harassed?... 3/3

B. Why It's Hard To Speak Up 3/5

C. Gray Areas of Behavior.. 3/10

D. Deciding Whether To Take Further Action 3/18

E. Confronting Your Harasser 3/23

F. What To Do If the Harassment Continues 3/31

CHAPTER 4

Workplace Policies and Programs

A. The Importance of a Sexual Harassment Policy 4/3

B. Evaluating Your Workplace 4/5

C. Effective Sexual Harassment Policies 4/8

D. Complaint Procedures and Investigations 4/17

E. Training Sessions 4/25

F. Sexual Harassment Monitoring Survey 4/32

G. Special Procedures for Some Employees 4/36

CHAPTER 5

A Look at the Legal Remedies

A. Legal Remedies: An Overview 5/2

B. Objective One: Stopping the Harassment 5/5

C. Objective Two: Recovering Wages and Other Losses 5/8

D. Objective Three: Compensation for Personal Injuries 5/9

E. Objective Four: Reforming the Company 5/12

F. Special Scenario: The Not-So-Rosy Case of Ms. Riveter 5/14

CHAPTER 6

The EEOC and the U.S. Civil Rights Act

A. When To Use the Civil Rights Act 6/3

B. Coverage and Remedies 6/4

C. The Importance of Counting Employees 6/5

D. How To Count Employees 6/7

E. Independent Contractors 6/12

F. Where To File an EEOC Claim 6/14

G. How To File a Claim 6/16

H. Time Limits for Filing a Claim 6/18

I. Contents of the Sexual Harassment Claim 6/21

J. EEOC Investigation of the Claim 6/30

K. EEOC Action After Completing the Investigation 6/32

L. Lawsuit By the EEOC or By the Employee 6/33

M. EEOC District Offices 6/37

CHAPTER 7

State Fair Employment Practices Laws

A. EEOC Relationship with State FEP Agencies 7/2

B. Excluding Certain Employees 7/5

C. Choosing a Remedy: The Importance of Damages 7/7

D. Monetary Damages: State Differences 7/8

E. Money Damages: State Summaries 7/11

F. FEP Laws and Procedures: State Summaries 7/14

CHAPTER 8

Common Law Tort Actions

A. When To File a Tort Action 8/2

B. Common Tort Actions Against Sexual Harassment 8/4

C. Disadvantages of Tort Actions 8/26

D. Workers' Compensation: Employers' Defense 8/28

CHAPTER 9

Lawyers and Legal Research

A. Hiring A Lawyer 9/2

B. Legal Research 9/9

Appendix

The Appendix is a comprehensive listing of resources on sexual harassment—including information and referral services, legal assistance, training, hotlines and special services for union and government workers.

Foreword

Striking a Nerve

Sexual harassment on the job took a dramatic leap into public awareness in October 1991, when Professor Anita Hill's charges against Judge Clarence Thomas became known after his nomination to the United States Supreme Court. When the U.S. Senate—98% of it men—appeared ready to confirm Thomas without airing the charges, an outpouring of protest from American women stopped the proceeding in its tracks and forced a public hearing. The ensuing days of revelations and testimony, charges and countercharges, played in front of a massive television audience that seemed mesmerized. And the spectacle was even more dramatic because the charges were leveled at the man who had been responsible for enforcing the laws against sexual harassment.

Suddenly, sexual harassment was featured on every talk show and debated in every workplace in America. Within a few days, the number of sexual harassment complaints filed with government agencies quadrupled. Well over one-half of the working women in America, according to public opinion polls, said they had been sexually harassed at some time during their careers. Female reporters, commentators and witnesses on both sides of the hearing began discussing the sexual harassment that they had suffered. A great many working women who had suffered silently from sexual harassment began to speak out.

It was one of those rare moments in American history when a major issue simmering below the surface boiled to the surface of public consciousness.

Anita Hill's charges demonstrated something else about sexual harassment: the depth of the pain it can cause and the risks and difficulties a woman faces when she comes forward. Although it was not a trial, the truth of Hill's charges were judged, first, by a panel of 14 men and then by the larger, nearly all-male Senate. The pattern of disbelief, dismissal and discrediting exhibited at the

Thomas hearing is one women frequently face when they report sexual harassment.

First the senators asked Hill why she didn't come forward earlier. When she tried to explain how sexually harassed women often repress the injury as a means of psychological protection, the committee stared at her in disbelief. When it was suggested that Hill might have held back to protect her career and not jeopardize future employment, several senators reacted with indignation. They implied it is wrong for working women to concern themselves with such things. And when the committee members scolded Hill for not having faith that the legal system would protect her, they demonstrated through their own actions how little protection the system offered.

Hill was forced to endure utterly baseless charges about her motives, her associations, her fantasies—even her sanity. For many working women who have had to endure sexual harassment, the pattern is all too familiar.

A Snapshot of a Moving Picture

This book explains what sexual harassment is and what you can do about it. We've attempted to explain the laws that prohibit sexual harassment on the job and to show you what you can do to assert your rights under those laws.

Today, in theory at least, laws protect against most workplace harassment. But don't expect your rights to be easily vindicated. In practice, sexual harassment laws are fraught with problems of interpretation, enforcement and inadequacy. Many of these problems are the result of an underfunded legal apparatus overstretched to cope with a growing problem. Other problems reflect serious rear-guard efforts to slow the thrust of social change.

Sexual harassment is a new area of law full of rough edges, anomalies and uncertainties. It yields less to logic and orderly development than it does to political pressure and counterpressure. The law against sexual harassment looks nothing at all like it did five years ago—and it will look entirely different five years, or even one year, from now.

What we are giving you is a snapshot of a moving picture.

Taking Charge of the Future

After talking with many women about sexual harassment, several things became clear: Women simply want to be left alone in the workplace to do their jobs. Women don't want to use the law to gain an advantage, to get revenge or to put themselves in positions of power. In virtually every case in which a woman has turned to the courts for help, she has done so in desperation after other efforts to solve the problem have failed.

We have premised this book on the assumption that working women want to use all available resources to persuade their employers and co-workers to end sexual harassment. Much of what we discuss is preventive—things a woman can do on her own, or together with other women and sympathetic men, to change their workplaces.

But we are not optimistic enough to think that all sexual harassment on the job will end any time soon. The problem is intricately linked to the larger problem of sexism in America and the unresolved power relationships between the genders. This has proven to be one of the more intractable problems of human history.

Now, at least, there are laws against sexual harassment to help women in the workplace fight back. Several chapters of this book explain how to use them. The laws protect men against sexual harassment as well, but because the problem is intrinsically tied to historical inequalities suffered by women, we have written from a woman's perspective.

One further thought: Sexual harassment on the job is deliberate, learned behavior; it can be unlearned. The relearning process may be difficult in many cases and efforts at change often are slow to yield results. But it's something that can—and should—be done.

We hope this book helps.

■ ■ ■

1

Background, Causes and Effects

A. Defining Sexual Harassment.. 1/2
   1. The range of behavior... 1/2
   2. Common misconceptions.. 1/4

B. The Causes of Sexual Harassment.. 1/7
   1. Violence and self-perceptions.. 1/7
   2. The economics of women's work 1/8
   3. Discrimination as a form of workplace control 1/9

C. The Effects of Sexual Harassment 1/10
   1. Job-connected injuries... 1/11
   2. Personal injuries... 1/14
   3. Injuries to women as a group.. 1/16

D. Sexual Harassment Laws: A Checkered History 1/19
   1. The First Hurdle: Making sex discrimination illegal 1/20
   2. The Second Hurdle: Equating harassment with discrimination 1/21
   3. The Third Hurdle: Putting teeth in sexual harassment laws 1/22
   4. The Fourth Hurdle: Fighting for changes in the Civil Rights Act............. 1/24

E. Ending Sexual Harassment: The Alternatives... 1/25
   1. Confronting the harasser 1/25
   2. Using a company complaint procedure... 1/25
   3. Filing a complaint with a government agency 1/26
   4. Filing a lawsuit under the Civil Rights Act or FEP laws........................... 1/27
   5. Filing a common law tort suit.. 1/27

A. Defining Sexual Harassment

In legal terms, sexual harassment is any unwelcome sexual advance or conduct on the job that creates an intimidating, hostile or offensive working environment.

That's a shorthand version of the definition used by the federal government and most states. But it's not necessary to couch the problem in legalisms. Simply put, sexual harassment is any offensive conduct related to an employee's gender that a reasonable woman or man should not have to endure.

1. The range of behavior

Sexual harassment covers a wide range of conduct—all of it illegal. An employee who has been led to believe she must sleep with her boss to keep her job has been sexually harassed, as has one whose co-workers regularly tell offensive, sex-related jokes and plaster their walls with pictures of nude women. An employee who is pinched or fondled against her will by a co-worker has been sexually harassed, as has one whose colleagues leer at her, block her path or act like they're going to grab her.

An employee who is constantly belittled and referred to by sexist or demeaning names has been sexually harassed, as has one who is subjected to repeated lewd or pornographic remarks. Sexual harassment occurs when a supervisor acts as if the women working under him owe him sexual favors, and it also occurs when a co-worker attacks or intimidates a woman because he doesn't think she should be doing what he considers Man's Work.

The forms that sexual harassment can take are as varied as a perverse imagination can create. They range from offensive sexual innuendos to physical encounters, from misogynist humor to rape. It occasionally derives from an excess of sexual desire by the harasser, but most often it is motivated by fear, power or hate.

Most cases of sexual harassment are never reported, because the harassed women are either too degraded, too uncertain of their rights and options or too fearful of retaliation to do anything about it. However, thousands of harassment claims have been filed through government agencies and company complaint procedures—and there is no evidence that any of them were faked or brought for revenge or spite.

While relatively few cases have gone all the way through a court hearing, those that have reveal a wide variety of harassing activity:

- Female office workers at AT&T Technologies in North Carolina who were "rated" by male employees as they passed the men's desks, followed by lascivious comments about their hips and breasts.[1]

- Women who were subjected to a dress code by their supervisor, established by him specifically so he could admire their legs.[2]

- An employee of a county sheriff's office who was taken for a country drive by the newly elected sheriff and told that she and her mother could only keep their jobs if she started "seeing him."[3]

- A Penthouse model whose employer coerced her into having sex with the company's financial advisor.[4]

- A waitress whose supervisor repeatedly exposed himself to female employees, passed around child pornography and gave choice working assignments to waitresses who cooperated with his sexual advances.[5]

- A woman who was obliged to dress in a scanty costume and stand in the lobby of a large office building in New York City, where she was ogled by passersby.[6]

- A machine operator in a Connecticut printshop whose employer refused to discipline or fire a supervisor who subjected her to repeated sexual solicitation and physical assaults.[7]

---

[1] *Wall v. AT&T Tech*, 754 F. Supp. 1084 (M.D.N.C. 1990).

[2] *Dias v. Sky Chefs*, 919 F.2d 1370 (9th Cir. 1990).

[3] *Simmons v. Lyons*, 746 F. 2d 265 (5th Cir. 1984).

[4] *Thoreson v. Penthouse Int'l, Ltd*, 563 N.Y.S. 2d 968 (N.Y. Sup. Ct. 1990).

[5] *Priest v. Rotary*, 634 F. Supp. 571 (N.D. Cal. 1986).

[6] *EEOC v. Sage Realty Corp.*, 507 F. Supp. 599 (S.D.N.Y. 1981).

[7] *Maturo v. Nat'l Graphics Inc.*, 722 F. Supp. 916 (D. Conn. 1989).

- A bank employee whose supervisor propositioned her, fondled her in front of the other employees, followed her into the women's restroom and forced her to have intercourse with him.[8]

- A student at the New York City police academy who had to fight off the assault of a male student by hitting him with a box of ammunition and who had her breasts fondled from behind by her instructor as she tried to fire her gun.[9]

- Two female workers for a construction firm in Iowa whose male colleagues repeatedly "mooned" them, flashed obscene photos, urinated in their water bottles, cornered them between trucks and reached out the windows of their trucks to rub the women's breasts and thighs.[10]

These examples only scratch the surface. Put almost any five working women in a room, and chances are three or more of them will have harassment stories—some as serious as the ones just listed.

2. Common misconceptions

One common misconception about sexual harassment is that the laws prohibiting it restrict normal socializing between men and women at work. The truth is that sexual harassment consists of unwelcome conduct of a sexual nature—and it in no way affects ordinary social contact between employees. The oft-repeated fear of many people—mostly men—that sexual harassment laws prevent them from complimenting a woman or asking her out for a date is simply misplaced. Nothing in the law prevents dating, as long as it is done in a reasonable manner that respects a co-worker's dignity and wishes. Office romances are not unlawful, as long as the relationship is welcomed by both employees.

---

[8] *Meritor Sav. Bank v. Vinson,* 477 U.S. 57 (1986).

[9] *Watts v. New York City Police Dep't,* 724 F. Supp. 99 (S.D.N.Y. 1989).

[10] *Hall v. Gus Constr. Co,* 842 F.2d 1010 (8th Cir. 1988).

Another misconception, at the opposite end of the spectrum, is the notion that anything goes in the workplace as long as there is no physical contact with another employee. That, too, is wrong. Sexual harassment can result from any verbal or physical conduct of a sexual nature. Many types of sexual harassment involve no touching, but they are nevertheless offensive or intimidating to the employee—as well as being clearly illegal.

THE SHOCKING AND PATHETIC RESPONSE OF THE U.S. SENATE TO CHARGES OF SEXUAL HARASSMENT AGAINST JUDGE CLARENCE THOMAS HAS TRIGGERED THE MOST SPONTANEOUS AND MASSIVE OUTPOURING OF WOMEN'S RAGE I HAVE WITNESSED IN MY LIFETIME. CLEARLY THE BOYS ON CAPITOL HILL JUST DON'T GET IT. AND JUST AS CLEARLY, MILLIONS AND MILLIONS OF AMERICAN WOMEN HAVE HAD IT.—ELEANOR SMEAL, PRESIDENT OF THE FUND FOR THE FEMINIST MAJORITY, IN AN OCTOBER, 1991 APPEAL TO MEMBERS

DISPELLING THE MYTHS

Myth: SOME WOMEN ASK TO BE SEXUALLY HARASSED.

Reality: Being subjected to sexual harassment is a painful and difficult experience. Defenses such as "she wore provocative clothes" and "she enjoyed it" are neither acceptable nor accurate.

■

Myth: IF A WOMAN REALLY WANTED TO DISCOURAGE SEXUAL HARASSMENT, SHE COULD.

Reality: Often, the harasser is in a position to punish the woman by withholding a promotion, or giving a bad evaluation. In this society, men often rationalize their behavior by claiming that a woman's "no" actually means "yes."

■

Myth: MOST CHARGES OF SEXUAL HARASSMENT ARE FALSE.

Reality: Women have little to gain from filing false charges. It is exceedingly difficult to file sexual harassment charges and confronting the harasser can be both physically and financially draining.

■

Myth: SEXUAL HARASSMENT IS INEVITABLE WHEN MEN AND WOMEN ARE WORKING TOGETHER.

Reality: While interaction between the sexes might be inevitable, uninvited sexual overtures are not.

■

Myth: IF YOU IGNORE SEXUAL HARASSMENT, IT WILL GO AWAY.

Reality: Only 29% of the women recently surveyed who said they tried to ignore the behavior said that it "made things better." Over 61% said that telling the person to stop made things better.[11]

---

[11] Adapted from "Combating Sexual Harassment: A Federal Worker's Guide," a pamphlet published by Federally Employed Women, Inc., 1991.

B. The Causes of Sexual Harassment

Sexual harassment results from a misuse of power—not from sexual attraction. Far too many cases of sexual harassment involve meanness, anger and abuse of power to blame it all on a dating ritual gone awry or an adult version of school boy pranks.

1. Violence and self-perceptions

The relationship between the sexes in modern America includes a great deal of violence against women. One out of every ten American women are raped or sexually assaulted during their lives, while more than half of all women living with men have experienced a battering or similar incident of domestic violence.

This volatile mixture of sex and violence is also played out in the workplace. Susan Faludi, author of *Backlash: The Undeclared War Against American Women*, suggests that one explanation for male hostility can be found in surveys that track male attitudes about the proper role of a man in society:

> *For twenty years [pollsters] have asked subjects to define masculinity. And for twenty years, the leading definition, ahead by a huge margin, has never changed. It isn't being a leader, athlete, lothario, decision maker, or even just being "born male." It is simply this: being a "good provider for his family."*
>
> *If establishing masculinity depends most of all on succeeding as the prime breadwinner, then it is hard to imagine a force more directly threatening to fragile American manhood than the feminist drive for economic equality.*[12]

---

[12] Susan Faludi, *Backlash: The Undeclared War Against American Women* p. 65, (Crown, 1991).

2. The economics of women's work

Focusing on the economics of men's and women's work exposes sexual harassment as something that has a perverse logic from the harasser's point of view: It is one way that many men express their resentment and try to reassert control when they view women as their economic competitors.

Despite the impediments working women face to obtaining jobs, the number of women working has steadily increased. In 1860, only 15% of American women were in the paid labor force. By 1947, their number reached 32% and jumped to 58% by 1990.

Women's entry into the workforce has been prompted by necessity, since many families cannot make ends meet if the wife and husband don't both work at full-time jobs. There is also a large and growing number of families in which a woman is the sole means of support. Between 1980 and 1990, the number of female-headed families in the U.S. increased by 27% until they now account for more than 21% of all families with children under 18—and the vast majority of all families on welfare.

As more women have tried to obtain wage-paying jobs, they have had to fight continuously for fair treatment. As recently as 1990, the median annual earnings for a full-time woman employee in the United States was $19,816 per year—only 71% of the median earnings of a full-time male employee.

Also, society's segregation of jobs into Man's and Woman's Work means most women work for low pay. The leading occupations for women in 1990 were still the traditional ones: secretaries, cashiers, account clerks, nurses and nurses' aides, schoolteachers, waitresses and sales clerks—all of them relatively low paying. A disproportionately large number of women work in part-time jobs, as domestic workers, or in piecework jobs where the pay is extremely low and the benefits non-existent.

And economic discrimination doesn't end when women move into what were traditionally higher paying jobs. Many jobs that are now held primarily by women paid more when men held them. For example, in 1950, most bank tellers were men—and their median salary was 120% of the median salary for wage earners nationwide. But by 1980, when 91% of bank tellers were women, the median salary had dropped to 79% of the median salary nationwide—and the women bank tellers still had a median salary that was only 78% of the median salary of the few remaining men in that occupation.

This is a distressing but familiar pattern: When the number of women in a particular job category increases, the pay rates lag.

3. Discrimination as a form of workplace control

If sex discrimination forces women into lower-paying jobs, sexual harassment helps keep them there. This may not be the intention of the harasser in every instance, but it is often the effect.

Seen in this context, male workers who harass a woman on the job are doing more than annoying her. They are reminding her of her vulnerability, creating tensions that make her job more difficult and making her hesitant to seek higher paying jobs where she may perceive the tension as even greater. In short, sexual harassment creates a climate of intimidation and repression. A woman who is the target of sexual harassment often goes through the same process of victimization as one who has suffered rape, battering or other gender-related crimes—frequently blaming herself and doubting her own self-worth.

There is no Typical Harassed Woman. Women of all ages, backgrounds, races and experience are harassed on the job. Women in traditional Woman's Work, such as waitresses and secretaries, are often given menial, degrading tasks. They are called "Honey," "Sweetie" and other demeaning names. And they are led to believe that a certain amount of male domination and sexism is normal. All of this reinforces the idea that women workers are of little value in the workplace. Women who try to break into traditionally all-male work, such as construction jobs, medicine or investment banking, often suffer even more intense harassment clearly aimed at getting them to leave. (See Section C.3.)

Thus sexual harassment often accomplishes informally what laws against sex discrimination theoretically prohibit: gender-based requirements for a job. A woman subjected to sexual harassment endures pressure, degradation or hostility that her male co-workers don't have to endure—making it just that much harder to compete for the job and for advancement.

Catharine MacKinnon, author of the 1979 book *Sexual Harassment of Working Women*, was the first legal scholar to draw attention to the connection between sex discrimination and sexual harassment:

> *... [W]omen tend to be in low-ranking positions, dependent upon the approval and good will of male superordinates for hiring, retention and advancement. Being at the mercy of male superiors adds direct economic clout to male sexual demands.... It also deprives women of material security and independence which could help make resistance to unreasonable job pressures practical....*
>
> *...[S]exual harassment of women can occur largely because women occupy inferior job positions and job roles; at the same time, sexual harassment works to keep women in such positions.[13]*

C. The Effects of Sexual Harassment

Sexual harassment on the job can have very serious consequences both for the harassed individual as well as for other working women who experience it secondhand.

The consequences to the individual employee can be many and serious. In some situations, a harassed woman risks losing her job or the chance for a promotion if she refuses to give in to the sexual demands of someone in authority. In other situations, the unwelcome sexual conduct of co-workers makes the working conditions hostile and unpleasant—putting indirect pressure on her to leave the job. In some cases, the employee is so traumatized by the harassment that she suffers serious emotional and physical consequences—and very often, becomes unable to perform her job properly.

The consequences to working women as a group are no less serious. Sexual harassment has a cumulative, demoralizing effect that discourages women from asserting themselves within the workplace, while among men it reinforces stereotypes of women employees as sex objects. Severe or pervasive sexual harassment in certain types of businesses creates a hostile or intimidating environment that causes women to leave their jobs and look elsewhere for work or discourages them from seeking those jobs in the first place.

---

[13] Catharine MacKinnon, *Sexual Harassment of Working Women,* pp. 9-10, (Yale University Press, 1979).

1. Job-connected injuries

Sexual harassment causes direct economic injury to many women. These are injuries directly related to her status as an employee and wage earner, and they include lost wages, lost promotions and other job benefits as well as loss of the job itself.

a. Loss of job

Sometimes the connection between sexual harassment and the injuries it causes is simple and direct: A woman is fired for failing to go along with the sexual demands of her employer. Usually the management uses some other pretext for firing her, but the reasons are often quite transparent.

> **Example:** A federal court found that a woman working in a Domino's pizza shop in Michigan was fired by her supervisor after she refused to have sex with him, even though the restaurant argued she was fired for some other reason.[14]

> **Example:** A California federal court found that a waitress was given unfair job as-signments and finally fired after she refused to go along with the manager's fondling, kissing and obscene humor. The court gave no credence to the man-ager's claim that she was fired because she failed to follow work rules.[15]

Sometimes the firing technically occurs because of some other event, but it is still clearly related to sexual harassment. For example, if a company down-grades an employee's job and assignments because of a harassment incident and then fires her for complaining about the demotion, her injury is legally caused by sexual harassment.

---

[14] *EEOC v. Domino's Pizza, Inc.,* 34 F.E.P. 1075 (E.D. Mich. 1983).

[15] *Priest v. Rotary,* 634 F. Supp. 571 (N.D. Cal. 1986).

Example: An employee of a Texas real estate development company was forced up against a wall by her supervisor while one of the salesmen slipped a camera under her dress and took a picture. She objected to this and other harassing incidents. When she came to work one morning, someone else was sitting at her desk without any explanation. She complained to her boss, and the ensuing argument led to her firing. A federal court found that although the argument was the incident that precipitated the firing, the entire set of events arose out of a sexual harassment situation.[16]

If an employee is temporarily unable to work as a result of the harassment and the management uses that as an excuse to fire her, this is also sexual harassment.

Example: A Philadelphia policewoman was subjected to sexual slurs and pornography, crank phone calls and dangerous pranks by her male co-workers, causing her to become emotionally upset and unable to work. The police department fired her for going beyond her allotted sick leave, but a federal court found that the firing was directly related to the sexual harassment.[17]

b.   Loss of wages and other benefits

If an employee is demoted or denied a promotion or raise because she resists sexual advances from her supervisor or objects to obscene humor and other sexual activity in the office, she suffers a serious loss.

But even if an employee doesn't suffer an immediate economic loss, a denial of a promotion or other adverse change in her job status can both harm her standing within the company and jeopardize future pay increases.

A loss of wages usually entails a loss of other job benefits as well, such as pension contributions, medical benefits, overtime pay, bonuses, sick pay, shift differential pay, vacation pay and participation in any company profit-sharing plan.

---

[16] *Ross v. Double Diamond, Inc.*, 672 F. Supp. 261 (N.D. Tex. 1987).

[17] *Andrews v. City of Philadelphia*, 895 F.2d 1469 (3d Cir. 1990).

c. Forced reassignment

Sometimes a company responds to an employee's complaint of sexual harassment by transferring her to a different department and leaving her harasser unpunished. This forced reassignment is another form of job-connected injury, and it may be compounded if combined with a loss of pay or benefits or reduced opportunities for advancement.

d. Constructive discharge

Sometimes the sexual harassment is so severe that the employee quits. If her situation was intolerable and she was justified in quitting, sexual harassment caused her to be "constructively discharged"—that is, forced to leave. This is the same as an illegal firing.

> **Example:** A female truck driver for the Celanese Corporation in South Carolina received frequent threats as well as blatant sexual solicitations from her co-workers. These co-workers also told her that they had established a "club" to determine which one of them would be the first to have sex with her. She complained to management but got nowhere. She finally quit her job to seek medical attention after one employee burst out of the restroom and exposed himself to her. A federal court hearing the case ruled that the woman employee had been constructively discharged—and was entitled to the same legal relief as if she had been fired.[18]

e. Retaliation for reporting sexual harassment

Employees are frequently fired or penalized for reporting sexual harassment, or otherwise trying to stop it. This is called retaliation. In such cases, her injury is legally considered to be a direct result of the sexual harassment.

---

[18] *Llewellyn v. Celanese Corp.*, 693 F. Supp. 369 (W.D.N.Y. 1988).

Example: A California office worker found the phrase "How about a little head?" flashed across her computer terminal from an unknown source within the company. She reported it to her supervisor, who was a woman, and the two women reported the incident to higher management. In response to their complaint the company embarked upon a campaign of downgrading their jobs and benefits until both women were forced to resign.

The court held that the injuries suffered by the two women were in retaliation for their reporting the sexual harassment incident. The legal consequences of these acts of retaliation were the same as if the injuries had resulted from the sexual harassment.[19]

2. Personal injuries

A sexually harassed woman often suffers personal injuries in addition to the job-connected losses just described. In many sexual harassment cases, these injuries—ranging from stress-related illnesses to serious physical and emotional problems—are the most serious and costly results.

a. Stress-related problems

A study by the Working Women's Institute showed that 96% of the women who were sexually harassed experienced emotional stress. Between 35% and 45% of these women also suffer physical and work performance stress that can affect the way they do their jobs.

The American Psychiatric Association recognizes stress-related problems resulting from sexual harassment as a specific, diagnosable medical ailment. It can produce symptoms such as distractions from tasks, dread of work or an inability to work at all.

---

[19] *Monge v. Superior Court (Crown Gibraltar Graphic Center, Inc.)*, 176 Cal. App. 3d 503 (1986).

b. Other physical and mental injuries

Sexual harassment also causes a great many other types of physical, mental and emotional injuries. Some of these injuries are stress-related, but others are caused by physical pranks or violent acts directed at the harassed worker.

A sampling of cases that have gone through the courts illustrates the types of injuries that can occur.

- A New York City police trainee who was harassed by her instructor and co-trainee suffered severe and persistent headaches and stomach pains as a result.[20]

- A truck driver who was subjected to constant solicitations and threats from her co-workers developed a seizure disorder similar to epilepsy.[21]

- A folder operator in a printshop who was constantly propositioned and touched by her supervisor suffered a high level of anxiety and stress, withdrawal symptoms and sleeping and eating disorders.[22]

- A federal employee whose supervisor made defamatory remarks about her sexuality and then continued to follow and telephone her put her in such fear of sexual abuse that she suffered a miscarriage.[23]

- A Philadelphia policewoman suffered severe burns when she put on a shirt from her locker that her co-workers had laced with a lime sub-stance.[24]

- Two women drivers suffered carbon monoxide poisoning when male mechanics ignored their complaints about leakage of that gas into the truck's cabin.[25]

---

[20] *Watts v. New York City Police Dep't*, 724 F. Supp. 99 (S.D.N.Y. 1989).

[21] *Llewellyn v. Celanese Corp.*, 693 F. Supp. 369 (W.D.N.Y. 1988).

[22] *Maturo v. Nat'l Graphics, Inc.*, 722 F. Supp. 916 (D. Conn. 1989).

[23] *Otto v. Heckler*, 781 F.2d 754 (9th Cir.), *modified on other grounds*, 802 F.2d 337 (9th Cir. 1986).

[24] *Andrews v. City of Philadelphia*, 895 F.2d 1469 (3d Cir. 1990).

[25] *Hall v. Gus Constr. Co*, 842 F.2d 1010 (8th Cir. 1988).

These personal injuries can be severe, long-lasting—and difficult and expensive to recover from.

3. Injuries to women as a group

In addition to the injuries suffered by the harassed employee, sexual harassment can also have pernicious consequences for other working women who may not be in the immediate line of fire. An atmosphere of sexual harassment tends to segregate the workplace and to limit the job options for working women.

Sexual harassment often has its harshest consequences where women are trying to break into previously all male occupations—firefighters, bankers, surgeons, welders, doctors, lawyers.

a. Limited job options

A 1989 study of 100 women working in a factory revealed that female machinists, a job traditionally held by men, were harassed far more often than assembly line workers, a job where women had worked for years, although both fields had roughly the same number of male co-workers. And harassment isn't confined to factory jobs. A high level of sexual harassment occurs in every non-traditional job category that women enter. In fact, women bankers and surgeons report the highest levels of harassment.

WHAT'S DOWN, DOC?

A 1991 survey of 200 doctors by the Massachusetts chapter of the American Medical Women's Association revealed that:

- 27% said they had been sexually harassed during a one-year period ending in 1990.

- More than half said they had received unwanted sexual attention during that time.

- 2/3 of those surveyed said they had received offensive comments about their gender.

- Half of the general surgeons and 37% of the interns said they had been harassed.

The simple explanation is that the more male-dominated the job, the more likely it is that men will be threatened when they see women moving into their workshoes. That threat is likely to be compounded during tough economic times when people worry about losing their jobs.

And women in non-traditional jobs are most often subjected to the most violent and egregious harassment. These acts of harassment would be highly improper and illegal in any situation, but they are particularly harmful in situations where women are trying to break into jobs from which they have been excluded.

b. Stereotyped workers

When sexual harassment occurs in jobs that are predominantly male, it reinforces patterns of discrimination and makes those patterns that much harder to break. In jobs where women workers are a rarity, a woman worker is very likely to be judged in stereotypical, sexual terms. This creates a burden that the male employees do not have, because women employees in such a situation must be constantly vigilant as to how their actions may be interpreted or misinterpreted. One court recently recognized this underlying historical struggle in the battle between the sexes:

Women must constantly monitor their behavior to determine whether they are eliciting sexual attention; they must conform their behavior to the existence of the sexual stereotyping either by becoming sexy and responsive to the men who flirt with them or by becoming rigid, standoffish and distant so as to make it clear that they are not interested in the status of sex object.[26]

The debilitating effects of such pressure are enormous. A woman working in an environment that has been traditionally closed to her group has a difficult enough time trying to adjust to a new situation and prove her worth to skeptical old-timers on the job. If sexual harassment is added to the situation, it often increases the pressure to the level where the job environment is no longer endurable.

At the same time that the tolerance of sexual harassment is demoralizing to a female employee, it reinforces stereotypical attitudes of male co-workers and management and makes them less open to the idea of female employees in their particular workplaces.

Sexual stereotyping creates a no-win situation for a woman who is sexually harassed. If, for example, a male co-worker squeezes her buttocks, she can either complain about it or do nothing. She loses either way. If she says nothing, she reinforces the idea that women really like such activity or, at the very least, accept their role as sex objects. If she objects, she reinforces the idea that women are complainers. In either case she is not likely to fit the mental image of what management is looking for when considering employees for advancement.

---

[26] *Robinson v. Jacksonville Shipyards, Inc.*, 760 F. Supp. 1486 (M.D. Fla. 1991).

◯N THE PLIGHT OF WOMEN FACTORY WORKERS IN THE EARLY
1900S: WHEREVER THEY WORKED, WOMEN WERE SEXUALLY
HARASSED BY MALE WORKERS, FOREMEN AND BOSSES. LEARNING TO
"PUT UP" WITH THIS ABUSE WAS ONE OF THE FIRST LESSONS ON THE
JOB. . . . IT WAS COMMON PRACTICE AT THE FACTORIES FOR MALE
EMPLOYERS TO DEMAND SEXUAL FAVORS FROM WOMEN WORKERS IN
EXCHANGE FOR A JOB, A RAISE, OR A BETTER POSITION.—FROM *A
HISTORY OF WOMEN IN AMERICA* BY C. HYMOWITZ & M. WEISSMAN
(1978)

D. Sexual Harassment Laws: A Checkered History

Today's laws against sexual harassment are a collection of pieces that don't
quite fit: a labyrinth of legal dead ends and pitfalls that have assumed their
present form because of historical reasons, rather than logical ones. Even if
you're not a history buff, it's worth taking a brief look at how the laws against
sexual harassment have evolved.

Prior to the 1980s, there were no federal or state laws prohibiting sexual
harassment on the job and few instances in which it was prevented or punished. A woman who was beaten, seriously molested or raped in the workplace might file an assault and battery lawsuit, for example, but that happened
only rarely. The term sexual harassment was unheard of—and sadly, the
problems that women experienced in their jobs were almost invisible to the
male legislators who wrote the laws.

Nothing was done about sexual harassment on the job, or the broader
problem of sex discrimination, until the re-fueled women's movement began

pushing the issues in the 1970s. "Pushing" is not really the right word: It was more like running the high hurdles.

1. The First Hurdle: Making sex discrimination illegal

Sexual discrimination in employment became illegal in the United States when the Civil Rights Act of 1964 was adopted. That Act established the Equal Employment Opportunities Commission (EEOC), which later issued important regulations and guidelines on sexual harassment. But there is a mountain of irony in this, because the virtually all-male Congress had no real intention of passing a law against sex discrimination or sexual harassment.

As originally introduced in Congress, the Civil Rights Act of 1964 only prohibited discrimination in employment based on race, color, religion or national origin. Discrimination on the basis of sex was not included. It was attached to the bill at the last moment, when conservative, Southern opponents of the measure introduced an amendment prohibiting discrimination on the basis of sex. They thought that adding sexual equality was so obviously preposterous that it would scuttle the entire bill when it came to a final vote.

The very idea of prohibiting sex-based discrimination engendered mirth on the floor of the Congress and on the editorial pages of major newspapers: Men, it was laughingly argued, could now sue to become Playboy bunnies. The Lyndon Johnson administration, however, wanted the bill passed badly enough that it decided not to oppose the amendment. So the Civil Rights Act, including the ban on sex discrimination, was voted into law. Only one of the proponents of the erstwhile bill-killing amendment on sexual equality actually voted for the final bill that included it.

With that less-than-ringing endorsement, discrimination in employment on the basis of sex became illegal. But for several years, the law was all but a dead letter. The first head of the EEOC—the agency charged with enforcing the statute—considered the sex discrimination provisions of the law a joke, saying that it was "conceived out of wedlock." The EEOC took no action against sexual discrimination in employment until several years later when it started to feel pressure from the women's movement. Finally, the agency realized it had to begin enforcing the law as it was written.

2. The Second Hurdle: Equating harassment with discrimination

After convincing the EEOC to begin enforcing the law against sex discrimination, women faced another problem: how to stop sexual harassment in the workplace. The term "sexual harassment" wasn't mentioned anywhere in the Civil Rights Act, nor was it found in the fair employment practices statutes enacted in most of the states within a few years of the U.S. Civil Rights Act. But many women cogently argued that sexual harassment was a form of sex discrimination—and that laws prohibiting discrimination should outlaw harassment as well.

Nevertheless, most courts considering the issue early on refused to pin down whether sexual harassment was prohibited by the Civil Rights Act. They characterized harassment cases as some sort of personal dispute between the woman employee and her harasser that was not covered by the law. For example, when Adrienne Tompkins, an employee at New Jersey's Public Service Electric and Gas Company, was physically detained, assaulted and then fired by her boss for refusing to have sex with him, a federal court judge ruled in 1976 that the Civil Rights Act was not intended to prevent a "physical attack motivated by sexual desire on the part of a supervisor" just because it "happened to occur in a corporate corridor rather than a back alley."[27]

Women's groups kept pressing the issue, however, urging the EEOC to rule that sexual harassment is a form of sex discrimination. Harassment, they argued, makes it impossible for women to work in certain types of situations, and so it discriminates against them as much as a Men Only employment policy. Finally, in 1980, the EEOC under the leadership of Eleanor Holmes Norton issued regulations defining sexual harassment and stating that it was a form of sex discrimination prohibited by the Civil Rights Act. It wasn't until 1986 that the U.S. Supreme Court acknowledged that progress, holding that sexual harassment on the job was a form of sex discrimination—and illegal.[28]

---

[27] *Tompkins v. Public Serv. Elec. & Gas Co.*, 422 F. Supp. 553 (D.N.J. 1976).

[28] *Meritor Sav. Bank v. Vinson*, 477 U.S. 57 (1986).

3. The Third Hurdle: Putting teeth in sexual harassment laws

After 1980, when EEOC regulations finally made sexual harassment on the job illegal, several states followed suit and enacted their own laws and regulations making sexual harassment illegal. But whether state fair employment practices (FEP) statutes provide decent protection for a sexually harassed employee depends upon where she works. Employees in a few states are pretty well protected, but those in other states are afforded little or no protection under state FEP laws.

State laws

All of the state fair employment practices (FEP) laws that were enacted after the U.S. Civil Rights Act have theoretically outlawed sexual harassment on the job, but in terms of enforcement they have ranged from the strong to the useless. Some states, like Alabama and Arkansas, have no statute at all. Others, like Georgia, set up an enforcement agency but enacted a law that only applies to public employees. Most states have done somewhat better, giving their enforcement agency or the courts the power to reinstate a sexually harassed worker who is fired or forced out of her job, as well as being able to award the worker any lost wages.

On the key issue of compensation for personal injuries, some states, like New York and Massachusetts, have relatively good programs that allow an employee to recover full compensation. Unfortunately, many state FEP laws do not allow compensatory damages for any personal injuries. (See Chapters 5 and 7 for a detailed discussion of state FEP laws.)

Common law tort cases

Since 1980, attorneys for employees who suffered severe emotional or physical injuries have taken well-established legal actions for personal harm, called torts, such as rape, assault and battery and intentional infliction of emotional distress, and adapted them to fit the specifics of a sexual harassment situation. In a number of these lawsuits, sexually harassed employees recovered large money awards.

But common law tort cases have not been a perfect solution, either. They are generally only available where the injuries are quite severe, and they are limited further by the practicalities of time and money required to pursue them. Moreover, some states have greatly hampered the use of common law tort lawsuits by restrictive interpretations of the state FEP law, workers' compensation law or the tort laws themselves. (See Chapters 5 and 8 for a full description of these legal theories and how they apply to a sexual harassment situation.)

As with state FEP statutes, the evolution of common law tort suits in the last decade has provided a good legal remedy for some sexually harassed women, but many are without adequate legal protection.

The EEOC and the Civil Rights Act

Even though the U.S. Equal Employment Opportunities Commission (EEOC) has been dealing with sexual harassment complaints since 1980, its enforcement powers have been limited and its record uneven. (See Chapter 6.)

For example, the EEOC can investigate harassment claims, subpoena witnesses, settle cases and, if necessary, take the matter to court. But funding limits and heavy caseloads have resulted in the EEOC taking well over a year for most investigations, rather than the six months prescribed in the law. And even when it has decided an employee's case has merit, the EEOC has only had the resources to file a lawsuit in a small percentage of the cases.

An even bigger problem throughout the 1980s was that even if a harassment case was proved in court, the only money a woman could recover under the Civil Rights Act was for lost wages. The statute did not allow for what would be the most effective remedy: compensatory damages for physical, emotional and other personal injuries. And even though the EEOC eventually issued extensive guidelines amplifying its rules against sexual harassment, its moral bark continued to be far stronger than its enforcement bite.

4. The Fourth Hurdle: Fighting for changes in the Civil Rights Act

In 1990, women's groups and others pushed a bill through Congress that would have allowed an employee to sue for compensatory damages for personal injuries in a sexual harassment case. That bill was vetoed by President Bush.

It wasn't until late 1991, in the wake of the Clarence Thomas-Anita Hill hearings, that the issue came up again before Congress. The Bush administration still opposed allowing employees to sue for damages—and it was set to scrap the bill again. But at the last minute, feeling the political heat, it agreed to a compromise version of the bill that allowed an employee to sue for damages but put a strict limit on the total amount of damages that an employee could recover in any case—$50,000 to $300,000 based on the number of employees in the company.

Women's groups and their supporters in Congress were quick to point out the unfairness of it: No other group is subject to such severe limits on the amount of damages that can be recovered in a personal injury action. But since the alternative was to stay with the status quo—with no right to recover money damages at all—they reluctantly supported the bill. It was then enacted into law.

THEY JUST DON'T GET IT. THOSE MEN JUST DON'T UNDERSTAND HOW INJURIOUS, HOW DEMEANING AND HOW FRIGHTENING SEXUAL HARASSMENT REALLY IS. SO IT TOOK A MASSIVE ERUPTION OF OUTRAGE FROM WOMEN ACROSS AMERICA—AND ACROSS PARTY LINES—TO SHOCK THOSE SENATORS INTO DELAYING THE VOTE ON THOMAS SO THE CHARGES COULD BE INVESTIGATED.—MOLLY YARD, PRESIDENT OF THE NATIONAL ORGANIZATION FOR WOMEN, IN AN OCTOBER 10, 1991 PLEA TO MEMBERS TO HELP FINANCE CAMPAIGNS OF WOMEN FOR CONGRESS

E. Ending Sexual Harassment: The Alternatives

An employee faced with a sexual harassment situation today has a variety of alternatives for dealing with the situation. No one of them is entirely satisfactory, and several of them are complex and overlapping.

If you face a sexual harassment situation that is serious enough that it could end up in a legal battle—or if you are interested in a basic legal definition of sexual harassment—take a good look at the legal issues of sexual harassment discussed in Chapter 2.

One way to look at the solutions for ending harassment discussed in this book is as a series of alternatives: In a few cases, only one approach may work. In most cases, you have clear choices as to how to proceed.

But these alternatives can also be viewed as a series of escalating steps. If the sexual harassment isn't ended by using one option, you can switch to other, increasingly formal strategies until you find an effective method.

Here are five alternatives for dealing with sexual harassment.

1. Confronting the harasser

Often the best strategy for the employee sounds the simplest: Confront the harasser and persuade him to stop. This is not appropriate or sensible in every case, particularly when you have suffered injuries or are in some danger. But many situations can be defused by a face-to-face conversation with the person who is creating the problem.

(Strategies for confronting a sexual harasser are discussed in Chapter 3.)

2. Using a company complaint procedure

Some companies have good policies against sexual harassment and effective complaint procedures to handle them. You can file a complaint under the company procedure immediately, or you can use that procedure as the next step if your face-to-face meeting with the harasser produces no satisfactory result.

(Chapter 4 discusses company sexual harassment policies and complaint procedures and gives guidance about how best to use them. The ideas in that chapter are helpful even if there is no immediate sexual harassment problem, because an employee or employee group can use such ideas to help convince management to adopt an effective policy.)

3. Filing a complaint with a government agency

If the sexual harassment does not end after face-to-face meetings or through use of the company complaint procedure, consider filing a complaint under the U.S. Civil Rights Act with the U.S. Equal Employment Opportunities Commission (EEOC) or filing a complaint under a similar state law with a state or local fair employment practices (FEP) agency.

Filing a complaint with the EEOC or a state FEP agency is important for two reasons:

1. It sets in motion an investigation by the EEOC or the state FEP agency that may resolve the employee's sexual harassment complaint, and

2. It is a necessary prerequisite under the U.S. Civil Rights Act and under some state FEP statutes if an employee wants to file a lawsuit.

Sometimes an EEOC or a state FEP agency can resolve a sexual harassment dispute at no cost to the employee and with relatively little legal involvement on her part. Almost all of these agencies provide some sort of help in negotiating an amicable settlement with the company. A few state FEP agencies also provide an administrative hearing panel that can compensate you for your personal injuries, although the EEOC and most other state agencies do not have this important additional power.

(Chapter 5 compares the EEOC and the state FEP agencies. The procedure for filing a complaint with the EEOC is described in Chapter 6 and similar state-by-state information about the various FEP agencies is included in Chapter 7.)

4. Filing a lawsuit under the Civil Rights Act or FEP laws

If all investigation and settlement attempts fail to produce satisfactory results, your next step may be to file a lawsuit for damages under the U.S. Civil Rights Act or under one of the state FEP statutes.

Even if you intend right from the beginning to file such a lawsuit, you sometimes must first file a claim with a government agency. For example, an employee pursuing a claim under the U.S. Civil Rights Act must first file a claim with the EEOC, and a similar procedure is required under some state FEP laws. At some point, that agency will issue you a document referred to as a right-to-sue letter that allows you to take your case to court.

What you can hope to win in such a lawsuit varies considerably from state to state. Generally, the right to obtain money damages under the U.S. Civil Rights Act is better than the rights available under the laws of about half of the states, because the FEP laws in such states don't allow money damages for personal injuries caused by the sexual harassment. By contrast, the Civil Rights Act allows the employee to recover some damages—out-of-pocket losses plus $50,000 to $300,000 in damages depending upon the number of employees in the company. However, about half of the states allow you to recover greater money damages than you could get under the U.S. Civil Rights Act.

(See Chapter 5 for a further comparison of federal and state statutes. See also Chapter 6 for a discussion of the EEOC and the Civil Rights Act and Chapter 7 for a state-by-state look at FEP statutes.)

5. Filing a common law tort suit

If the sexual harassment has resulted in severe injuries, consult an attorney. You may then decide to skip all of the above steps and instead file a lawsuit for damages based on any one of several common law tort theories such as the intentional infliction of emotional harm or wrongful discharge. Generally, common law torts are best suited for harassed employees who have been seriously injured, because you must prove the conduct was truly outrageous—and such actions are costly in time and in money.

Torts are significantly different from state to state. Not every sexual harassment case will fit within a common law tort theory. However, in the appropriate case where a tort is proved successfully, a judge or jury is free to award large sums in damages.

(See Chapter 8 for a detailed discussion of tort actions most often filed in sexual harassment cases.)

When filing a tort action, you will almost always need to hire a lawyer for help. (See Chapter 9, Section A.)

CHAPTER

2

The Legal View

A. Conduct of a Sexual Nature 2/4
   1. Sexual advances or demands 2/5
   2. Hostility related to sex 2/11
   3. Pornographic and vulgar behavior 2/14

B. Conduct That Is Unreasonable 2/15

C. Conduct That Is Severe or Pervasive 2/18
   1. EEOC guidelines 2/18
   2. The totality of the circumstances 2/19

D. Conduct That Is Unwelcome 2/21
   1. Voluntary but unwelcome 2/22
   2. The employee's appearance 2/23
   3. Coping strategies 2/24
   4. Breaking off a relationship 2/25
   5. The employee's limited consent 2/26

This chapter focuses on the basic issues of sexual harassment as defined by law and interpreted by the EEOC and the courts. It will give you the working knowledge you need to prove your case of sexual harassment.

Of course, not all sexual harassment disputes will end up as courtroom battles. Many women deal each day with harassment that is not severe enough to warrant a lawsuit—and many more feel the need to approach the problem from a different direction. If you are more interested in workplace strategies for stopping harassment than in whether what's happening to you meets the legal definition of harassment, skip to the next chapter.

Chapter 3 discusses sexual harassment from a more personal perspective—looking at the practical problems it can create and stressing what a woman can do on her own to deal with the situation.

Certain basic legal issues are involved in most sexual harassment, and in this chapter we will be focusing on four of them:

- Was the conduct sexual in nature?

- Was the conduct unreasonable?

- Was the conduct severe or pervasive in the workplace?

- Was the conduct unwelcome?

These are the factors that a government investigating agency or a court will look at to determine whether you have been sexually harassed. All four factors are usually present in every case—and it is important to keep in mind that they usually relate to one another.

EEOC REGULATIONS ON SEXUAL HARASSMENT

Legal definitions of sexual harassment vary from state to state, but almost every state extends the minimum protection found in the regulations of the U.S. Equal Employment Opportunities Commission (EEOC). EEOC definitions and standards are the most influential throughout the United States in defining the parameters of sexual harassment.

The EEOC definition of sexual harassment is found in 29 Code of Federal Regulations (CFR) 1604.11(a):

Harassment on the basis of sex is a violation of [the law]. Unwelcome sexual advances, requests for sexual favors and other verbal or physical conduct of a sexual nature constitute sexual harassment when:

1. *submission to such conduct is made either explicitly or implicitly a term or condition of an individual's employment,*

2. *submission to or rejection of such conduct by an individual is used as the basis for employment decisions affecting such individual, or*

3. *such conduct has the purpose or effect of unreasonably interfering with an individual's work performance or creating an intimidating, hostile or offensive working environment*

The EEOC regulations also make clear that most sexual harassment cases can only be resolved by looking at all the facts in context (29 CFR 1604.11(b)):

In determining whether alleged conduct constitutes sexual harassment, the [EEOC] will look at the record as a whole and at the totality of the circumstances, such as the nature of the sexual advances and the context in which the alleged incidents occurred. The determination of the legality of a particular action will be made from the facts, on a case-by-case basis.

A. Conduct of a Sexual Nature

Conduct of a sexual nature that may be legally considered to be sexual harassment includes:

1. Sexual advances, propositions or attempts to get sexual favors from an employee. These are the situations that most people probably think of first when they hear about sexual harassment on the job. (See Section A.1.)

2. Outright hostility toward women employees or a particular woman employee. This most often occurs in jobs that have not been traditionally open to women. These types of situations range from pranks, threats and intimidation, to highly dangerous attacks. (See Section A.2.)

3. Lewd, sexual or pornographic pictures, language and jokes permeating the workplace, creating an environment—or a "sexually poisoned workplace"—that is offensive to many women employees. The sexual commentary and lewd humor in such cases may or may not be directed at the particular employee, but she may nevertheless find the sexually-charged atmosphere to be intimidating and offensive—and that it puts her at a distinct disadvantage with respect to her male co-workers. (See Section A.3.)

Because it may be essential to you in evaluating whether the problems you are encountering in the workplace qualify as illegal sexual harassment, each type of sexual conduct will be discussed in more detail below.

SEXUAL HARASSMENT IS HIERARCHICAL. THE SAME MAN WHO IS PATTING THE FANNY OF THE WOMAN WHO WORKS FOR HIM IS NOT PATTING THE FANNY OF THE WIFE OF THE PRESIDENT OF THE COUNTRY.—ELIZABETH EVANS, PSYCHOTHERAPIST, BERKELEY, CALIFORNIA

QUID PRO QUO OR HOSTILE ENVIRONMENT

The terms "quid pro quo" and "hostile environment" are frequently used in the cases and literature about sexual harassment.

Quid pro quo describes a situation in which an employee is confronted with sexual demands to keep her job or obtain a promotion. As the Latin term quid pro quo suggests, you have to do "this" to get "that." In more familiar vernacular, this is called a sex-for-jobs situation.

Hostile environment is frequently used to describe other types of cases in which the threat—or the trade-off—is not as blunt. This typically involves sexually offensive conduct that permeates the workplace, making it difficult or unpleasant for an employee to do her job.

Courts often confuse the type of harassment with the type of injury resulting from it. For example, you will sometimes find sex-for-jobs cases described as hostile environment cases—presumably because the woman employee was not fired of forced out of her job. And some serious sexual harassment cases are referred to as quid-pro-quo even though they involve no sex-for-jobs solicitation.

1. Sexual advances or demands

Unwelcome sexual advances and propositions are one of the most common forms of sexual harassment. Whether a particular sexual advance is illegal sexual harassment usually depends on who is making the advance and how he is doing it.

a. By supervisors or others in authority

Here the focus is on who is making the sexual advance. Sexual advances from a supervisor or other person in authority will be scrutinized far more closely than those of other co-workers because of the strong possibility of intimidation and abuse of power. Supervisors are in unique positions of power in the workplace. It is usually presumed that the employer has knowledge of any sexual harassment committed by supervisors, and so the employer is almost automatically responsible for their actions.

Sexual advances by supervisors frequently involve the classic sex-for-jobs situation. The EEOC regulations state that sexual advances under these circumstances are unlawful if they are "explicitly or implicitly a term or condition of an individual's employment." In other words, if a woman must put up with these demands as part of her job, they may qualify as harassment.

Example: A sales manager invites a saleswoman on his staff to dinner. While eating dessert, he says softly: "Let's go up to my apartment after dinner, have a drink and get comfortable. If you want, we can discuss the performance reports and the salary recommendations that I have to make next week."

Although the sales manager makes no explicit reference to sex, it is strongly implied. By mentioning "getting comfortable" and "salary recommendation" in the same conversation, he creates a strong link between the two. This is a sex-for-jobs or quid pro quo situation.

In a supervisor-subordinate relationship, very little conduct of a sexual nature is needed to support a finding of harassment. Even a relatively polite request for a date by an employer or supervisor can be the basis of a sexual harassment charge if it appears to be connected to future work assignments, promotions or raises.

Sexual harassment can arise from an unwanted sexual advance even if the person in authority makes a favorable employment decision on behalf of the employee. If a woman submits to an unwelcome sexual advance because of a promise from her supervisor, he is guilty of sexual harassment—whether he delivers on his promise or not. It's the act or threat of using sexual conduct as the basis for making employment-related decisions that gives rise to the sexual harassment.

The same rules apply to anyone with real or apparent power over the employee who threatens to use such power as the basis for making an employment decision—even if the person in authority is not in the employee's immediate chain of command.

Example: A secretary has a raise application pending. A senior staff member of the personnel department invites her several times to go out for dinner and dancing, but she refuses him. Finally he tells her: "I've got a lot of recommendations on my desk for raises, and it usually takes me quite a while to get around to processing someone's raise if she isn't a little more friendly." His conduct qualifies as sexual harassment.

b. By co-workers

Unwelcome sexual advances or demands from a co-worker can also be the kind of conduct giving rise to sexual harassment. However, since these cases do not involve a supervisor or someone in authority, the threat to the woman employee is not as direct. These cases require a greater look at all the surrounding circumstances.

There is another important practical difference between a situation involving a co-worker and one involving a supervisor or someone in authority. As mentioned, with a supervisor or someone in authority, the company is presumed to know what's going on and therefore to be legally responsible for the situation. However, this presumption of knowledge does not apply to co-workers.

PROVING YOUR CASE

To hold the employer—as opposed to the individual—responsible for sexual demands by a co-worker, you must usually prove that the company knew about the harassing acts and did nothing effective to stop them. It is important, therefore, to tell the co-worker that his advances are unwelcome and, if he persists anyway, to tell someone in authority. (See Chapter 3, Sections E and F.)

Sometimes an employer's reaction makes the sexual harassment situation worse and may result in the company being liable when it might not otherwise have been.

Example: An office worker in California received an anonymous, unwanted sexual solicitation from a co-worker on her office computer screen and reported it to her woman supervisor. The company responded to the complaints from the two women by demoting both of them, cutting back on their privileges and eventually forcing them to leave. Whether the company would have been held responsible for the original solicitation by the co-worker is unclear, but the act of retaliating against the two women employees made the company clearly liable for what later happened.[1]

If the sexual solicitation comes from a co-worker and management is not involved, directly or indirectly, the focus is on the nature of the sexual advance. The emphasis is less on the "who" and more on the "how." Many facts are important in determining whether a co-worker has crossed the line from friendly bantering into sexual harassment: the frequency of the solicitation, the nature of the proposition, the language used, the physical gestures and proximity and the behavior of the co-worker. There is no hard and fast rule as to how much is too much.

Example: Arthur Brown approaches Clara Davis, a co-worker, at her desk in the office. In polite, non-threatening language he asks, "Would you like to try that new Chinese restaurant Saturday night?"

That alone would not be sexual harassment. It could either be argued that such a request is not conduct of a sexual nature or that a reasonable woman would not find it offensive. Either way, the result is the same: There is no sexual harassment.

But if a polite request for a date is made in sexually explicit terms or in a highly suggestive tone, it could give rise to a sexual harassment claim unless the female employee had previously indicated that such an overture was welcome.

---

[1] *Monge v. Superior Court (Crown Gibraltar Graphic Center, Inc.)*, 176 Cal. App. 3d 503 (1986).

Example: Arthur asks Clara for a dinner date, but in this instance he leans over her desk, winks at her and makes suggestive movements with his tongue.

Not only is his conduct explicitly sexual, but a reasonable woman would also be more likely to find it offensive. With these two factors strongly present, this is likely to be considered sexual harassment.

The strength of the woman employee's initial response is often the key to showing that the sexual advance is unwelcome. If she firmly rejects a co-worker's initial request for a date and makes it clear that no further solicitation is welcome, any subsequent advances by him, whether in polite language or not, might constitute sexual harassment. "No" should definitely be taken to mean "no."

Example: Arthur asks Clara for a dinner date in polite language. She says no—and she makes it clear that she is not open to dating him. He persists in coming by her desk every workday for the next month and asks her if she's changed her mind and will go out with him, and each time she firmly tells him no. Arthur's request has crossed over the line from polite to harassing.

c. By customers and others

An employer can be legally responsible for sexual harassment if it creates or allows a situation where an employee will be sexually harassed by customers, salespeople, visitors or even passersby. This can happen where the employer puts an employee in a situation where it knows or should know that unwelcome sexual advances are likely to occur—for example, when a company requires an employee to dress in provocative clothing where customers or passersby are likely to make sexual advances to her.

A more serious situation occurs when the employer tries to force an employee to have sex with a client or someone else it wants to please.

Example: A Penthouse model successfully sued the magazine and Robert Guccione, the publisher, for $4,000,000 in damages under the New York Human Rights Law based on Guccione's coercive efforts to make her have sex with the company's financial advisor and others. The court viewed that situation as the equivalent of one in which the employer attempted to get sexual favors for himself.[2]

d. Showing preferences

A sexual harassment claim may also arise when sexual advances are made to two or more women with differing results. For example, if the office Lothario denies a promotion to Ms. A because she won't sleep with him and then gives the same promotion to Ms. B because she will, both women have experienced the kind of unwelcome sexual conduct that amounts to sexual harassment. Ms. A would obviously have a sexual harassment claim based upon the improper denial of her promotion by a person in authority in a sex-for-jobs situation. Ms. B would also have a claim if his sexual advances were unwelcome and she submitted only out of fear of losing the promotion.

But what if a supervisor has a consensual affair with one of his employees and gives her promotions and raises in preference to other employees? This type of nepotism combined with abusive behavior toward other employees can be a form of sexual harassment. While the supervisor is looking for someone willing to say "yes," he is frequently harassing the women who say "no."

---

[2] *Thoreson v. Penthouse Int'l, Ltd*, 563 N.Y.S.2d 968 (N.Y. Sup. Ct. 1990).

Example: A male supervisor made the rounds of the office, propositioning several of the female employees. He then boasted that he was giving one woman a promotion because "she knew how to make him feel good." Although he had never specifically promised anyone else a promotion in exchange for sex, the court nevertheless held that his preferential treatment for his new girlfriend was part of an overall discriminatory treatment of women employees.[3]

Sometimes it is not the preferential treatment that amounts to sexual harassment so much as the retaliation against the women who complained about it.

Example: In a crackdown on harassment in a government workplace, the court found that the U.S. Securities and Exchange Commission had created a hostile environment for women who complained about male supervisors giving preferential treatment to women with whom they were having affairs.[4]

PROVING YOUR CASE

If you feel you have been passed over in favor of your employer's paramour, carefully examine your working environment. If the employer's favoritism arises out of sexual conduct in the workplace, creates an atmosphere of intimidation or sets a different standard for female employees, it may also qualify as sexual harassment. Here, the strongest proof may be evidence that other women workers feel the same way you do.

---

2. Hostility related to sex

Hostile acts related to an employee's gender are another type of prohibited conduct of a sexual nature, even though they may not involve sexual overtures at all.

---

[3] *Toscano v. Nimmo*, 570 F. Supp. 1197 (D. Del. 1983).

[4] *Broderick v. Ruder*, 685 F. Supp. 1269 (D.D.C. 1988).

Many cases of sexual harassment are based on outright hostility toward a particular woman employee or toward women employees in general. Sometimes the hostility comes from the reaction of a rejected lover. Other times a supervisor may be hostile toward a particular woman employee right from the outset and indulge his hostility in ways that he wouldn't think of doing if she were a man. In most of these situations, however, the hostility stems from men's opposition to women in previously all-male jobs—and it manifests itself against any woman worker who happens to come upon the scene.

Some employers have argued that sexual harassment is not involved if a co-worker treats a woman employee with hostility. Sexual harassment, they argue, requires some evidence of sexual overtures to the female employee who registered the complaint. Fortunately, the courts have firmly rejected this argument, finding instead that sexual harassment can exist without sexual misconduct.

Example: A Washington D.C. court found that a supervisor who blocked the doorway and forcefully twisted a woman employee's arm had sexually harassed her. She conceded that he wasn't after sexual favors, but the court ruled in her favor anyway, reasoning that her supervisor wouldn't have treated a man in that manner.[5]

Hostile conduct is often a thinly disguised effort to force a woman employee out of the workforce.

Example: A supervisor at a bakery plant stated that he didn't think a woman should be foreman and then boasted that he would make it "rough enough for her to leave." He then went on a campaign of yelling at her, ridiculing her and giving her impossible tasks to do. Although he didn't demand sexual favors, the court ruled in the woman's favor anyway, holding that "threatening, bellicose, demeaning, hostile or offensive conduct by a supervisor in the workplace because of the sex of the victim" was enough to state a claim for sexual harassment.[6]

It is sometimes easier to visualize cases involving overt hostility as sexual discrimination cases rather than sexual harassment. If a supervisor subjects his

---

[5] *McKinney v. Dole*, 765 F.2d 1129 (D.C. Cir. 1985).

[6] *Bell v. Crackin Good Bakers, Inc.*, 777 F.2d 1497 (11th Cir. 1985).

female employees to ridicule and abuse because he would prefer to have men working for him, he is treating them differently than he treats his male employees and, therefore, discriminating against them. Fortunately, the conceptual difference between a sexual discrimination case and a sexual harassment case is not important, because both are subject to the same legal prohibitions. In fact, the laws against sexual harassment are largely derived from the laws against sexual discrimination.

HOSTILE ACTS AGAINST LESBIANS

Most sexual harassment laws contain no specific provision prohibiting hostile acts against lesbians—although there are some state and local ordinances that offer some protection. A good argument can be made, however, that such hostility is illegal under the general laws prohibiting sexual harassment against women.

Hostile acts directed at a lesbian are likely to contain elements of animosity toward the woman's gender as well as her sexual orientation. Hardcore woman-haters consider "lesbian" to be a derogatory epithet—and they use it against any woman they don't like. Sometimes this type of blind hatred can be turned against the harasser. If, for example, a lesbian is subjected to repeated abuse, hostility and derogatory names from a co-worker, she should take a close look at how he treats other, non-lesbian women employees. It's likely that he calls all independent women lesbians and treats them all badly. If that's true, she may be able to show that his animosity is really directed at her assertiveness and independence and that it would have existed regardless of her sexual orientation.

A lesbian faced with hostile conduct should stress those elements of her claim that she has in common with other harassed women to fit within the protection of the sexual harassment laws. Her best strategy is to try and show that the hostility toward her is a subspecies of a more general animosity toward all women employees.

3. Pornographic and vulgar behavior

There is a growing recognition by the EEOC and the courts that pornographic material and vulgar behavior in the workplace can create an offensive working environment or "sexually-poisoned" workplace for women employees.

Here, the offensiveness is not always directed at a specific individual; it usually derives from the cumulative effect of a lot of offensive and demeaning acts that may seem relatively innocuous when viewed in isolation.

Often the main injurious effect of this type of sexual conduct is to create a working atmosphere that is hostile to working women as a group. The sexually-poisoned workplace creates a situation where discrimination against women commonly flourishes.

Example: In one case, a court concluded that a proliferation of pornographic magazines, vulgar employee comments about them, sexually oriented pictures in a company sponsored film and slide presentation and offensive sexual commentary during the film all contributed to a hostile working environment, because it creates "an atmosphere in which women are viewed as men's sexual playthings rather than as their equal co-workers."[7]

Lewd and vulgar behavior is often sexist and woman-hating as well, making the potential discriminatory effect on women's careers even more clear— and often revealing a very clear double standard for male and female employees.

Example: A woman employee in a Florida shipyard complained that the walls displayed pictures of a woman's pubic area with a meat spatula, a nude woman wearing high heels and holding a whip, and a dartboard with a drawing of a woman's breast and nipple as the bull's eye. There were no pornographic pictures of men pinned up. The court noted that: "Pornography on an employer's wall or desk communicates a message about the way [the employer] views women, a view strikingly at odds with the way women wish to be viewed in the workplace."[8]

---

[7] *Barbetta v. Chemlawn Servs. Corp.*, 669 F. Supp. 569 (W.D.N.Y. 1987).

[8] *Robinson v. Jacksonville Shipyards, Inc.*, 760 F. Supp. 1486 (M.D.Fla. 1991).

PROVING YOUR CASE

Although more courts are recognizing that lewd and vulgar behavior in the workplace is a form of sexual conduct that can amount to harassment, these are often difficult cases for an employee to win. The harassed employee must be prepared to show that the conduct is severe or pervasive throughout the workplace: isolated instances, unless they are particularly offensive, will not be enough. (See Section C.)

To help clear this hurdle, look carefully at the entire working environment to see if an offensive atmosphere can be linked to other, more specific harm. For example, if an anti-woman joke makes the rounds of the office, it may seem to have no immediate ill effect. But if the same joke is repeated by someone who is about to recommend employees for promotion, it is an important indication of a possible bias against women employees. It is crucial in these cases to look for that type of linkage.

B. Conduct That Is Unreasonable

The second legal factor is unreasonableness. The law only prohibits unreasonable sexual conduct in the workplace. Some harassing conduct is obviously unreasonable. For example, if a supervisor makes sexual demands on an employee as a condition of getting a raise or a promotion—a sex-for-jobs demand—this is clearly unreasonable. It is also always unreasonable for an employer to physically assault or attack women employees.

Reasonableness typically only becomes important where the conduct may be ambiguous or subject to misinterpretation. Courts want to make sure that the employee bringing the case is not complaining about conduct that other people wouldn't find offensive. As the EEOC Compliance Manual, the handbook for personnel investigating harassment states, somewhat pompously, the law should not "serve as a vehicle for vindicating the petty slights suffered by the hypersensitive."

THE COMING OF AGE OF THE REASONABLE WOMAN

In assessing whether conduct is unreasonable, courts have traditionally used an objective test—asking whether a reasonable person would find it offensive. In sexual harassment cases, the reasonable person test seemed particularly inadequate. Is this hypothetical person a man or a woman? Will the conduct be judged from a male perspective or that of a female?

Courts have begun to recognize that there is often a big difference in how men and women view the same facts. As one court put it: "A male supervisor might believe, for example, that it is legitimate for him to tell a female subordinate that she has a 'great figure' or 'nice legs.' The female subordinate, however, may find such comments offensive."[9] (See Chapter 3, Section B.1 for a further discussion of gender differences in perception.)

The EEOC Compliance Manual strongly suggests that the conduct should be judged from the viewpoint of the woman employee: "The reasonable person standard should consider the victim's perspective and not stereotyped notions of acceptable behavior." More recent cases have been more explicit, stating that conduct in the workplace should be viewed from the standard of a reasonable woman. As one court noted:

> ...[M]any women share common concerns which men do not necessarily share. For example, because women are disproportionately victims of rape and sexual assault, women have a stronger incentive to be concerned with sexual behavior. Women who are victims of mild forms of sexual harassment may understandably worry whether a harasser's conduct is merely a prelude to violent sexual assault. Men, who are rarely victims of sexual assault, may view sexual conduct in a vacuum without a full appreciation of the social setting or the underlying threat of violence that a woman may perceive.[10]

---

[9] *Lipsett v. University of P.R.*, 864 F.2d 881 (1st Cir. 1988).

[10] *Ellison v. Brady*, 924 F.2d 872 (9th Cir. 1991).

How a woman employee responds to a situation may, within certain limits, determine what conduct is reasonable or unreasonable within her own workplace.

To a certain extent, a woman employee makes her own rules as to what is—and is not—acceptable workplace behavior. Once a woman reasonably defines the boundaries of what is personally offensive to her, it will often be considered sexual harassment for a co-worker to cross such boundaries.

Example: A married woman works as a stock broker. She shares a desk with another broker. He never asks her out, but he frequently prefaces remarks to her with the phrase, "If you weren't married..." and mentions how he can't find a woman he likes as much as her.

It's not clear whether a reasonable woman would find the man's comments offensive or not. However, if this particular employee tells her co-worker that she is bothered by his remarks and asks him to stop, she in effect creates a standard of conduct that applies to their relationship. As a reasonable woman, she has defined what conduct she finds offensive.

Of course, a woman employee can't impose unrealistic or unworkable standards on her co-workers. But there are grey areas in determining what kind of conduct is reasonable and what is not. By speaking up and explaining what is offensive to her, a woman has some control over the standards that will apply in her own work environment. (See Chapter 3, Section E for a discussion of confronting your harasser.)

ALTHOUGH IT IS USUALLY WOMEN WHO ARE THE VICTIMS, UNLESS AND UNTIL MEN SEE THE ERADICATION OF SEXUAL HARASSMENT AS THEIR CONCERN, IT WILL NOT BE EFFECTIVELY CURTAILED.—BARBARA M. WHITE, GOLDEN GATE UNIVERSITY LAW REVIEW VOL. 10:879

PROVING YOUR CASE

If you have been harassed by unreasonable conduct, the most important evidence you can present is that you let the harasser know that you found his conduct unreasonable—and that he persisted to violate the standard you set. Two kinds of documentation will be most persuasive in such a case. One is evidence that you told the harasser he was behaving unreasonably—a dated entry in your journal, a copy of any letter you sent him asking him to desist. Also important would be dated documentation that he kept up the harassing behavior even after you notified him it was unacceptable—again, dated journal entries or your statements to co-workers or others.

C. Conduct That Is Severe or Pervasive

The third factor to consider in evaluating sexual conduct is whether it is so severe or so pervasive throughout the workplace that it creates an intimidating, hostile or offensive working environment.

Although important, this factor is often assumed or left unstated in certain types of cases. For example, if a co-worker physically molests or endangers a woman employee, the situation is obviously severe.

However, the severe or pervasive factor is important in less obvious situations, such as those involving sexual advances by a co-worker other than a supervisor. Here, it is usually necessary to weigh all of the circumstances to determine whether the particular conduct was severe in and of itself or so pervasive as to create a hostile or intimidating environment.

1. EEOC guidelines

The EEOC Compliance Manual sets out guidelines for investigators to follow in determining whether any sexual conduct is severe or pervasive. According to the EEOC, investigators should consider:

- *whether the conduct was verbal or physical, or both*
- *how frequently it was repeated*
- *whether the conduct was hostile and patently offensive*
- *whether the alleged harasser was a co-worker or a supervisor*
- *whether others joined in perpetuating the harassment, and*
- *whether the harassment was directed at more than one individual.*

The EEOC Compliance Manual explains how conduct should be evaluated using these factors. According to the EEOC, unless there is a single, "quite severe" incident, the investigator should go through a weighing process to determine whether the conduct gives rise to a sexual harassment claim. No weighing process is necessary in a sex-for-jobs situation, however, because the EEOC says that "a single sexual advance may constitute harassment if it is linked to the granting or denial of employment benefits." In other words, a sex-for-jobs situation is always considered severe without anything further.

Cases involving intrusive types of touching or fondling are also usually considered severe, even if the offensive behavior only occurs once. This is true whether or not it involves a supervisor.

In general, the EEOC considers physical actions by a co-worker to be much more serious than words, because "even a single unwelcome physical advance can seriously poison the victim's working environment."

And the EEOC Compliance Manual takes the position that "the more severe the harassment, the less need to show a repetitive series of incidents. This is particularly true when the harassment is physical."

2. The totality of the circumstances

In the case of persistent sexual advances from co-workers or a sexually-poisoned workplace, it is usually important that the harassed employee build her case fact by fact, with an eye toward showing the totality of the working environment.

No one fact may be decisive, but the sum total of them all might be. Here is how one court looked at it: "A play cannot be understood on the basis of some of its scenes but only on its entire performance, similarly, a discrimination analysis must concentrate not on individual incidents but on the overall scenario."[11]

The case from which that quote was taken is a good example of how the cumulative effect of offensive behavior worsens the work environment. Lois Robinson testified that there were groups of pornographic pictures displayed at nearly 40 sites throughout the Jacksonville Shipyard where she worked—and that she found them to be offensive.

But she also took the case one step further, directly connecting the pornographic photos to her working conditions. She testified that several male co-workers made suggestive remarks to her when they were in the presence of the pornographic photos. One told her: "I'd like to get in bed with that." Another said: "Hey pussycat, come here and give me whiff."

The connection between the pornographic workplace and Robinson's individual harassment went still further. When she objected to the pictures, her co-workers increased their sexual taunting. When she objected to a sexist joke in which sodomous rape was referred to by the term "boola-boola," her co-workers started calling her by that name. It was the cumulative effect of all this interrelated behavior that created a hostile and intimidating working environment.

Even behavior that a woman worker does not witness can still have a cumulative, pervasive effect in creating an abusive working environment.

HARASSMENT HAS MORE TO DO WITH DOMINATION THAN IT DOES WITH LOVE OR SEX.—GEORGE LEONARD, AUTHOR OF *THE END OF SEX*

---

[11] *Robinson v. Jacksonville Shipyards, Inc.*, 760 F. Supp. 1486 (M.D.Fla. 1991).

Example: A woman works in an office where pornographic pictures are passed around by the male employees and where they persist in telling obscene, sexist jokes. She tells them that she is offended by their conduct. The next time she walks into the room one of her co-workers says, "Look out—here comes Snow White. Let's go in the other room so I can finish this story."

Here, the joke that the woman's co-workers tell out of earshot just "among the boys"is relevant to her claim that she is working in a sexually-poisoned workplace. The co-workers' condescending attempt to protect her from one particular joke makes little difference, because her sensitivity to that joke is not the real point. The main issue is the cumulative impact of pornographic and obscene behavior in the workplace, and her co-workers' furtive manner doesn't change the situation.

PROVING YOUR CASE

Courts that have ruled against women employees in sexually poisoned work-place cases have often done so because there was insufficient proof that the of-fensive sexual conduct was severe or pervasive. An employee bringing such a case must usually show that such conduct permeates the workplace to over-come the inertia of a less-than-sympathetic judge.

In presenting a case, be prepared to list as many sexual or hostile incidents as possible, including dates, places and witnesses. Look for other witness who can testify as to other similar incidents. Search hard for connections that link the overall atmosphere (the prevalence of pornographic pictures) to specific hostile incidents (sexual taunting when you object). Focus on whether supervisors par-ticipated in creating or tolerating the sexually-poisoned atmosphere.

D. Conduct That Is Unwelcome

The EEOC regulations prohibit "unwelcome sexual advances, requests for sex-ual favors and other verbal or physical conduct of a sexual nature." This is a subjective test. The sexual conduct must actually be unwelcome and offensive to the employee bringing the complaint.

At first glance, it would seem that this factor would be easy to fulfill in any situation: If the conduct wasn't personally offensive and unwelcome, why would the employee bother to complain about it? The problem is timing. The woman must show that the conduct was unwelcome and offensive to her at the time it occurred. Sometimes that can be difficult.

In a sex-for-jobs situation, the supervisor or employer will frequently claim that the employee welcomed the sexual advances at the time and that the relationship was purely consensual. Likewise, in the case of the sexually-poisoned workplace, an employer will often argue that the employee was a willing participant in the rough humor and sexual pranks and that she didn't really seem offended by it. The issue of unwelcomeness can be a problem in any kind of situation where there is no clear evidence of the subjective attitude of the employee when the events occurred.

1. Voluntary but unwelcome

In the past, employers have argued that if a woman voluntarily submits to her employer's sexual advances, she has consented to them. The legal rule, however, is more favorable to the employee: She is only deemed to have welcomed the sexual advance or conduct if it can be shown that it is something she wanted to do at the time.

The best example is taken from the first case involving sexual harassment that the U.S. Supreme Court decided. In that case, Mechelle Vinson testified as to what happened shortly after she was hired by the Meritor Savings Bank:

> *[Her supervisor] invited her out to dinner and, during the course of the meal, suggested that they go to a motel to have sexual relations. At first she refused, but out of what she described as fear of losing her job she eventually agreed. According to [Vinson], Taylor [her supervisor] thereafter made repeated demands upon her for sexual favors, usually at the branch, both during and after business hours; she estimated that over the next several years she had intercourse with him some 40 or 50 times. In addition,...Taylor fondled her in front of other employees, followed her into the women's restroom when she went there alone, exposed himself to her and even forcibly raped her on several occasions.*

Almost unbelievably, the lower court judges thought that this was not sexual harassment because they characterized the relationship between Vinson and her supervisor, Taylor, as "a voluntary one." The U.S. Supreme Court, however, held the behavior was clearly harassment.[12]

PROVING YOUR CASE

A woman who gives in voluntarily to sexual demands out of fear of losing her job does not forfeit her right to raise a claim of sexual harassment. The test is whether the employee welcomed the sexual advance or conduct—not whether she felt compelled under the circumstances to go along with it.

Your strongest evidence in such a case is any proof that you found the behavior repugnant and felt apprehensive about the stability of your job at the time.

---

2. The employee's appearance

The U.S. Supreme Court has stated that a court can consider evidence of the employee's "sexually provocative speech or dress" along with other facts in determining whether the employee really welcomed any sexual advances.

There is justified criticism of this rule. It's virtually impossible to know what the Supreme Court is talking about when it referred to provocative speech or dress: provocation, like beauty, is in the eye of the beholder. We must assume, however, that a woman employee who dresses in a way that might stimulate a man's fantasies has to be particularly careful.

---

[12] *Meritor Sav. Bank v. Vinson,* 477 U.S. 57 (1986).

PROVING YOUR CASE

Courts' emphasis on a harassed woman's wardrobe places an unfair burden on women who choose to dress in certain ways. But, fair or not, women in that position should be particularly explicit in telling a co-worker that his sexual advances are unwelcome in offsetting his own misplaced mindset. (See Chapter 3, Section C.2 for a further discussion of work clothes.)

---

3. Coping strategies

Speaking out against harassment, while preferrred, is not always possible. Frequently, an employee is fearful of what will happen if she does. A woman faced with harassing conduct in the workplace often adopts a coping strategy—behavior that sometimes gives the appearance that she is a willing participant but in fact may only be her way of dealing with an unpleasant situation.

According to one expert on coping strategies:

> *[W]omen respond to sexually harassing behavior in a variety of reasonable ways. The coping strategy a woman selects depends on her personal style, the type of incident, and her expectation that the situation is susceptible to resolution.*
>
> *Typical coping methods include:*
>
> - *denying the impact of the event, blocking it out*
> - *avoiding the workplace or the harasser, for instance, by taking sick leave or otherwise being absent*
> - *telling the harasser to stop*
> - *engaging in joking or other banter in the language of the workplace in order to defuse the situation, and*
> - *threatening to make or actually making an informal or formal complaint.*[13]

---

[13] *Robinson v. Jacksonville Shipyards, Inc.,* 760 F. Supp. 1486 (M.D.Fla. 1991).

PROVING YOUR CASE

If your coping strategy has been to go along with the language of the workplace, you can still pursue a claim for sexual harassment. But this strategy, although understandable, can create a difficult proof problem: you act one way while the events are occurring and later make the claim that you felt quite the opposite.

Fortunately, even a woman who reasonably believes that she cannot tell her harasser to stop without jeopardizing her job or facing worse harassment usually has ways to establish that she did not welcome the sexual advances or conduct when it occurred.

Example: A young woman works in a stock brokerage, and a co-worker tries to sit close to her and put his arm around her at office social events or informal gatherings. One time another employee saw him trying to kiss her as the elevator door opened. She is afraid to tell him to stop because he has a bad temper and their supervisor is his best friend and tennis partner.

Here, the woman's coping strategy is to go along with the sexual conduct, but she must somehow establish facts that will show that the situation is really unwelcome to her. Probably the best way to do that is to tell as many people as she can trust, such as other co-workers, friends outside the business and counselors that the relationship is not what it appears to be and that she is only putting up with it out of fear. She needs to develop contemporaneous, corroborating evidence of her true attitude toward his sexual advances, even if that proof is outside of company channels.

4. Breaking off a relationship

Sometimes there are situations where it is important for a harassed woman to take affirmative steps to show that sexual conduct is unwelcome. This may be particularly true if there has been a close relationship between the woman and her harasser.

An employee does not forfeit her right to protection from sexual harassment if she was romantically involved with a co-worker, but she has to make it clear to him that any further sexual advances are unwelcome. The prudent thing in this situation may be to tell everyone, including management and her fellow employees, that the relationship is over, so as to dispel any appearance that she is still welcoming his advances.

WE DON'T TALK [ABOUT HARASSMENT] BECAUSE WE ARE USED TO MAKING EXCUSES FOR MEN'S BEHAVIOR. WE'RE TAUGHT TO DO IT FROM THE TIME WE ARE LITTLE GIRLS. "YOUR FATHER HAD A HARD DAY AT THE OFFICE, THE FACTORY, THE HOSPITAL, THE COURTROOM" WE WERE TOLD TO EXPLAIN AWAY THE KIND OF BEHAVIOR BY OUR FATHERS THAT WE'D NEVER ACCEPT FROM OUR MOTHERS.—SANDRA THOMPSOM, *ST. PETERSBURG TIMES*, APRIL 4, 1991

5. The employee's limited consent

Employers frequently argue that an employee has welcomed certain sexual advances or conduct because she willingly participated in some similar type of activity. An employer might try to generalize from the mild to the severe—citing instances in which the woman told an off-color joke or participated in a relatively harmless sexual prank as evidence that she must have no objection to the working environment as a whole. But often that working environment includes hard core, misogynist pornography, dangerous pranks and demeaning sexual comments that go well beyond the type of conduct that she did not find offensive. In tolerating certain types of mild sexual conduct she does not forfeit her right to challenge other, more serious forms of sexual harassment.

Even if a woman is hired to do a highly sexualized job, she does not waive her right to object to other forms of sexual conduct that she finds offensive. A leading case on this point involved a woman hired as Pet of the Month by *Penthouse* magazine and whose job involved movie and personal appearances in highly sexualized settings. Despite the nature of her job, the magazine and its publisher were held liable for coercing her into having sex with business associates and others that the publisher wanted to please:

> *The offensiveness of defendants' conduct is not mitigated by the fact that plaintiff's job as a model and actress for Penthouse involved, in part, the commercial exploitation of her physical appearance. Sexual slavery was not a part of her job description.... Protections against sexual harassment are arguably more necessary in a workplace permeated by conceptions of women as sex objects. When there is a significant potential for discriminatory abuse of power by an employer, the need for an effective deterrent to enforce public policy and protect employees is even greater.*[14]

To many harassed women, it will be obvious that they have been sexually harassed within the meaning of the law. Others may conclude that one or more technical factors may be weak or missing from their cases. That needn't signal hopelessness. The definitions explained here are intended only as an introduction to the law.

---

[14] *Thoreson v. Penthouse Int'l, Ltd*, 563 N.Y.S.2d 968 (N.Y. Sup. Ct. 1990).

3

First Steps To Stopping Harassment

A. Have You Been Harassed? 3/3

B. Why It's Hard To Speak Up 3/5
   1. Men and women: different perceptions 3/6
   2. Much ado about the sterile workplace 3/8

C. Gray Areas of Behavior 3/10
   1. Office romances 3/10
   2. Work clothes and behavior 3/12
   3. Pin-ups 3/13
   4. Jokes 3/15
   5. Innuendos 3/17

D. Deciding Whether To Take Further Action 3/18
   1. Sizing up the situation 3/19
   2. What to do when you need to do more 3/22

E. Confronting Your Harasser 3/23
   1. Tell him what you don't want 3/24
   2. Put it in writing 3/25

F. What To Do If the Harassment Continues 3/31
   1. Collect evidence 3/31
   2. Keep a detailed journal 3/32
   3. Talk with friends 3/34
   4. Talk with co-workers 3/34

5. Organize a group.. 3/35
6. Get a copy of your work records.. 3/35
7. Build your own strength 3/37
8. Consider filing a formal action... 3/37
9. Use formal complaint procedures 3/38

Having read Chapter 2, you are now familiar with how the law attempts to define sexual harassment on the job. While that is essential knowledge in evaluating any uncomfortable workplace situation, we now ask you to briefly suspend that legal knowledge.

This chapter analyzes sexual harassment from a strictly personal perspective—how it feels, what you can do about it, why it is so difficult to combat. Unfortunately, a large part of the burden of stopping harassment still often lies with the woman who is being harassed. But this chapter provides help— strategies for how to speak up to your harasser, how to report harassment, how to make it stop.

Surveys of women who have been sexually harassed indicate that less than 7% of them file a formal legal complaint or seek legal help.[1] Most women most of the time stop harassment by taking direct action against it in the workplace, rather than in a courtroom or through a wrangling administrative procedure.

---

[1] From "The Impact of Sexual Harassment," a factsheet published by the Women's Legal Defense Fund (October 11, 1991).

A. Have You Been Harassed?

Despite the language of the Civil Rights Act, EEOC regulations and many court opinions interpreting both, sexual harassment can be very difficult to define. In all but the more outrageous instances, whether particular conduct is sexual harassment often turns on the individual facts, the sensitivities of those involved and the sensibilities of those investigating it.

Years ago, when asked in a case to define pornography, the U.S. Supreme Court justices hedged, ruling that while they couldn't define pornography, they knew it when they saw it. Sexual harassment is much the same. While a woman is rarely able to fit her situation neatly into a formula or definition, she knows she's being sexually harassed when she feels it.

This gut-check is your best barometer in knowing whether you have been sexually harassed at work. But deciding whether to take action against it—and what action to take—is often a more problematic decision. Start by learning about your possible legal actions and other options. (See Chapters 5 and 7.) Then with the help of this chapter, focus on what you can do now.

SOMETHING HIGHLY OFFENSIVE TO MINNIE PEARL MIGHT BE AN INVITING DARE TO MADONNA.—JONATHAN A. SEGAL, A BALTIMORE LAWYER WHO ADVISES EMPLOYERS ON HOW TO AVOID HARASSMENT LAWSUITS

ONE WOMAN'S STORY

I've never told anyone this before, not even my husband—and we've been married almost 50 years:

It was 1943 and I was 20 years old when I started teaching school—I had to get a special license from the state. It was prestigious then to be a schoolteacher. That was something to be very proud of.

I got nothing but compliments the first two years.

Then one night, the school's head football coach told me he thought we could do more at pep assemblies. "I'd like to talk to you about it," he said. "But I wouldn't be comfortable in your home." We got in his car and he drove about 45 minutes out of town, finally stopping at a bar. He kept urging me to have a rum and Coke, something to drink.

When we got in the car to leave, the wrestling began. He told me he was grieving because his wife was very sick. I'll never forget that he said: "I just want to feel your underwear"—and he put his hand up my skirt. I told him to drive me straight home. He said: "I don't think you understand what can happen here. I'll just make one phone call—and you'll never work again." I wept all the way home. I really believed this was something I might have to go along with to keep my job. It was a small town and he was a local boy. The school board, principal and superintendent all revered him like an absolute saint—maybe even more powerful, since he was a coach, after all.

He avoided me after that. But my boss called me in and said my contract wouldn't be renewed for the next term. I had a permanent license that said I could teach forever. But I couldn't get a job anywhere without good recommendations. I became terribly disillusioned. I thought, if he can do this to me, then anyone else can, too. I left teaching.

It would have never occurred to me to tell my parents or my friends what happened. I hate hearing myself say this, but I just wonder if my parents would have thought I had done something to cause it. As immigrants, they believed so strongly you could come to America and be treated fairly. I think women friends, too, would have thought I was a hussy somehow.

Now it seems so sad. I loved teaching. It was the thing that I felt I did best. I feel that I was cheated and in some ways, I hope I don't sound immodest, but I think the students were cheated, too. They needed a younger person about.

I don't feel pain. I feel anger. I know now, given that it's 1991, that I would do something about that kind of behavior.

B. Why It's Hard To Speak Up

The statistics about workplace harassment, although often repeated, still have the power to shock: Most women who have been sexually harassed on the job never speak up about it. Only a small minority take informal action against harassment using company procedures. And only a miniscule number ever make a formal legal complaint with the EEOC or state enforcement agency. Why this heavy blanket of silence in the face of such abusive behavior?

There is no simple answer.

A number of feelings often combine to keep women's lips sealed: guilt, shame, embarrassment, fear of being labeled a troublemaker, too sensitive, bossy or humorless. Upbringing or experience may make the subject of harassment seem too painful or laden with other taboos for some women to come forward. Young or inexperienced workers may even assume harassment is all in a day's work. And of course, many women keep silent because they distrust the procedures for handling their harassment complaints, or don't believe they'll be effective. And some women simply say it is demeaning to have to turn to authorities for personal protection at work.

These reasons, although powerful, don't explain all of the hesitancy.

The answers may lie more in what is often overlooked. Traditional cultural programming also helps explain the silence. Women have long been socialized to be the sexual gatekeepers, responsible for setting the bounds of closeness in their relationships with men. The foremost thought on the minds of many women who have been harassed is: *What have I done wrong?*

This, perhaps, helps get at the deeper explanation of the meaning of silence. Sexual harassment is not about sexual attractiveness or a testosterone-induced urge to get close. It's not about sex at all. Sexual harassment on the job is almost always an abuse of power designed to discourage women from continuing in the workforce or getting more desirable, better paying jobs. Sexual harassment is a male tactic to make a woman vulnerable in the workplace.

It often works.

Experience shows that women who feel vulnerable and violated often have little strength to fight back, especially when they know the system is stacked against them.

IT WAS HORRENDOUS. I WOULD GO HOME AND THINK "HOW CAN MY HUSBAND LOVE ME" MY SELF-ESTEEM... THEY WOULD MAKE ME FEEL LIKE A SLUT. I WOULD THINK "WHY ARE THESE PEOPLE DOING THIS TO ME?"—A MILWAUKEE WOMEN WHO WON A LAWSUIT AFTER MALE CO-WORKERS SEXUALLY HARASSED HER FOR OVER FIVE YEARS, INCLUDING POSTING PICTURES OF ANIMALS IN CRUDE SEX ACTS AND REGULARLY DROPPING THEIR PANTS IN FRONT OF HER

1. Men and women: different perceptions

But it's not just women's socialization to silence that stands in their way of re-porting workplace harassment. The fact that some men seem willfully blind to what harassing behavior is can sometimes be a greater barrier. According to one telephone survey of 1,200 Los Angeles residents: 67% of the men said they would be complimented if propositioned by a female co-worker; only 17% of the women said a workplace proposition would be a compliment. And 63% of the women but only 15% of the men said they would be insulted by it.[2]

In another recent poll, men and women workers were asked how they would respond to sexual advances at work. Only 15% of the men said they would be offended; 75% said they would be flattered. In contrast, over 75% of the women said they would be offended by the advances.

---

[2] Conducted by Dr. Barbara Gutek, psychologist at the University of Arizona Business School, 1980-81.

WALK A MILE IN OUR PUMPS

Ellen Wells, testifying at the 1991 Senate hearings on the confirmation of Clarence Thomas to the U.S. Supreme Court, when questioned about why a woman wouldn't talk to other people about being harassed:

You blame yourself. Perhaps it's the perfume I have on. . . . I remember one sister [in Catholic school] telling us that you have to be careful with the kind of perfume that you wore because the title indicated the kind of emotions you would generate in a gentleman...

And so you try to change your behavior because you think it must be me. You ask yourself: What did I do? I must be the wrong party here. And then I think you perhaps start to get angry and frustrated. But there's always that sense of powerlessness.

And you're also ashamed. What can you tell your friends and family, because they ask you: What did *you* do?

And so you keep it in. You don't say anything. And if someone says to you: You should go forward, you have to think: How am I going to pay the phone bill if I do that? And yes, perhaps this job is secure, but maybe they'll post me in a corner with the *Washington Post* to read from. And that won't get me anywhere.

So you're quiet. And you're ashamed. And you sit there and you take it.

More subtle behavior is eyed differently, too. In another recent study, workers were asked to assess the actions of a man who suggestively eyed female co-workers up and down. At least 24% of the women in the survey characterized the behavior as harassment; only 8% of the men did.[3]

Many men say they find it easiest to relate to women flirtatiously. Add to this the fact that when many men entered the workplace, teasing women with various types of sexual remarks and innuendo were common on the job—and seemed to win them approval. They simply don't consider such behavior to be wrong.

---

[3] Reported in *Harvard Business Review,* March-April, 1981.

These differing gender responses to sexual harassment, borne out by many of life's daily experiences, come as little surprise. It should be even less surprising that they directly contribute to women's reluctance to report acts of harassment in the workplace. After all, if the male workers don't perceive their conduct as harassing in the first place, it seems futile to complain about it through a male-established power structure.

Many sociologists and other communications experts dismally portend that the differences in how men and women perceive harassment won't go away soon. They remind us that since men's workplace behavior is so tied to traditional socially-enforced patterns of behavior and often based on a deeper desire to keep women out of the workplace, change is sure to be slow and difficult.

2. Much ado about the sterile workplace

While the spotlight's focus on sexual harassment is long overdue, it has also prompted a new feeling of timidity in many workplaces. Some men claim that the increasing awareness of workplace harassment and the increasing likelihood of actions against it will cause them to become increasingly stifled and uncertain. For example, some men fret about whether they can freely compliment women co-workers on their work or appearance without running the risk of a lawsuit. They worry that if they tell a risque joke in what we quaintly used to call mixed company, they'll lose their footing on the corporate ladder.

Other men trumpet more dire predictions:

- "Women are going to lose their femininity. It used to be that when a fellow left for another job or a vacation, you could kiss a woman goodbye at the office. You can't do that anymore. It's sad," lamented one 38-year-old office worker in California recently.

- A college professor complained that because of his school's new policy against sexual harassment, he would no longer be able to perform his job effectively. His biggest fear: He could not discuss his female students' dissertations with them over lunch.

- Citing the growing number of legal actions against clergy members for sexual misconduct—over 2,000 pending in 1990—Wisconsin minister James D. Eckblad told those attending his Law Day for Clergy seminar that the increased reporting is preventing the lending of aid and comfort to parishioners: "It becomes almost impossible to give a caring hug spontaneously when you're worried about somebody else accusing you of being a criminal," he said.

The impending peril of the sterile workplace is greatly exaggerated. And of course, from a woman's point of view, there is a huge upside to such male agonizing: It should result in more would-be harassers reigning in their obnoxious workplace behavior. Awareness, coupled with education about sexual harassment, can go a long way toward increasing equality and decreasing discomfort in the workplace.

But there is also a downside: Excessive male handwringing over what is and what is not acceptable behavior may once again be engineered to make women feel foolish and intimidated—to still their tongues about harassment.

A LITTLE GUIDANCE FOR MEN

For men who now wonder if they will be overly-hampered by the sudden attention to Proper Workplace Behavior, there is little reason to be fearful. The super-cautious advice—don't say anything to women at work except name, rank and serial number—is surely overkill.

The better advice is to use common sense. There is plenty of room to be friendly and personable without behaving in a way that is likely to offend workers of either gender.

Some rough guides for evaluating your own workplace behavior:

- Would you say or do it in front of your spouse or parents?
- Would you say or do it in front of a colleague of the same sex?
- How would you feel if your mother, wife, sister or daughter were subjected to the same words or behavior?
- How would you feel if another man said or did the same things to you?
- Does it need to be said or done at all?

C. Gray Areas of Behavior

In some situations, it can be truly difficult to know whether particular behavior by a male co-worker amounts to harassment. Here, we look at the most troublesome borderline behavior from a personal perspective. (Chapter 2 analyzes the legal considerations of some of this behavior.)

Many women have the greatest difficulty in assessing and knowing how to handle the less blatant examples of male behavior—touching a co-worker on the shoulder, pinning up some kinds of less graphic pictures, looking a woman up and down. To some women, these things may feel like harassment; to others, they're innocuous.

Even worse, within the gray areas are often more shades of gray: Whether some conduct is harassment may depend on who does it. One request for a date by a co-worker may be OK, but one such request by a manager a week before a performance review may be harassment. Whether telling an off-color joke qualifies as harassment depends on whether it's welcomed by the listener. And sometimes, it depends on how off-color the off-color joke is— and the context in which it's told.

For both women and men, there is a benefit in knowing when they are treading upon shaky ground.

1. Office romances

As many as 70% of all male and female workers have either dated or married someone they met in the workplace.[4] Those are far better odds than you have of meeting someone at a bar, party or other social gathering specifically engineered to be a meeting place.

Some people point to this likelihood of meeting a date or mate at work to justify the prevalence of harassment there. This badly confuses the issue. Sexual attraction is a natural outgrowth of people working together—and is in

---

[4] 1991 statistics by the California-based Employment Development Department, which conducts workplace training seminars.

no way illegal. Sexual harassment is unwanted, non-mutual, unacceptable conduct.

It's that simple.

Some employers have adopted a strict policy that prohibits supervisors from dating people they supervise. While this may be understandable given the relatively low legal threshold for a supervisor's conduct to be considered harassment, it is as unnecessary as it is impossible to enforce. Far better to remember that since workplace harassment is almost always about an abuse of power—not about romance gone sour—the focus should be on preventing intimidation.

Still, becoming romantically involved with someone you work with—especially a person you supervise or report to—requires caution. If you date someone at your workplace, it may be best to keep your socializing to after-work hours. If the relationship ends while the two of you still work together, be sure there is as clear an understanding as possible about it. If you have any indication that a former paramour may turn antagonistic or hostile to you at work, try at least to let a friend or office confidante know about it.

LOVE & WORK: SOME ADVICE FOR THE STARRY-EYED

1. Be honest. Don't ask someone out under the guise of talking business, when what you're really after is a social relationship.

2. If your overtures to a co-worker are rebuffed once, back off. Even if the reasons stated for not going out seem neutral—my mother's in town, my child is sick—assume that no means no. Let the other person initiate any further social invitations.

3. If you start seeing someone socially, meet outside the workplace.

4. Pay attention to the way the person you are interested in responds to you and tailor your behavior around that. When in doubt, go slowly.

5. Speak up if you feel put upon.

---

2. Work clothes and behavior

Wrongful behavior—especially behavior that harms women—is often explained away by blaming the victim.

> *It's no wonder she was raped, working so late at the office when she knows what a rough neighborhood it is.*

> *She should have expected to be ogled at the convention, she was the only woman there.*

> *She practically asked to be harassed, the way she dressed for work.*

The simple response is that no one has the right to abuse another person.

But the convenient explanation of blaming a woman for her own harassment at work is much alive and deep-rooted—and crosses gender lines. About 49% of the women and 53% of the men polled by *Time* magazine in 1986 agreed with the following statement: Women who complain about sexual harassment have often asked for trouble by the way they dress or behave. Paradoxically, this attitude prevails even though there is absolutely no evidence that harassers are put off by conservative attire.

Wear whatever you feel is appropriate to work. But know that the issue may be more important than it seems at first glance. Many people are bothered when their co-workers wear tight-fitting, provocative clothes. It makes them feel uncomfortable—as if a vague sexual aura has pervaded the workplace. Some men may even wrongly interpret sexy clothes such as a low-cut blouse or short skirt as an invitation to act inappropriately.

If the clothes you usually wear to work are provocatively styled, take an honest moment to ask yourself why. In some workplaces, women workers are motivated to dress in certain ways because of some subtle expectancy that they are supposed to look like sex objects. Double-check to be sure that you are not playing into this type of sexist game.

So the bottom line is in a sort of limbo: There's no need to become a fashion victim by sacrificing your imagination in clothes for a wardrobe of button-down shirts and bowties. At the same time in this age of heightened sensitivity as to Proper Workplace Conduct, a definite—albeit nebulous—standard indicates you should dress differently for work than you might for a night of nightclubbing.

THE LAW LOOKS AT YOUR HEMLINE

As offensive and irrelevant as it may seem, if you do decide to take formal action against your harasser, what you wear to work and how you act there will likely be examined by the person investigating your complaint or evaluated by a court.

PORNOGRAPHY ON AN EMPLOYER'S WALL OR DESK COMMUNICATES A MESSAGE ABOUT THE WAY HE VIEWS WOMEN, A VIEW STRIKINGLY AT ODDS WITH THE WAY WOMEN WISH TO BE VIEWED IN THE WORKPLACE.—FROM *ROBINSON V. JACKSONVILLE SHIPYARDS*, 760 F. SUPP. 1486 (1991)

3. Pin-ups

As long as "cheesecake" or "girlie" pictures have been around—nude and semi-nude, sexually provocative pictures of women—so has raged the debate over whether they are smut or art.

Some people are unbothered by them and will defend anyone's wish to see and display nude or pornographic pictures as a constitutional right. Others find them acceptable only in private. Not surprisingly, many women find all such displays demeaning in the workplace.

Displaying highly suggestive pin-ups that some employees find offensive is almost always harassment. A good example is the recent *Robinson* case,[5] already famous in the annals of sexual harassment history for being among the first to recognize that harassing behavior should be evaluated according to a reasonable-woman, not a reasonable-man, standard. (See Chapter 2, Section B.)

In that case, a female welder in a Florida shipyard complained that cartoons, magazines, calendars, graffiti, posters, plaques and drawings featuring partially clad or nude women, most in sexually suggestive or submissive poses, were displayed throughout the workplace. Just a few of the more obnoxious examples from the hundreds that made up visual assault in the shipyard included:

- a picture of·a woman's pubic area with a meat spatula pressed on it
- a sketch of nude female torso with "USDA Choice" written on it
- a dartboard picturing a woman's breast with the nipple as the bull's eye
- a lifesize drawing of a nude woman on a workspace divider
- a drawing of a nude woman with fluid coming from her genital area
- graffiti painted prominently on the workplace walls including: "lick me you whore dog bitch," "pussy," "cunt" and "eat me."

The court found that while the displays would not interfere with some men's abilities to get their jobs done, they could understandably seem offensive and distracting to a reasonable woman worker. It ordered the shipyard to implement at once a detailed sexual harassment policy which included a comprehensive procedure for making, investigating and resolving sexual harassment and retaliation complaints. In addition, the company was ordered to train all female employees how to resist and prevent sexual harassment and to train all supervisors and managers how to handle harassment complaints.

And if, as some men protest, pin-ups are a constitutionally protected artform, one might wonder why only women are the only subject. Men do appear on pin-ups, too, but it is rare that they are displayed in workplaces. In fact, one foreman in the Florida case testified that he did not know of a ven-

---

[5] *Robinson v. Jacksonville Shipyards, Inc.,* 760 F. Supp. 1486 (M.D.Fla. 1991).

dor distributing a calendar of nude men, but if one did, he would "think the son of a bitch was queer."

WHEN THE ARTWORK ISN'T ART

If there are pictures or graffiti displayed in your workplace that you find offensive, there are a number of steps you can take.

- If the pin-ups are displayed in a public area that is not part of another person's workspace, take them down.

- If only one person has posted pictures you find offensive, take him aside and tell him so. Ask him to stop doing it.

- If your company has regular staff meetings, bring up the matter of the unwanted office decor there.

---

4. Jokes

Humor, by its nature, walks a fine line between delighting and offending—and perceptions of it are intensely personal. While the prospect of a workplace devoid of humor is as bleak as a workplace devoid of paychecks, it's also true that humor can hurt.

Because jokes are often used both to reinforce and deflect strong feelings, many are built around racist, homophobic and sexist punchlines. Parrying back with a witty retort may occasionally feel good, but it runs the risk of reinforcing the behavior—and may even cause it to escalate.

Whether a joke told in the workplace crosses the line from good-humored to mean-spirited depends first on its content. If a joke is not obviously directed at a particular person or not obviously raunchy, it's more likely to be acceptable for the workplace. And whether a joke is acceptable for the workplace also depends on the audience and context.

Example:

Q: How do you make a blond laugh on Monday?

A: Tell her a joke on Friday.

As they wait alone for an elevator at the end of the week, Debby tells this joke to her boss Robin, with whom she has a fairly close relationship. Both women are blond. Both laugh. No harm done.

Suppose Ted uses the same joke to close his Friday night speech at the real estate developers symposium. Robin is one of only three women in the large audience— and the only one with blond hair. Robin is embarrassed as the titters and stares focus on her. Ted should have held his tongue. Robin should call him on his unfortunate behavior privately, after he has finished his speech.

If you often feel like the butt of an unwelcome joke, there are good ways to show your disapproval and, hopefully, put an end to having them uttered in your presence.

Simply don't laugh. Stronger stuff than it sounds. Consider that nothing makes a stand-up comic sit down more quickly than the din of silence. If the harasser's aim is to make you uncomfortable or to catch you off-guard, a bored, unresponsive look may quickly show him he's off his mark.

Leave the room. While not always a practical solution, this can also act as a strong antidote for many wannabe comedians. The truth is, you don't want to go on 24-hour surveillance of the office buffoon to make sure he doesn't tell the one about the guy who goes to the whorehouse. But you don't have to encourage him by being among his listening audience.

Firmly but politely tell the jokester that you don't appreciate the remark. The first two responses may work best for one-on-one encounters, but if many others are present, your silence or leaving may not be noticed or may even be turned against you to add to the levity.

- You may need to be more upfront. You might say: "I'm sorry, but rape is not at all funny to me." Here, your own timing can be crucial. Don't take the jokester to task in front of his boss or other employees; you're likely to antagonize him completely and cause the discomfort to escalate. Call him aside and tell him how you feel. If you are uncomfortable speaking to him alone, do it with others who share your feelings.

- A repeat performance or two usually signals that more than good-natured fun is intended: You're being harassed.

- A complaint to your supervisor or through your company's grievance procedure is your next logical step. (See Chapter 4.)

- If the offensive behavior does not stop after that, you may decide to file a complaint with your state fair employment practices agency or the EEOC. (See Chapter 6, Section G and Chapter 7, Section A.)

5. Innuendos

Sexual and sexist innuendos are usually less direct than jokes, but no less damaging. While at their mildest, they are merely the annoying trademark of the office oaf, they can also be uncomfortably suggestive or even intimidating.

Example: Harry, the newly-hired vice president of a large architectural firm, spots a co-worker, Roya, at the office water cooler. She has a pencil in her hand. "Sure wish you'd help *me* with some dictation," he says.

Roya is annoyed by his remark and finds it demeaning. To stop this sexist behavior from becoming a way of life at the office, she should firmly and clearly tell him so.

Example: Harry and Roya are in Harry's office discussing the site of a planned project. "Sure wish you'd help me with some *dictation*," he says, picking up the microphone to his dictaphone and waving it suggestively in his lap.

The same sentence, but this one far more loaded with sexual innuendo, may justifiably feel like harassment to Roya. Not only should she be upfront about telling him she finds his behavior offensive, it would be wise for her to begin keeping a written record of his unwanted behavior in case he repeats or escalates it. (See Section F.)

There are also many variations of sexist innuendos—a slightly different breed of quip that focuses on some real or imagined difference between the sexes. Some such common quips:

> *Don't even try to talk to Leslie today. She's got a whopping case of PMS.*

> *The only reason Toni got a good performance review is because she'd cry if she didn't.*

> *Mary can't handle that union contract. She's not hard-nosed enough.*

> *It would be a waste to give that promotion to Sarah. Her husband's rich, so she doesn't even need to work.*

Such comments may feel demeaning or embarrassing. Taken at their worst, they reinforce the societal prejudice that women are less capable and less dependable workers because of their gender and all their hormonal swings and surges. Innuendos may also feel particularly hard to combat because women are often chided for "being too sensitive" or for not being able to "keep up with" the men in the office.

If any comment makes you feel uncomfortable, do not laugh or respond with a quip of your own. Take the speaker aside and tell him how you feel. He just might not have known that he was being offensive. If nothing else, he'll be put on notice.

If he persists—or his comments take on the distinct tone of putdowns—consider taking more formal action against him.

D. Deciding Whether To Take Further Action

The truth is frustrating to hear: There is no one right way to respond to sexual harassment on the job. Despite the urgings of people who are leading the fight to ban harassment in the workplace and of books like this one, there still can be valid reasons not to speak up about being sexually harassed. Any complaint may make your harasser agitated, causing him to retaliate against you by making it still more difficult for you to do your job. Your co-workers may suddenly shun you, deciding that it's not worth their while to associate with a troublemaker.

Also, if you take legal action against your harasser, you will probably have to hire a lawyer, spend lots of time and money and be required to publicly air some personal matters such as your mental and physical health. Harassment investigations, whether within your company or through your state or EEOC procedure, often take a long, wearying time—and there is no assurance that they will end the unwanted behavior. So some women don't report harassment because they simply want to get on with their lives.

If the harassment you're experiencing is fairly mild and occasional, you may be able to perform your job effectively and to live with yourself comfortably without complaining about it. It may mean you will spend time and energy at work in the effort to skirt your harasser. Or you may even decide to leave your job to avoid him, although, obviously, this is a practical choice only if you have other equivalent or better job options.

Asserting your right to be treated with dignity and respect is usually your best course. One fact alone should motivate you: Men have traditionally relied on the fact that women often feel too vulnerable and violated to speak up. If you remain mum, you not only acquiesce in this strategy of male dominance, you all but guarantee that it will continue to infect your workplace.

1. Sizing up the situation

The first step in deciding whether to take informal or formal action against sexual harassment is to take a hard and honest look at the behavior that is making you uncomfortable, angry or frustrated. Be as objective as possible about the situation, weeding out the facts from any emotion you feel. It is often helpful at this stage to discuss your situation with a fair-minded friend, asking for a candid evaluation of your perceptions. Use his or her assessment to help you sort out what might be genuine harassment from what may be other workplace politics and life frustrations. This is especially helpful where the workplace behavior that's giving you cause for worry is not seriously threatening.

Example: The head of your department, a man about your age, acts uncomfortable around you, avoiding eye contact. He often fails to send you copies of memos or invite you to meetings that discuss projects in which you're involved. You know that he invited other co-workers to social events at his home and this, too, makes you feel cast out. You feel that you are treated differently than your co-workers, and that the difference may lead to you doing your job less well than you could. But you're not sure if you're being subjected to sexual harassment.

The best assessment that a knowledgeable friend could give you in this situation is to be wary. Although the lack of eye contact and lack of social invitations may make you feel excluded and shunned, they should not affect your job performance. However, consistently cutting you out of workplace information is more serious—and may amount to sexual harassment if it deprives you of the means you need to do your job well. It's sensible to begin to keep notes as to how your work is made more difficult and may be less effective. Spend some time thinking about how you and your supervisor can work to reduce the tension between you.

ALAS, I WAS NEVER SCUTTLED. SOMETIMES I WOULD LOOK UP HOPEFULLY FROM MY TYPEWRITER TO SEE THREE OR FOUR SCUTTLERS SKULKING IN THE DOORWAY, MULLING IT OVER, BUT THE DECISION WAS ALWAYS THE SAME—TOO YOUNG, TOO PALE, TOO FLAT-CHESTED. CLEARLY UNSCUTTLABLE.—HELEN GURLEY BROWN, EDITOR IN CHIEF OF *COSMOPOLITAN* MAGAZINE, RECALLING SCUTTLING—A RITE AT A FORMER WORKPLACE IN WHICH MALE HIGHER-UPS CHASED SECRETARIES AND TORE THEIR PANTIES DOWN

Example: You used to be the only person working in Accounts Receivable. Recently, two new employees have been hired. You think they may take over your job responsibilities completely, and you will be demoted back to your old position as a secretary.

To make matters worse, one of the new hires, John, has twice asked you on dates—once for a drink after work and another time to a cafe for lunch. You turned him down both times, the second time telling him you are engaged. John acted surprised. He said that at his old workplace, employees often ate lunch and socialized together; he meant nothing untoward. You suspect that he really wanted to get you alone to pick your brain about the specifics of your job so he could take it over.

In this situation, a friend might best tell you to lighten up. If you are insecure about the status of your job, talk with your supervisor, but don't blame John. His behavior isn't unreasonable so far; he may have merely been attempting to be friendly. You've made it clear that you don't want to socialize with him, so it's probably best to assume he will take you at your word. But just in case he doesn't, restate your reasons for wanting to keep the relationship strictly professional.

Example: Your co-worker, Frank, seems to spend an inordinate amount of time in your office. Each time, he closes the door behind him—and closed doors are not de rigueur at your workplace. Frank claims he needs to talk with you "because he respects your opinion" on how to package new compact discs for your employer, a music production company. You work as a film editor and have no real expertise or interest in packaging—and you resent the need to stay late to make up for the worktime you lose during Frank's frequent visits.

While Frank has made no sexual overtures, you are vaguely bothered by his too-frequent attention, recurring questions about your social life and lingering eye contact. You have not confronted him because you don't want to make an enemy or be seen as a someone who doesn't care about the company's success.

Here, a wise friend would encourage you to speak up to Frank to firmly let him know that his behavior is making it more difficult for you to do your job. If he persists, consider writing him a concise letter or telling a supervisor how you feel. (See Section F, below.)

2. What to do when you need to do more

For some women in some situations, the strategies discussed for fighting back against harassment may not suffice. They may need to take extra steps, such as:

- Making a special effort to educate themselves about how to recognize and fight back against harassment. This book, as well as a number of recently published pamphlets can help in this effort. (See the Appendix.)

- Meeting with other similarly situated women to discuss the common harassment problems and ways to deal with them. In many communities, particularly medium to large cities, there are ongoing support groups established expressly for this purpose. (See the Appendix.)

- Trying to educate management about the perils, pitfalls and seriousness of sexual harassment on the job. If your employee handbook makes no mention of the company's stance against harassment and defining how to recognize it, ask management to add one. If there is no sexual harassment policy, lobby for one. (See Chapter 4, Sections C and D.)

- Taking immediate legal action under your state laws (see Chapter 7) or with the EEOC (see Chapter 6)—especially if the harassment involves violence or the threat of it.

IF PERTICULIAR CARE AND ATTENTION IS NOT PAID TO THE LAIDIES WE ARE DETERMINED TO FOMENT A REBELION, AND WILL NOT HOLD OURSELVES BOUND BY ANY LAWS IN WHICH WE HAVE NO VOICE, OR REPRESENTATION.—ABIGAIL ABIGAIL ADAMS, IN A LETTER TO HER HUSBAND JOHN, MARCH 31, 1776

CONSULTING THE PROFESSIONALS

Results of an October 10, 1991, poll by the National Association of Female Executives:

- 77% of all those polled said that sexual harassment was a problem in the workplace

- 53% responded that they had been sexually harassed at work

- 64% of those did not report it

- Of the 36% who did report it, most felt that the problem was not addressed satisfactorily. They were made to resign, quit or transfer to a position they didn't want.

E. Confronting Your Harasser

The key in assessing whether behavior is sexual harassment is whether it is unwanted. If it is, ask that it be stopped. Surprisingly often—some experts say up to 90% of the time—this works.

When confronted directly, harassment is especially likely to end if it is at a fairly low level: off-color jokes, inappropriate comments about your appearance, repeated requests for dates, tacky cartoons tacked onto the office refrigerator.

Saying no in a tangible way does more than assert your determination to stop the behavior. It is also a crucial first step if you later decide to take more formal action against the harassment, whether through your company's complaint procedure or through the legal system. And give serious thought to documenting what's going on; your case will be stronger if you can later prove that the harassment continued after you confronted the harasser.

PROCEED CAUTIOUSLY IF THERE'S VIOLENCE

Sexual harassment is sometimes associated with violent behavior. If you fear your harasser, do not confront him alone. Alternatives include getting the support of co-workers who will agree to confront him with you, filing a complaint with your company (see Chapter 4), filing a confidential harassment claim with your state agency or EEOC (see Chapter 6) or filing another court action (see Chapter 8). If his behavior is truly frightening, consider reporting it to local police.

---

1. Tell him what you don't want

If possible, deal directly with the harassment when it occurs. But if your harasser surprises you with an obnoxious gesture or comment that catches you completely off-guard—a common tactic—you may be too flabbergasted to respond at once. Or if you did respond, you may not have expressed yourself clearly. Either way, talk to him the next day.

Keep the conversation brief. Try to speak to your harasser privately—out of the hearing range of supervisors and co-workers. At the same time, avoid giving the appearance that you want a social meeting. Asking him to meet you away from work in a bar or restaurant is likely to give the wrong impression.

Do not smile, touch your harasser or give any other mixed messages when you speak.

This is not a good time to use humor to make your point. Joking may be too easily misunderstood or interpreted as a sign that you don't take the situation seriously yourself. For example, if a male co-worker flashes you a picture of a couple having sex in an unusual position and you find the picture offensive, do not say: "Unfortunately, I'm not that flexible." A better response might be: "I'm offended by these kinds of pictures. In the future, please respect my privacy."

It is usually better to make a direct request that a specific kind of behavior stop, rather than to describe to your harasser how you feel. For example, saying: "I am uncomfortable with this," may be enough to get the point across to some, but the subtlety will surely be lost on others. And of course, making you uncomfortable may be just the effect the harasser was after.

Make your point with simple, direct sentences like these:

Please do not touch me when we talk.

I will gladly discuss the BFT account with you during workhours, but I'm not interested in having dinner with you.

Please remove that picture you left on my desk—that's my private workspace.

I'm not at all interested in that kind of movie.

Keep in mind that you're not the one whose behavior is inexcusable. There is no need to offer excuses or apologies, such as: "My boyfriend wouldn't like it if we met at your apartment to discuss our new project."

If the thought of speaking up to your harasser makes you nervous, rehearse. Ask a friend to stand in for the harasser and attempt to anticipate how he might respond to you; practice your response.

If the harasser persists after you have said no, or changes tacks to performing other annoying and unwanted behavior, repeat your request that he stop, using stronger language. You may want to point out to him that his behavior is illegal—and that it is seriously affecting your ability to do your job. Let him know that if he persists, you are prepared to take action against the harassment—such as reporting the situation to company authorities or filing a legal action. Begin preparing for a formal action by documenting the situation. (See Section F.2.)

2. Put it in writing

If your harasser persists, write him a letter, spelling out what behavior you object to and why. Also specify what you want to happen next. If you feel the situation is serious or bound to escalate, let him know that you will take action against the harassment if it doesn't stop at once. If your company has a written policy against harassment, you may want to attach a copy of it to your letter.

SAMPLE LETTER

February 1, 199X

Charles Gazda
McNulty Company
Thiscity, Thisstate 00000

Mr. Gazda:

During this morning's meeting, you twice interrupted my sales presentation to comment on the way I was dressed.

I found this demeaning and feel that it detracted greatly from the overall professionalism of our pitch.

During your portion of our presentation, and in all our time at work, I have treated you with respect. In the future, please show me the same respect by confining your comments to business matters.

Sincerely,

Marcia Malini

I CAN'T IMAGINE ANY MOTHER NOT TEACHING HER DAUGHTER HOW TO TELL SOMEONE "NICELY" TO BACK OFF. TO SAY, "THAT'S NOT MY TASTE," "I DON'T APPRECIATE THAT KIND OF HUMOR," OR "WHY DON'T YOU SAVE THAT FOR THE BOYS." YOU DON'T HAVE TO GET HUFFY. — RESPONSE OF LISA MAC, 40, WHEN ASKED THE QUESTION "HAVE YOU EVER EXPERIENCED SEXUAL HARASSMENT?" IN AN ON-THE-STREET INTERVIEW, *SAN FRANCISCO CHRONICLE*, NOV. 17, 1991

SAMPLE LETTER

February 10, 199X

Frank Stroh
Booktale Corporation
Thiscity, Thisstate 00000

Mr. Stroh:

Two weeks ago, you commented about my legs, told me I'd look better and "more accessible" in shorter skirts and asked me to meet you after work for a drink. I told you I was not interested in a social relationship and that I'd prefer that you didn't comment about my body and clothing.

Today, you brushed up against me as we passed in the hallway--and again said you "were anxious to see more of me" and asked me to meet you in the bar on the first floor of our office building "during the time after work and before my husband is expected home."

Your persistent comments on my clothing and requests to meet socially are upsetting to me and, as I have made clear, are unwelcome. I want our relationship to be purely professional, as it was during the first six months I worked at Booktale.

Should you be unwilling to comply with my request to conduct yourself more acceptably in the workplace, I will ask our Human Resources Department to investigate.

Sincerely,

Lizanne Romanowski

SAMPLE LETTER

October 1, 199X

Ernest Configliano
Consulters, Unlimited
Thiscity, Thisstate 00000

Mr. Configliano:

This morning, while reviewing the draft of the complaint
in the Kyler case, you brushed against my breast and twice
touched my buttocks while ostensibly reaching for other
office materials.

As I told you last week, I am offended by you touching me
in these suggestive ways and find it to be totally inappropriate workplace behavior.

I have attached pages of our company's policy against sexual harassment. Note that your behavior not only clearly
violates the letter and intent of our policy, it is also
prohibited by both state and federal law.

Should you persist in your behavior, I will take action
against it at once by bringing a copy of this letter when
I discuss this distressing matter with your supervisor,
Cathy Henderson.

Sincerely,

Rachel Bornstein

Before you send the letter to the person you feel is harassing you, ask the
opinion of someone you trust as to whether your letter is clear and to the
point. Experience indicates that a surprising number of women have been too
nice, too indirect—and therefore not very effective in writing down what they
mean.

Make a copy of your letter before you send it. Keep your copy in a safe place away from work, preferably at home. If the situation remains or escalates, the letter will be great evidence that you were forthright and prompt in letting the harasser know that his behavior was wrong.

In most cases, the recipient of your letter will not respond or write back to you—but he may express surprise or shock about your view of his behavior. He will likely be concerned about the possibility that you will go public with the charges. But his reaction to your letter is not as important as the fact that you have sent it—making your feelings and intentions clear and beginning to document the unpleasant situation.

Best of all, in a great many situations, this will stop the harassment.

RESULTS OF A RECENT RANDOM TELEPHONE SURVEY OF 1,000 LOS ANGELES RESIDENTS CONDUCTED BY DR. BARBARA GUTEK, PSYCHOLOGIST AT THE UNIVERSITY OF ARIZONA BUSINESS SCHOOL:

- 67% OF THE MEN SAID THEY WOULD BE COMPLIMENTED IF PROPOSITIONED BY A FEMALE CO-WORKER; ONLY 17% OF THE WOMEN SAID A WORKPLACE PROPOSITION WOULD BE A COMPLIMENT.

- 10% OF THE WOMEN QUESTIONED SAID THEY LEFT A JOB BECAUSE OF SEXUAL HARASSMENT.

HOW TO SAY NO—AND BE HEARD

Elizabeth Evans, a psychotherapist in private practice in Berkeley, California, also has extensive experience teaching classes in assertiveness and communication skills, primarily aimed to help women in the workplace. She urges the following formula for a woman who wants to speak up to her workplace harasser.

Take the scenario where you are being pestered by a male co-worker or supervisor for a lunch date you don't want. I recommend starting out with a rather benign statement the first time you speak to him. You might say: "I am comfortable with our business relationship, but I'm not comfortable carrying it any further—even for lunch."

But even more important than your words is how you say them. Pay special attention to your body as you speak—posture, vocal tone, eye contact, facial expression, personal distance.

Aim for a relaxed, confident stance. Do not hunch or strut. Take time to adjust your position so that you're neither looking up at nor down at him. The tone of your voice should be even and firm. Look him in the eye. If standing, stand at a distance that feels comfortable—not too close, not so far that you have to raise your voice unnaturally. Make only appropriate gestures. Do not wring your hands, look down, stare, move in toward the person, or shake your finger under his nose.

If he persists in the unwanted behavior, make an escalated assertion, something like: "I've told you three times that I am not interested in any other relationship. I would like you to stop asking me."

If the harassment persists: "The answer is no and please don't ask again."

Another thing a woman can do is to reward the behavior that she wants repeated. For example, at the end of a meeting, you might say: "Thanks, John, for letting me express my opinions. I noticed you really listened to me."

F. What To Do If the Harassment Continues

Serious harassers will persist in their behavior—even after you have clearly made known that their advances or other wrongful conduct are unwanted. You will need to consider your next move.

You can choose to remain on the job, keep your mouth shut and hope that the harassment will stop. In some cases, the harassers simply wear themselves out or move on to another target. But most do not. In fact, sensing an easy target, many hardcore harassers escalate their obnoxious behavior.

It is impossible to offer foolproof advice on how to respond to every situation involving serious sexual harassment. But it's usually best to get official help either from your employer or a state or federal agency. Prepare to do this by collecting as much detailed evidence as possible about the specifics of your harassment.

Two areas are especially important.

Your reactions to the advances. You will want to be able to show as clearly as possible that the advances were unwanted, and

The timing of your complaint. The more quickly you confront your harasser—and if the harassment continues, make an official complaint—the more credibly your complaint is likely to be treated.

Here are some practical suggestions.

1. Collect evidence

Be sure to save any offensive letters, photographs, cards or notes you receive. And if you were made to feel uncomfortable because of jokes, pin-ups or cartoons posted at work, confiscate them—or at least make copies. An anonymous, obnoxious photo or joke posted on a bulletin board is not anyone else's personal property, so you are free to take it down and keep it as evidence. If that's not possible, photograph the workplace walls. Note the dates the offensive material was posted—and whether there were hostile reactions when you took it down or asked another person to do so.

2. Keep a detailed journal

Write down the specifics of everything that feels like harassment. Include the names of everyone involved, what happened, where and when it took place. If anyone else saw or heard the harassment, note that as well. Be as specific as possible about what was said and done—and how it affected you, your health or job performance.

Also include details of harassing or annoying phone calls you receive at work or home—including dates, times, lengths of time that the calls lasted and summaries of what was said. Again, keep this journal in a safe place, preferably at home.

THE ONLY REASON I PUT UP WITH IT AS LONG AS I DID IS I REALLY WANTED TO ADVANCE. YOU PUT UP WITH A LOT TO TRY AND BE ONE OF THE CROWD. I FEEL VERY GUILTY FOR HAVING PUT UP WITH IT.— DR. FRANCES CONLEY, A NEUROSURGEON WHO RESIGNED FROM STANFORD UNIVERSITY'S MEDICAL SCHOOL AFTER 25 YEARS, CITING HARASSMENT AND DEMEANING ATTITUDES BY MALE COLLEAGUES

SAMPLE JOURNAL ENTRIES

April 24, 199X

On his way in to work today, my supervisor Robert Neeson
stopped by my office. As I took off my coat, he stepped
behind to help, then clasped me against him with one arm.
He said: "You look so sexy with your hair down--just like
the star of a really hot movie I saw last night. Do you
like to watch porno movies?" I felt a little scared, but I
said no, took his arm off my shoulder and sat down at my
desk and began to return phone calls. It was early--about
7:45--and no one else was at work yet.

April 26, 199X

When I came back from lunch today, there was an
interoffice memo left on my chair that said: "Here's your
look-alike. Please see me about this.--Bob" Attached was a
picture of a nude woman with long brown hair and the
caption Pleasure Me. The woman was on her hands and knees.
A man was holding a gun to her head. This afternoon, I
told Mr. Neeson that I found the picture offensive and
asked him not to show me any more. He said: "It's too bad
for you. Debby really went for that flick in a big way."
This was the week after Deborah Utner had been promoted
from my position to become Neeson's assistant.

April 27, 199X

At midnight, Mr. Neeson came to my apartment door with a
bouquet of flowers in his hand. He looked drunk and
slurred his words. When I refused to let him in, he became
angry and shouted: "You don't know what you're missing"
and "You little bitch, I'll make sure your life gets
harder." He shouted and swore for about ten minutes, until
Burt Griffith, my upstairs neighbor, called down to ask
whether he should call the police.

3. Talk with friends

Sexual harassment usually takes place in private—with no witnesses—and a later legal action will often turn on how reliable the person complaining is considered to be. Promptly telling other people you trust about the harassment is an excellent way to create potentially valuable witnesses to verify that you were angry or upset about the harassment. And of course, telling another person about the harassment is likely to make it seem less threatening or scary, less like a terrible secret.

If you do not complain to or confide in someone when the harassment occurs, an investigator, judge or jury evaluating the situation later may conclude that you were not really offended by the incident—or that it didn't occur as you claim.

4. Talk with co-workers

Talking with co-workers can be somewhat trickier than talking with friends. You don't want to jeopardize their jobs or bring down their morale at work, but you may need to enlist their help. This is especially important if the co-workers have seen or heard your harasser at work and can back up your claim. Being familiar with your office innerworkings, he or she might also be in the best position to discuss your options in dealing with the harassment.

Finally, if you want additional seasoned advice about how to deal with your situation and protect your safety, or want an experienced assessment of whether you are being sexually harassed from a legal standpoint, contact a sexual harassment hotline or support group. (See the Appendix for contact details.)

BEWARE OF RETALIATION

In possibly volatile cases in some workplaces, do not overlook the possibility that some company witnesses may be blackmailed with the threat—often unspoken—of losing their jobs or being demoted if they cooperate with you in documenting or investigating a sexual harassment complaint. While retaliation is illegal, it is often difficult to prove. If possible, try to document the harassment by talking with witnesses both inside and outside the company.

---

5. Organize a group

If sexual harassment is pervasive and taken for granted and management appears oblivious to it, communicate your concerns to other employees. You may find that several of your co-workers have been subjected to a similar kind of harassment. Certainly if your workplace is poisoned by sexual materials, comments and jokes, you should have little difficulty rounding up allies. You can then provide a great support network for one another.

If several of your co-workers have been harassed by the same person or in the same way, several simultaneous complaints about the behavior will speak more loudly than a single one. If you are still considering whether you want to take action, you will likely find it empowering to have witnesses: If your harasser uses verbal harassment, try to make sure there are other people within hearing range when he is likely to speak to you.

But when talking with other co-workers, be discreet. Talk at first only with those who may have been harassed by the same person or who you know are likely to be sensitive to the issue. Meet in private, away from work—and preferably before or after work hours.

6. Get a copy of your work records

If your employer has conducted periodic evaluations of your work, make sure you have copies. In fact, you may want to ask for a copy of your entire personnel file—before you tip your hand that you are considering taking action against a harassing co-worker. Your records will be particularly persuasive evidence if your evaluations have been good and your employer later retaliates by trying to transfer or fire you, claiming poor job performance.

If the atmosphere becomes particularly negatively charged at your workplace, you may want to guard against your records being changed or destroyed. To do this, mail a copy of your records to yourself, but do not open it. Save the sealed, postmarked envelope for evidence.

GETTING STRENGTH FROM NUMBERS

Here are some practical ideas for organizing allies in your workplace.

Find out who else cares about the problem. Sexual harassment is an issue that affects many people. Talk with co-workers you know and ask them to talk with the people they know who may also be concerned about it.

Agree on a plan. Get together—at lunch, after work, or in the evening at someone else's home. Identify who in the company you need to deal with. List concrete suggestions to improve the situation. Figure out how to get more information if you need it. Decide whether the best tactic is a letter, a petition, a meeting with the boss or some other work action.

Take action. Involve as many people as you can, and act as a group.

Spread the word about your successes. When others see you have made a difference, they'll want to join in. Once you've gotten started, you might decide to have an ongoing group to learn more about the issues at your workplace and continue to win improvements.

Keep it going. A support or advocacy group can give workers a collective voice to raise issues of concern. Since such a high percentage of women workers have been sexually harassed at some time, it is likely that in any organization of women, several members will be able to share experiences, help you plan a course of action, deal with day-to-day stresses of the situation, reinforce your attitudes and otherwise advise and support you.

If you belong to a book group, church group, professional women's group or some other organization, you might also find help among the members. Local chapters of special interest groups, such as 9 to 5, National Association of Working Women, or Federally Employed Women have many resources for their members who want to start these type of groups. (See the Appendix for contact details.)[6]

---

[6] Adapted from "The New 9to5 Office Worker Survival Guide," published by 9to5, National Association for Working Women (1990).

7. Build your own strength

Acknowledge that you are in the midst of a very trying situation. It is wearying to put up with harassment on the job—and going forward with a complaint about it will also require a great deal of energy.

Make a special effort to spend time with friends or family members who will support and encourage you without being judgmental. Help reduce the increased stress in your life by setting aside time for activities you enjoy that help you feel calm and strong—exercise, yoga, massage, reading, other hobbies.

Learn more about assertiveness and effective communication principles—many of them offer simple ways to help build your confidence and get you centered on solving your workplace problems. There are several good books now out on the subjects; browse through a bookstore for one that appeals to you. Many companies offer workshop or courses in assertiveness or workplace communication. If your employer does not, check at a local adult school or community college. And, as discussed above, many communities have support groups you can join.

8. Consider filing a formal action

If you have sent your harasser a letter demanding that he stop (as discussed in Section E.2), but he hasn't been deterred, you may want to take more forceful action. Consider giving a copy of your letter to his supervisor—along with a memo explaining that his behavior has become more outrageous.

If the harassment still does not abate, send the letter to the next-ranked worker or official at your workplace. Include a cover letter in which you offer your own remedy for the situation—something realistic that might help end the discomfort, such as transferring the harasser to a more distant worksite.

If it's your own supervisor who has been harassing you, consider asking to be assigned a different supervisor.

9. Use formal complaint procedures

If you have followed the steps suggested in this chapter that seem feasible to you but the harassment continues, your next option is to pursue any procedure your company has established for handling harassment. (See Chapter 4 for guidance.)

> **I**T IS ONLY AFTER A GREAT DEAL OF AGONIZING CONSIDERATION THAT I AM ABLE TO TALK OF THESE UNPLEASANT MATTERS TO ANYONE EXCEPT MY CLOSEST FRIENDS.—PROFESSOR ANITA HILL, TO A SENATE JUDICIAL PANEL DURING OCTOBER, 1991 CONFIRMATION HEARINGS FOR U.S. SUPREME COURT NOMINEE CLARENCE THOMAS

CHAPTER

4

Workplace Policies and Programs

A. The Importance of a Sexual Harassment Policy 4/3
   1. Benefits to employees 4/3
   2. Benefits to employers 4/4

B. Evaluating Your Workplace 4/5
   1. Evaluate the sexual hostility 4/6
   2. Measure the comfort level 4/6
   3. Take a reading of the office gossip quotient 4/6
   4. Look at the professional acceptance level for women employees 4/6
   5. Compare the promotion records 4/7
   6. Look at whether sex is traded for preferential treatment 4/7

C. Effective Sexual Harassment Policies 4/8
   1. Hallmarks of a good policy 4/9
   2. Sample sexual harassment policy 4/13

D. Complaint Procedures and Investigations 4/17
   1. Sample complaint form 4/17
   2. Workplace investigations 4/21

E. Training Sessions 4/25
   1. Tips on choosing workplace training 4/27
   2. Effective training programs 4/29

F. Sexual Harassment Monitoring Survey 4/32

G. Special Procedures for Some Employees 4/36
   1. U.S. government employees 4/36
   2. Union members 4/37

This chapter sets out the policies and procedures an employer can adopt to monitor, root out and deal with sexual harassment on the job. It also guides employees who wish to lobby for a sexual harassment policy in their workplaces—or to check the strengths and weaknesses of an existing policy.

In the past, most employee manuals were little more than puff pieces—welcoming new employees, extolling the company's virtues and, occasionally, spelling out a few specifics, such as vacation and fringe benefits and the company stance on smoking in the workplace.

Now, however, employee manuals are used both to define and obtain workplace rights. And they also act as subtle legal contracts: An employer can set out the conditions of employment in a manual. And an employee can legally enforce them: insurance benefits, pay for overtime and, increasingly, a firm policy against sexual harassment and a procedure to enforce it.

Courts occasionally require a company to write up a comprehensive policy as part of the legal relief ordered in a sexual harassment case. But more often these days, the impetus to rid the workplace of sexual harassment comes from within. The link between decreased productivity and workplace harassment is now well-documented. As a result, more companies are taking an active role, adopting formal policies to prevent sexual harassment where possible and to deal with it when it occurs.

But not all employers are this enlightened. Some, especially smaller companies, still act as if ignoring the problem of sexual harassment will make it go away. Experience demonstrates that where an employer's feet drag on this issue, employees—especially if they band together—can initiate or improve policies and procedures for enforcing them. And this is not only true at huge corporations: car dealerships, plant nurseries and school districts can and should respond with action.

A. The Importance of a Sexual Harassment Policy

A well-crafted sexual harassment policy, which can be incorporated as part of an employee manual or set out separately, can offer both employees and employers guidance and certainty in dealing with harassment in the workplace.

1. Benefits to employees

If an employer has a clear written policy prohibiting harassment, all who work there will have a firmer idea of what behavior will not be tolerated in the workplace. If a woman is harassed, a strong policy can guide her as to how to take action against it.

Despite some paranoid perceptions, very few women who bring complaints about sexual harassment on the job are seeking big bucks or vengeance. Their goal, at least initially, is to make the harassment stop—and to take all practical steps to see that it stays stopped. It is typically only where an employer offers no fair way to resolve the problem that sexual harassment complaints evolve into lawsuits.

But if an employer doesn't take heed of complaints, a woman armed with a sexual harassment policy that has been ignored will often be in a better position to pursue more formal legal options to end the harassment.

TO END SEXUAL HARASSMENT IS TO SEPARATE WORK AND SEX AND THUS IMPROVE BOTH.—FROM "SEXUAL HARASSMENT IN THE WORKPLACE," A PAMPHLET PUBLISHED BY THE FEDERALLY EMPLOYED WOMEN LEGAL AND EDUCATION FUND

2. Benefits to employers

Women who are sexually harassed on the job often become distressed, depressed, frightened or angry. It's not easy to hold a job while also working full-time to keep a harasser at bay. And the challenge often takes its toll: Sexually harassed workers often become demoralized and miss work—and even while on the job, are much less able to concentrate and to work efficiently.

All of this runs counter to every employer's prime goal: workplace productivity. A number of recent workplace studies show the high cost of tolerating sexual harassment:

- Over 25% of women who are sexually harassed on the job use leave time to avoid the uncomfortable work situation.

- At least 15% of women who are harassed at work quit their jobs because of it.

- Nearly 50% of those harassed try to ignore it—and they suffer about a 10% drop in productivity. The harassed woman's peers who know of the situation also suffer a 2% drop in productivity.

But perhaps money talks most loudly: Ignoring sexual harassment can cost the average company up to $6.7 million a year in absenteeism, employee turnover, low morale and low productivity.[1]

In addition to these indirect costs, an employer that tolerates sexual harassment risks the high administrative costs involved in EEOC and other agency complaint investigations, as well as the pricey possibility of a successful lawsuit against it. Since many employers hire expensive corporate lawyers at the first scent of legal trouble, the costs of defending a sexual harassment lawsuit are extremely high.

And of course, if the harassed employee wins, costs to the employer will be even higher—sometimes a lot higher. Several employers have been hard hit with jury verdicts ranging into several million dollars for emotional distress, lost wages and wrongful discharge. (See Chapter 8, Section A.)

---

[1] Sandroff, R., "Sexual Harassment in the Fortune 500," *Working Woman* (Dec. 1988), pp. 69-73.

IS AN EMPLOYER LIABLE FOR WORKPLACE HARASSMENT?

The federal law and many state laws make employers liable for sexual harassment in the workplace. However, this is not always true.

Harassment by a co-worker. Managers are responsible for sexual harassment by one employee against another if they knew about it or should have known about the harassment and did nothing to stop it. If you are being harassed by a co-worker, report it to a supervisor. That is an essential step for the employer's awareness—and liability.

Harassment by a supervisor. Employers are almost always held responsible for sexual harassment by the supervisors and managers who work there, whether the heads of the company knew about it or not. If the supervisor is the one who's harassing you, it's not as critical to report the offensive behavior to another person, but the better approach is to tell some higher-up in the company, if possible.

B. Evaluating Your Workplace

In a campaign against sexual harassment, it is not enough for employers simply to adopt a sexual harassment policy from a book. And it is not enough for employees to go about their daily work as if the written policy had solved the problem.

For a sexual harassment policy to be effective, it must be tailored to the needs and sensibilities of the employees. And it must be respected and enforced by the employer, not merely given lip service.

If your employer does not yet have a policy against sexual harassment, or has a poor or inadequately enforced one, use the following list to assess whether the damaging effects of harassment may be taking their toll. The checklist should also help flag the particular trouble spots you most need to address in creating or updating a policy.

1. Evaluate the sexual hostility

Is there friction between individuals or groups that seems sex-based? Are there complaints or grievances about promotions or work performance that often pit men and women against each other? Do you often hear jokes that might be considered sexist? Check the walls. Are there pin-ups, cartoons or jokes posted that are aimed at one sex or another—and that could seem demeaning?

2. Measure the comfort level

Is there a lack of camaraderie between males and females? Do employees tend to cluster in groups of the same gender during breaks and lunchtime? Even the chosen seating arrangement at a meeting or office party may be telling. If men and women typically head for opposite sides of the room, it may signal that there is sexually-based discomfort beneath the surface.

Overly friendly office behavior can signal a problem, too. Check whether there is an inordinate amount of hugging, kissing or other touching that seems out of place or that seems to make anyone uncomfortable.

3. Take a reading of the office gossip quotient

How much backbiting and mudslinging with a sexual content goes on in a business day? For example, are there a lot of whispered conversations and averted glances when members of the opposite sex walk by? Is there an un-due amount of talk about employees' personal lives? Is there frequent boasting about sexual exploits and dates?

4. Look at the professional acceptance level for women employees

Are there some tasks that are consistently labeled Woman's Work and others that are automatically assigned to men? Do men congregate in Old Boy Networks and freeze out the women?

Are men and women equally represented—and given equal credit and recognition—on important projects and on the workplace committees with real clout, such as those that target new projects that will determine the company's growth? And how about the gender division on the more drudging tasks, such as planning holiday parties or stocking the company lunchroom?

5. Compare the promotion records

Are men promoted faster than women with similar skills and seniority? Are competent women routinely placed in lower-level jobs because of sexual stereotyping?

Take a look at the numbers of men and women who hold the best-paying or most responsible positions in the company. Pay special attention to the employees promoted to those positions recently. While it is arguably possible for an employer to have a cadre of mostly senior male employees who got started with the company before a significant number of women worked there, it is plainly inexcusable for that pattern not to change.

6. Look at whether sex is traded for preferential treatment

Do women who flirt or act in other sexually suggestive ways seem to be on a fast track, while others are consistently passed over for better jobs? Are some employees routinely called in to closed door sessions that seem overlong or unnecessary?

■ ■ ■

If your workplace scores low in its sexual harassment IQ, your strongest tack may be to meet with others who share your concerns. Take the time to let everyone voice their concerns. Assuming you eventually reach common ground on what needs to be done to combat sexual harassment in your workplace, request a meeting with the personnel manager or a person in a similar position in management.

Alert him or her to the problem and urge that an excellent sexual harassment policy be adopted at once—or your current one changed. (See Section C for guidance and a sample policy.) Suggest that the most effective policies against harassment are collaborative efforts by both employers and employees. Savvy managers will grasp your point. After all, a policy handed down by management without any input from employees is likely both to fall short of meeting the needs of the workplace, and to be met with resentment as a dictate from on high. (See Section F for a Sexual Harassment Monitoring Survey—an additional method that can be used for evaluating the workplace.)

C. Effective Sexual Harassment Policies

An effective sexual harassment policy discourages harassment. And it should also encourage employees to report all serious incidents of harassment promptly—with an eye to eliminating them. Employees cannot be required to report sexual harassment; that would be coercive and illegal. But if there is a sensible and sensitively written policy against harassment, backed by good policies to deal with it as confidentially as possible and to prevent retaliation against the person making the complaint, most employees will gratefully comply.

A model policy is offered here (see Section C.2), but keep in mind that a sexual harassment policy will be effective only if it is appropriate and realistic for your workplace. A conservative, multi-tiered accounting conglomerate based in New York City, for example, may find it reasonable to have more buttoned-down strictures on permissible workplace behavior than a small computer graphics company based in San Francisco or a tractor dealership in Pocatello, Idaho.

Also, to be effective, a sexual harassment policy must be clear and comprehensible. A growing number of employers pridefully point to the fact that they have written sexual harassment policies. However, a quick look at most policies reveals that they are so replete with legalese and cross-references to other workplace documents that they are more confusing than curing. Be sure your company adopts a policy that is meaningful and written so that it can be easily understood by everyone.

Finally, a sexual harassment policy should be seen by all as a work in progress. It will surely need to be changed with the times and perhaps even altered to reflect the changing roles and numbers of employees. To make sure that this happens, the policy should be reviewed and amended regularly. One good way to do this is to pass it around to all employees each year for comments and suggestions.

1. Hallmarks of a good policy

The most effective sexual harassment policies have a number of common elements.

A statement that sexual harassment will not be tolerated. A short, direct statement that sexual harassment will not be endured is most effective. In addition, let employees know that sexual harassment is against the law.

Define what behavior is prohibited. This used to be no small task. Fortunately, after struggling for years to come up with meaningful definitions of prohibited harassing behavior, the EEOC, legislatures and courts have made considerable progress. Today, it is possible to provide a number of clear definitions and rules. For example, it is clearly sexual harassment to suggest that future promotions will be bestowed in exchange for sexual favors.

While even the best policy cannot set out every kind of prohibited behavior, a good one should go beyond declarative language to list some specific examples. For example, a sexual harassment policy may ban:

- Verbal harassment, including making sexual comments about a person's body, telling sexual jokes or stories, spreading rumors about a co-worker's sex life, asking or telling about sexual fantasies, preferences or history

- Non-verbal harassment, such as giving unwanted personal gifts, following a person, staring at a person's body, displaying sexually suggestive material such as pornographic photos

- Physical harassment, including touching yourself in a sexual manner in front of another person, brushing up against another person suggestively.

Spell out what action will be taken for first-time offenses and repeated unacceptable conduct. Punishments should be appropriate, certain and reasonably strict. Appropriate action can range from a written warning in the employee's personnel file to counseling, suspension from work, transfer to a different position or dismissal.

STATES ACT AGAINST EMPLOYER INACTION

A few states have taken the initiative against sexual harassment in the workplace by passing laws that require employers to take action against it.

- California makes it unlawful for employers, labor organizations or employment training programs to fail to take all reasonable steps necessary to prevent discrimination and harassment (Cal. Govt. Code §12940(i)).

- In Minnesota, all state schoolboards must develop policies against sexual harassment and sexual violence and post them conspicuously (Minn. Stats. Ann. §127.46 (1992 Supp.)).

- Maine requires all employers to display a poster defining sexual harassment, giving examples of harassing behavior and describing the state's complaint process. It also requires employers with 15 or more employees to train all new employees on how to recognize and take steps against against harassment at work (Maine Rev. Stat. Ann. Ch. 47 §§806 & 7, subchapter IV-B).

Give guidelines on how to report harassment. Detail how, when and where employees can complain about harassment. For example, if the first step is to contact a particular person within the company, make clear exactly how to do that. The complaint process should be as confidential as possible. If a form is required to initiate a complaint, a copy should be included in every employee handbook—or at least be easily accessible. (See Section D.1 for a sample.)

Provide an alternative to employees who do not wish to file the complaint with their own supervisors, some of whom may either be responsible for the harassment or guilty of ignoring it. Make it possible to report the harassment to any other supervisor—or to anyone on a panel of employees designated to handle company grievances.

Provide for prompt and confidential investigations. Despite all best intentions to keep the matter hushed, news of a harassment investigation tends to circulate fast. And people often take sides quickly. Proceeding speedily and appropriately with the investigation helps take the strain from the workplace, stems the tides of worry and gossip and, above all, is the best way to get at the truth of the matter. During the investigation, as during the initial complaint filing, every effort should be made to respect the confidentiality of all involved.

If possible, appoint an outside investigator to look into the harassment complaint—or at least someone from outside the department where the problem was reported. During the investigation, both the accused and the accuser should be promptly interviewed, along with any potential witnesses to the alleged harassment and anyone who may have experienced similar behavior. (Investigations for sexual harassment are discussed in detail in Section D.2.)

BEWARE OF GAG RULES

Some harassment policies require the person making the complaint to sign a statement swearing not to discuss the matter with anyone inside the company during the investigation. Be leery of such requirements. Should your case later go to court or to the EEOC, proof that you discussed the harassment with others while it was going on may be some of the most powerful evidence in your favor. Harassment policies that prohibit confiding in others are often cynically penned by company lawyers who are trying to bottle up legitimate harassment complaints.

Make the results known. A report of the findings of a harassment investigation and a notation about whether any action is to be taken should be given to both the harassed employee and the accused harasser.

Take a strong stand against retaliation. The fear of retaliation is what keeps many employees from reporting even the most egregious workplace harassment. The retaliation may come from the harasser who, as a manager or supervisor, transfers an employee to an undesirable position, changes her work duties to be either mundane or overwhelming or fires her.

Co-workers, especially friends and supporters of the harasser, sometimes retaliate against a woman who has rocked the boat by reporting harassment. They may refuse to cooperate with the employee—so it becomes evermore difficult for her to work—or they may shun her, excluding her from workplace social functions and just plain refusing to be cordial.

A good harassment policy should also assure employees that there will not be any retaliation for filing a complaint against workplace harassment or for co-operating in the investigation of another's complaint. The policy should also spell out the kinds of discipline—reprimand, suspension, transfer, dismissal— that will be imposed against those who retaliate.

Provide training sessions and monitoring. A sexual harassment policy should also provide for regular education and training—and for periodic monitoring of the workplace. (See Sections E and F.)

IF THE FIRST WOMAN GOD EVER MADE WAS STRONG ENOUGH TO TURN THE WORLD UPSIDE DOWN ALL ALONE, THESE WOMEN TOGETHER OUGHT TO BE ABLE TO TURN IT BACK, AND GET IT RIGHT SIDE UP AGAIN. AND NOW THEY IS ASKING TO DO IT, THE MEN BETTER LET THEM.—SOJOURNER TRUTH, ADDRESS TO THE OHIO WOMEN'S RIGHTS CONVENTION, 1851

A LOOK AT HOW HARASSMENT COMPLAINTS ARE HANDLED

Results of a November 1991 survey of 524 firms belonging to the American Management Association:

- 52% of the companies polled have dealt with allegations of sexual harassment in the past five years.

Only half of the sexual harassment situations came to the employer's attention through a formal complaint. Just as often, cases developed through informal report or anonymous communications from employees to management. Of the total sexual harassment claims handled:

- 17% were dismissed without action

- 27% resulted in a formal reprimand

- 14% resulted in probation or suspension

- 6% resulted in the harasser being transferred to a new position

- 14% resulted in the harasser being dismissed.

2. Sample sexual harassment policy

Here is a good start for a sexual harassment policy that can be modified to fit the needs of most workplaces.

SAMPLE SEXUAL HARASSMENT POLICY

[Employer name] is committed to providing a work environment where women and men can work together comfortably and productively, free from sexual harassment. Such behavior is illegal under both state and federal law—and will not be tolerated here.

This policy applies to all phases of employment—including recruiting, testing, hiring, upgrading, promotion or demotion, transfer, layoff, termination, rates of pay, benefits and selection for training, travel or company social events.

Prohibited Behavior

Prohibited sexual harassment includes unsolicited and unwelcome contact that has sexual overtones. This includes:

- written contact, such as sexually suggestive or obscene letters, notes, invitations
- verbal contact, such as sexually suggestive or obscene comments, threats, slurs, epithets, jokes about gender-specific traits, sexual propositions
- physical contact, such as intentional touching, pinching, brushing against another's body, impeding or blocking movement, assault, coercing sexual intercourse, and
- visual contact, such as leering or staring at another's body, gesturing, displaying sexually suggestive objects or pictures, cartoons, posters or magazines.

Sexual harassment also includes continuing to express sexual or social interest after being informed directly that the interest is unwelcome—and using sexual behavior to control, influence or affect the career, salary or work environment of another employee.

It is impermissible to suggest, threaten or imply that failure to accept a request for a date or sexual intimacy will affect an employee's job prospects. For example, it is forbidden either to imply or actually withhold support for an appointment, promotion, or change of assignment, or suggest that a poor performance report will be given because an employee has declined a personal proposition.

Also, offering benefits, such as promotions, favorable performance evaluations, favorable assigned duties or shifts, recommendations or reclassifications in exchange for sexual favors is forbidden.

Harassment by Non-Employees

In addition, [Employer name] will take all reasonable steps to prevent or eliminate sexual harassment by non-employees including customers, clients and suppliers, who are likely to have workplace contact with our employees.

Monitoring

[Employer name] shall take all reasonable steps to see that this policy prohibiting sexual harassment is followed by all employees, supervisors and others who have contact with our employees. This prevention plan will include training sessions, ongoing monitoring of the worksite and a confidential employee survey to be conducted and evaluated every six months.

Discipline

Any employee found to have violated this policy shall be subject to appropriate disciplinary action, including warnings, reprimand, suspension or discharge, according to the findings of the complaint investigation.

If an investigation reveals that sexual harassment has occurred, the harasser may also be held legally liable for his or her actions under state or federal anti-discrimination laws or in separate legal actions.

Retaliation

Any employee bringing a sexual harassment complaint or assisting in investigating such a complaint will not be adversely affected in terms and conditions of employment, or discriminated against or discharged because of the complaint. Complaints of such retaliation will be promptly investigated and punished.

Complaint Procedure and Investigation

[Title of person appointed] is designated as the Sexual Harassment Counselor. All complaints of sexual harassment and retaliation for reporting or participating in an investigation shall be directed to the Sexual Harassment Counselor or to a supervisor of your choice, either in writing, by filling out the attached Complaint Form, or by requesting an individual interview. All complaints shall be handled as confidentially as possible. The Sexual Harassment Counselor will promptly investigate and resolve complaints involving violations of this policy and recommend to management the appropriate sanctions to be imposed against violators.

Training

[Employer name] will establish yearly training sessions for all employees concerning their rights to be free from sexual harassment and the legal options available if they are harassed. In addition, training sessions will be held for supervisors and managers, educating them in how to keep the workplace as free from harassment as possible and in how to handle sexual harassment complaints.

A copy of the policy will be distributed to all employees and posted in areas where all employees will have the opportunity to freely review it. [Employer name] welcomes your suggestions for improvements to this policy.

D. Complaint Procedures and Investigations

A good harassment policy is a crucial first step in ridding a workplace of offensive, unwanted behavior. But it won't count for much unless an employer also adopts a trustworthy and energetic procedure for handling and investigating complaints.

> **N**O TOUCHES, NO POSTERS, NO SEXUAL REMARKS OF ANY KIND.
> PATS ON THE BACK MAY BE FINE IN A BASEBALL DUGOUT, BUT ARE
> NOT APPRECIATED IN THE WORKPLACE. A MANAGER IS IN THE BEST
> POSITION TO STOP SEXUAL HARASSMENT BEFORE IT GETS STARTED.
> —FROM "WHAT EVERY MANAGER MUST KNOW TO PREVENT SEXUAL
> HARASSMENT," A BOOKLET PUBLISHED BY THE ALEXANDER HAMILTON
> INSTITUTE, INC.

1. Sample complaint form

A helpful attachment to a sexual harassment policy is a complaint form to record important dates, facts, names and flag important follow-up procedures.

SAMPLE SEXUAL HARASSMENT COMPLAINT FORM
Name:
Department:
Job Title:
Immediate Supervisor:
1. Who was responsible for the harassment?
2. Describe the sexual harassment.
First incident:
Approximate date, time and place:
What was your reaction?
Second incident:
Approximate date, time and place:
What was your reaction?

Subsequent incidents:
Approximate date, time and place:
What was your reaction?
3. List any witnesses to the harassment:
I UNDERSTAND THAT THESE INCIDENTS WILL BE INVESTIGATED, BUT THIS FORM WILL BE KEPT CONFIDENTIAL TO THE HIGHEST DEGREE POSSIBLE.
Employee:
Date:
FOR ADMINISTRATIVE USE
Dates of investigation of complaint:
Date of final report:

Copy sent to employee:

Action taken:

Date of follow-up conference with employee:

Results:

Date of follow-up conference with employee:

Results:

Date of follow-up conference with employee:

Results:

2. Workplace investigations

The tone and tenor of the investigation of a harassment complaint often means the difference between achieving a prompt and satisfactory resolution of the problem or having it escalate into an expensive legal battle. A shoddy, lip-service investigation not only fails to end the workplace problem, but risks becoming key evidence of the employer's failure to take harassment seriously in a later lawsuit.

A key component to resolving complaints is promptness. Not only is it extremely demoralizing to all concerned to have an unresolved harassment complaint hanging in the air, but a delayed investigation means that everyone's recollection of the events is likely to become unnecessarily hazy. A good rule is that the investigation should begin within 48 hours after a complaint is received.

BEWARE OF FILING DEADLINES

Federal and state laws impose fairly tight deadlines from the date the harassment occurred to the time in which you must file a complaint. Although deadlines vary, 180 days is a common cut-off. If you decide to use your employer's internal complaint procedure first, a logical argument can be made that these deadlines should be suspended while you await the outcome from your employer's investigation.

However, this is often not the case. If you think you may wish to file a complaint either with your state fair employment practices agency or the EEOC, file your complaint within the 180 day EEOC time limit (see Chapter 6, Section H) or the relevant state time period (see Chapter 7, Section F) even if a workplace investigation is still in progress.

It is also essential that whoever investigates the complaint be perceived by all within the workplace to be fair and objective. Depending on your workplace, it may be better to bring in an outside investigator once a complaint is filed. You may find a referral for one by contacting your state FEP agency. In other situations, especially for larger employers in which an impartial person can be brought in from another part of the company, it may work well to conduct the investigation internally.

And there are a number of subtleties inherent in conducting a good investigation. For example, some women feel uncomfortable discussing a harassment situation with a male investigator. A woman who feels this discomfort should have the option of being assigned a female investigator—or at least have a female personnel employee with her during investigation interviews.

A thorough investigation will have the following earmarks.

■ The complaining employee will be interviewed

The woman filing the complaint will be asked to recount details of the behavior she found offensive—including names, dates, places and specific behavior. This process can be painful, so referring to prepared notes can sometimes be helpful. In addition, a preprinted Complaint Form (such as the one set out in Section D.1), can help the interview be more organized and focused and less intimidating.

Confidentiality should be stressed. The investigator should assure the employee that the matter will be kept private and discussed with no more people than is necessary. And while the employee must be free to discuss the harassment incidents with confidantes and friends, once a complaint has been filed, she should not discuss specifics of the investigation too freely with co-workers.

It is likely that the employee will not be able to remember all details or incidents of harassment during the initial interview. A good procedure will make it easy for her to supply more information later.

■ The alleged harasser will be interviewed

The investigator should explain the substance of the complaint filed against the harasser, interview him thoroughly—and obtain a signed, written statement detailing his recollection of the events. If he refuses to sign—or acknowledges his behavior—that should be noted on the statement, which will later be put in his personnel file.

■ Witnesses will be interviewed

Witnesses to be interviewed include employees, former employees and anyone else who may know about the workplace behavior being investigated. It is particularly helpful if a witness has seen or heard the harassment on which the complaint is based. Anyone who claims to have been subjected to similar behavior by the same person should also be interviewed as part of the investigation.

■ The evidence will be evaluated

If the versions of what happened are different—as they often are—the investigator may have to make an effort to search for relevant facts. Objective proof of the charges, such as an eyewitness to the harassment, would likely be persuasive evidence, although such evidence is often impossible to gather, since much harassment takes place in private.

The investigator may need to delve into the reputations for truthfulness of those involved and any possible motivation behind the inconsistent stories— such as a bad performance review or a broken romance. Other complaints against the same employee should also be carefully evaluated.

■ Prompt action will be taken

A decision as to whether harassment occurred should be issued as quickly as possible to avoid prolonging the angst and damaging speculation that often accompanies an investigation in even in the most gossip-free workplaces.

If no harassment is found

If the situation has been thoroughly investigated and no harassment is found, the accused employee should be notified at once. Allegations of harassment are likely to be personally stressful and damaging to his work productivity, too.

The needs of the person bringing the complaint should also be considered. A finding that harassment has not been established may leave the employee feeling angry, frustrated or scared. She should be encouraged to discuss her feelings with a willing ear—a sympathetic co-worker or supervisor, company counselor, workplace specialist, psychologist or psychiatrist. In some situations, it may be sensible to make workplace changes that separate her from the person she accused of harassment.

Also, the employee bringing the complaint should be informed that the employer's decision is not the last legal word on the matter. Whatever the decision reached during the employer's investigation, she is free to go forward with federal or state complaints or file other legal action against the workplace behavior. (See Chapters 5, 6, 7 and 8.)

If harassment is found

If the investigator is convinced that there has been sexual harassment, management should promptly issue a written apology to the harassed woman. For many women, this is extremely welcome, as it signals the employer's understanding and acknowledgment of the problem.

The employer should also take quick disciplinary action against the harasser. What is appropriate will depend on the type and severity of harassment and on whether it is a first time or repeated offense. Appropriate action against the harasser may include: a verbal or written warning accompanied by the request to attend sexual harassment training sessions, or, in more serious cases, transfer to a different position, suspension or dismissal.

Ideally, where emotions are running high, it may be best to try to separate the employee and the harasser, giving either or both the option of transferring to a different position within the company. If it is the harassed employee who is to be transferred, there must be total assurance that the transfer is not done in retaliation for making the complaint. This means that the transfer must be acceptable to the harassed employee, and must not be to a lower paying, geographically isolated or otherwise less desirable position.

■ A follow-up plan for monitoring will be established

Old habits may die hard. Even prompt and strict action against the harasser may not end his bad behavior. And there may also be delayed retaliation against the person filing the complaint, coming from the alleged harasser or from his friends or co-workers who harbor a grudge.

To guard against these possibilities, a sexual harassment investigation procedure should make clear that the situation will be monitored for an extended period. Follow-up meetings at regular intervals—two weeks, one month, three-months, six-months and yearly—should be scheduled with the employee who originally complained to be sure both that the harassment has been eliminated and that there has been no retaliation for taking action against it.

S EXUAL HARASSMENT IS ENVIRONMENTAL POLLUTION OF THE WORST KIND.—SECRETARY OF LABOR LYNN MARTIN IN A STATEMENT ISSUED OCTOBER 10, 1991

E. Training Sessions

Sexual harassment in the workplace can be curbed or even eliminated by training supervisors and employees to recognize its signals and head it off. Doing this will end the need for harassment-related lawsuits, increase productivity and make the workplace more comfortable for everyone. Often, such training requires guidance from experts.

Sexual harassment training can take many different forms, depending on the size and budget of a company. The best training programs involve all levels of employees so that the entire workplace gets a better understanding of sexual harassment—why it happens, who it happens to, typical reactions of both the harasser and harassed woman and effective ways to make the harassment stop.

Typically, a trainer will visit a workplace and diagnose what is needed there. Most trainers offer:

- Help with writing a sexual harassment policy and a procedure for enforcing it—both tailored to the individual workplace.

- Seminars to increase staff awareness of sexual harassment, including strategies for preventing and addressing workplace harassment.

- Programs specifically geared to teach managers how to investigate and deal with sexual harassment complaints, so that everyone in the workplace will have some confidence in the process.

- Additional training for managers and supervisors in how to lead periodic sexual harassment prevention workshops in their own workplaces.

Large employers often require a full range of training services. Smaller employers without the resources for full-blown training and follow-up programs can still get expert, cost-effective help in designing a good sexual harassment policy. Also, for a reasonable cost, a few employees can attend one of the growing number of seminars offered by outside workplace consultants. Many trainers offer discount rates if a number of employees, such as three or more, attend their training.

IN RESEARCH WITH 832 WORKING WOMEN, DR. BARBARA GUTEK, A PSYCHOLOGIST AT THE UNIVERSITY OF ARIZONA BUSINESS SCHOOL, FOUND THAT:

- NEARLY HALF OF THE WOMEN SURVEYED SAID THEY HAD BEEN SEXUALLY HARASSED.

- NONE OF THOSE WHO SAID THEY HAD BEEN SEXUALLY HARASSED SOUGHT LEGAL HELP.

- ONLY 22% SAID THEY HAD TOLD ANYONE ELSE OF THE HARASSMENT.

TRAINING VIDEOS: THE SEMI-SILVER SCREEN

One widely touted training resource is videotapes defining and giving examples of sexual harassment on the job. While videotapes can efficiently reach a great number of employees, they have many drawbacks.

Most are of questionable quality. They offer little more than cursory, often condescending, glimpses of harassment on the job.

Many are outdated. Beware of training films that have not been updated within the past couple years; laws controlling sexual harassment have changed substantially.

Most are expensive. Only the largest employers are likely to find it cost-efficient to purchase a harassment training film. And even the costs of renting the films vary dramatically—from $50 to $200 for a 24-hour rental. Here, too, you do not always get what you pay for.

Many offer little further guidance. Some films are accompanied by manuals that have useful examples and devices to help employees remember the fine points of the training. However, while truly interested employees may take the time to read the information, many of those who could benefit the most from it will pitch the paperwork soon after showtime. Also, films and manuals alone will often not answer more specific questions employees may have—leaving them "trained" but frustrated.

Before investing in a training video, get information on the company producing it and whether those involved with the content have any experience in sexual harassment training. Try to get a preview copy—or at least get the names of similar employers that have used a particular training video and ask whether employees there found it useful.

1. Tips on choosing workplace training

A confusing array of workplace training experts have sprung up recently—some less expert than others. Training resources run the range from books such as this one, to seminars outside the office, to tailored in-house training programs. Match your specific needs with available resources.

A word to the wise is to start slowly: A solid policy against harassment may be the best first step, followed by more ambitious training as employee interest and awareness grows. If you decide to use some outside expertise, first do some research on how to spend your training dollars wisely.

Define your training needs. Focus first on the type of help that is needed most—a good sexual harassment policy, raising employee awareness about what harassment is, refreshers for employees on the changing legal options for dealing with harassment or advice for conducting investigations for the personnel manager and supervisors. Depending on the size and type of employer, an informal survey of employees may help define the workplace needs. Employees should be urged to be frank and specific about the company's current needs and shortcomings.

Put together a list of workplace consultants. You can get referrals for local training experts from the EEOC and from many women's groups. (For contact details, see the Appendix.) You can also get advice and ideas by talking with friends and business contacts in other companies.

Choose expert help that meets your needs and budget. Do not sign on at once for more than your budget can handle. Among the questions to ask potential trainers are:

WHAT SERVICES DO YOU OFFER?
Get details on the specific services. Note that in addition to training, many workplace consultants offer seminars, on-site investigation services, dispute mediation and other employment services.

WHAT IS YOUR EXPERIENCE IN SEXUAL HARASSMENT TRAINING?
Avoid companies that have little experience or have just recently jumped on the sexual harassment training bandwagon, spotting it as a good money-making scheme—for example, career development firms that primarily offer help with job searches and resumes, but which have become sexual harassment experts overnight.

Also, look for companies that have worked with employees, and have not been limited to training managers. A trainer who can see both sides of the sexual harassment issue is often best. And again, it's essential that the trainer is up to date on sexual harassment laws and court cases.

WHAT TYPES OF EMPLOYERS HAVE YOU TRAINED IN THE PAST?
Government agencies? Large corporations? Small businesses? Training
needs differ greatly. Specifically, look for trainers experienced in
working with employers similar to yours in size and type of work.

GIVEN OUR COMPANY'S NEEDS, WHAT TYPE OF TRAINING DO
YOU SUGGEST—AND WHAT WILL IT COST?
Make sure the consultant can offer practical, down-to-earth
suggestions tailored to your workplace, not just generalized
information that is readily available from many other sources. And
look for training services that aim at preventing harassment on the
job, such as monitoring complaints in-house.

2. Effective training programs

A typical sexual harassment training seminar lasts from four hours to two days,
depending on its scope. The number of employees attending ranges from a
small group at the workplace to an anonymous group of hundreds from various
employers who gather away from work in a conference room. Currently,
the best training programs use a number of different methods—including
videos and group discussions and written materials.

The first step in a training session is to get people comfortable enough to
discuss sexual harassment openly and honestly. Many trainers break the ice by
asking participants for examples of the kinds of behavior they consider to be
sexual harassment. This usually works best in small discussion groups, where
people are much more likely to bring up current workplace concerns rather
than make abstract comments or refer to events that happened at a previous
job.

Trainers should then take the lead in explaining the legal definition of
sexual harassment. All participants should get a list of prohibited behavior, including that set out in the sexual harassment policy (discussed in Section C),
supplemented by examples of behavior that is and is not considered harassment. The greatest concentration should be on the gray areas of behavior
(discussed in Chapter 3, Section C) that give most employees the most difficulty. The best lessons to be learned come from actual court cases—and train-

ers should cover more subtle kinds of harassing behavior along with more outrageous examples.

Trainers should then bring the point home to employees by getting them involved in how harassment feels. Some trainers show videos of re-enacted harassment scenes. Roleplaying is another popular technique with employees taking turns imagining that they are both the harassed and the harassing employees. This technique is especially effective in shifting the focus of awareness from what might happen to an accused harasser to what does happen to a harassed employee.

I'VE HAD WOMEN I'VE WORKED WITH MAKE COMMENTS ABOUT MY PHYSICAL ATTRIBUTES. IF I HAD WANTED TO ASSUME THEY WERE TREATING ME AS A SEX OBJECT, I COULD HAVE, BUT ACTUALLY, I WAS FLATTERED. I DIDN'T FEEL HARASSED. I FELT FLATTERED.
—RESPONSE OF ROSS MADDEN, 41, WHEN ASKED THE QUESTION "HAVE YOU EVER EXPERIENCED SEXUAL HARASSMENT?" IN AN ON-THE-STREET INTERVIEW, *SAN FRANCISCO CHRONICLE*, NOV. 17, 1991

PROGRESSIVE EMPLOYERS CONFRONT HARASSMENT

Some employers have demonstrated not only exemplary sensitivity and flexibility in dealing with sexual harassment on the job, but have come up with creative ways of dealing with the problem.

Among those employers who have gone the extra miles:

■ *U.S. West, a Colorado-based communication services company with about 65,000 employees, over half of them women.*

The company has long had a strong harassment policy, reviewed annually. It offers training to employees and designates individuals within each department to help employees with harassment problems. During and after the Senate hearings on harassment charges against Clarence Thomas, U.S. West sent notices to employees reminding them of the policy against harassment and of the company's ongoing training and workshops on stereotypes.

■ *E.I. Du Pont de Nemours & Co., a Delaware-based chemicals and energy company with about 105,000 employees, about one-quarter of them women.*

Recently, the company revised its sexual harassment training program, which used to concentrate on managers and supervisors to include all employees. The program now includes a four-hour workshop discussing harassment led by both a male and female facilitator—and a 24-hour confidential hotline staffed by trained Du Pont employees who respond to questions about workplace harassment.

■ *Ceradyne Inc., a California-based technical ceramics company with about 135 employees, 40 of them women.*

The company president periodically issues a strongly-worded statement to all employees that sexual harassment is not tolerated. All employees are informed that they can take complaints to the established complaint committee made up of four employees. Management's visible and strong open-door policy wards off potential harassment problems. There are regular "Breakfast with the president" sessions, in which several employees meet informally with the company president over coffee and donuts to discuss what's on their minds. Ceradyne employees took up a collection to send Anita Hill flowers during the Senate confirmation hearings of Clarence Thomas.

F. Sexual Harassment Monitoring Survey

In addition to adopting a sexual harassment policy and complaint procedure and providing employees with training, employers who are truly committed to eradicating sexual harassment should actively monitor their workplaces. The best way to do this is to regularly remind employees that sexual harassment is illegal and will not be tolerated—and to urge them to assess whether it is a problem in the workplace. A quick and confidential method is to ask each employee to complete a Sexual Harassment Survey every six months.

The survey that follows is a sample.

SAMPLE SEXUAL HARASSMENT SURVEY

To all employees:

We are committed to making every effort to have our workplace be free of sexual harassment, as defined in our sexual harassment policy. This survey is designed to assess whether sexual harassment is currently a problem here. Your answers will be used to develop policies to assure that the workplace feels safe and comfortable for everyone.

Please take a few minutes to complete this questionnaire and return it in the enclosed envelope. You need not sign your name. However, if you are now dealing with a sexual harassment problem, we urge you to report it promptly as discussed in our Sexual Harassment Policy. Thank you.

1. *I am a*

    ☐   woman
    ☐   man

2. *Do you believe you have ever been subjected to sexual harassment while employed here?*

    ☐   No.
    ☐   Yes

    If your answer is no, please go to question 10.

PLEASE ANSWER QUESTIONS 3 THROUGH 9 FOR THE MOST RECENT INCIDENT OF HARASSMENT.

3. *When was the most recent incident?*

    ☐   I am currently experiencing a sexual harassment problem.
    ☐   less than six months ago
    ☐   more than six months ago

4. *Who harassed you? Check all that apply.*

    ☐   my immediate supervisor
    ☐   higher management official
    ☐   union official
    ☐   co-worker
    ☐   clients, vendors or other non-employees

☐ other (specify)

_____

_____

5. *What was the nature of the harassment? Check all that apply.*

☐ unwelcome sexual relations

☐ unwelcome physical contact (touching, pinching, brushing against your body)

☐ commenting about your appearance or body

☐ obnoxious or unwanted telephone calls

☐ obnoxious or unwanted letters or other correspondence

☐ sexual propositions

☐ sexually suggestive objects or photographs displayed in the workplace

☐ offensive jokes or innuendos

☐ other (specify)

_____

_____

6. *What was your response to the harassment? Check all that apply.*

☐ nothing

☐ resolved the problem by talking to the harasser

☐ left the job by quitting or demanding a transfer

☐ complained to management

☐ complained to the personnel office

☐ filed a grievance through the union

☐ filed charges with the state anti-discrimination agency

☐ filed discrimination charges with the federal Equal Employment Opportunity Commission

☐ consulted an attorney and filed a lawsuit

7. *Was any adverse action threatened or taken against you because you complained about the harassment or because you refused to submit to it?*

☐ No

☐ Yes. Check all that apply.

    ☐ denied promotion

    ☐ denied salary increase

☐ reprimanded
☐ given a poor performance evaluation
☐ involuntarily transferred
☐ discharged
☐ other (specify)

_____

8. *If your answer to Question 6 was any but the first two options, did you find the assistance you sought helpful?*

☐ Yes
☐ No

If no, please explain why you found the assistance lacking or ineffective. If you used several types of assistance, specify which ones you found unhelpful:

_____
_____
_____
_____
_____

9. *What was the outcome of your effort to stop the harassment?* _____

_____
_____
_____
_____

10. *Do you have any suggestions about how we can respond more effectively to problems of sexual harassment?*_____

_____
_____
_____
_____

Date survey completed: _____

(Survey adapted from "Stopping Sexual Harassment," an AFSCME Guide, 1988.)

G. Special Procedures for Some Employees

When it comes to being sexually harassed on the job, all women are created equal. Each one is free to attempt to end the harassment by confronting the harasser, complaining to company management, filing a complaint with a government agency or bringing a private legal action. But some workplaces, by design, also provide more comprehensive resources to deal with the problem.

1. U.S. government employees

Each federal employer has an Equal Employment Opportunity (EEO) office set up to handle complaints about sexual harassment on the job. The formal complaint procedure for federal employees differs somewhat from other harassment complaint procedures.

Most importantly, the complaint process must be started within 30 days of the most recent incident of harassment. Harassed employees should initially contact an EEO counselor, whose name and location should be posted on your agency's bulletin board. If you are unable to find such a posting, call your local EEO office and ask that a counselor be assigned to you.

If the counselor cannot resolve your problem to your satisfaction, file a formal complaint with your agency through its EEO process. In the usual progression, there will be an investigation and a hearing on your charges to determine whether harassment has occurred. The agency head will then issue a final decision in the matter. If you are not satisfied with the decision, you may appeal it—first to the EEOC (see Chapter 6) and then to the local federal district court.

See the Appendix for listings of organizations that offer advice, attorney referrals and other services to government employees who have questions about sexual harassment on the job.

UP AGAINST UNCLE SAM

In a study of 10,648 women working for the federal government in 1988, 42% said they had been harassed. Of those instances of workplace harassment:

- 35% involved unwanted sexual remarks

- 28% involved leers and suggestive looks

- 26% involved being touched

- 15% involved being pressured for dates

- 9% involved being pressured for sexual favors

- .8% involved being raped or sexually assaulted

Additional lowlights of the report included statistics on the source of the reported harassment:

co-worker	41%	immediate supervisor	12%
other employees	37%	other	10%
higher level supervisor	19%	subordinate	2%

2. Union members

Harassed women workers who are also union members may have a potentially potent ally in fighting workplace harassment: the weight and authority of their union contract.

Under the National Labor Relations Act, your union has the duty to make a good faith effort to stop employment discrimination—and to represent you on issues of sexual harassment.

While few union contracts specifically prohibit sexual harassment on the job, many contain anti-discrimination clauses. Keep in mind that harassment is simply one form of discrimination—and that a broad anti-discrimination clause also protects against harassment. In some unions, this may require you to do a certain amount of fancy lipwork, but you will be well within legal bounds.

Because of their relatively long history of providing some organized assistance to workers, a number of progressive unions and their lobby groups, such as the American Federation of State, County and Municipal Employees (AFSCME) and the United Auto Workers (UAW), have been particularly successful recently in fighting workplace sexual harassment among members by:

- Establishing strong sexual harassment policy through local or council resolutions

- Educating union members about harassment by conducting seminars and workshops and distributing literature

- Expanding training on handling sexual harassment grievances by making it a mandatory part of all steward training, and

- Negotiating anti-sexual harassment language in collective bargaining units and formulating complaint procedures.

a.   Getting your union involved

If you are a union member who is being sexually harassed at work, your first course of action is usually to inform your union steward. Under most union agreements, a harassed union member will have the option of submitting her claim of harassment to the union's established grievance procedure. In a typical resolution of a harassment grievance, the union member, union representative, employer and alleged harasser will all work together to attempt a solution that ends the harassment and punishes the wrongdoer.

b.   What to do if your union is hostile

Just as women are relative newcomers to many workplaces, they are new arrivals in many unions. The sad truth is that you may find yourself up against The Old Boys' Network with a vengeance if you complain about sexual harassment to your union representative.

If you feel that your grievance about sexual harassment is falling on deaf ears, take a hard look at how your union is structured. Do women hold positions of trust? Does the union take an active stand on sexual harassment? Is there a woman trained and sensitive to the problems of workplace harassment who is involved in the complaint and investigation process? If your union comes up short when measured by this yardstick of questions, keep careful note. Your union's lack of responsiveness may become part of your harassment complaint—or form the basis for a later grievance against the union.

If your union steward or other grievance-taker shrugs off your complaint or labels it as a non-grievable issue, do not become discouraged and drop your complaint. Exercise every right to appeal. Unions in some workplaces have already recognized that not all stewards are equally adept at handling sexual harassment complaints. So some have designated specific stewards—who are most often women—to handle sexual harassment grievances. If your union offers this alternative, take advantage of it.

If the result of workplace investigation is not satisfactory to you, you may file a complaint directly with the state FEP agency or federal EEOC, or go directly to court to file common law action.

If your union refuses to aid you in investigating and prosecuting sexual harassment charges, you may also file an unfair labor practices lawsuit with the National Labor Relation Board (NLRB) for breach of its duty of fair representation. However, beware of this: Filing an NLRB charge against a union may later bar state and federal courts from considering the issues you raise there.

See the Appendix for listings of organizations that offer advice, attorney referrals and other services to union members who have questions about sexual harassment on the job.

THERE'S A BIG DIFFERENCE BETWEEN SAYING, "YOU LOOK GREAT" AND "WOW! WHAT A FIGURE!"—ABIGAIL VAN BUREN, AKA DEAR ABBY

5

A Look at the Legal Remedies

A. Legal Remedies: An Overview... 5/2
    1. The U.S. Civil Rights Act and the EEOC 5/2
    2. State Fair Employment Practices Statutes 5/3
    3. Common law torts 5/4
    4. Linking the harassment with a remedy 5/5

B. Objective One: Stopping the Harassment.. 5/5
    1. The Civil Rights Act and the EEOC.. 5/5
    2. State Fair Employment Practices Statutes 5/6
    3. Common law torts 5/7

C. Objective Two: Recovering Wages and Other Losses... 5/8
    1. The Civil Rights Act and the EEOC.. 5/8
    2. State Fair Employment Practices Statutes 5/8
    3. Common law torts 5/9

D. Objective Three: Compensation for Personal Injuries.. 5/9
    1. The Civil Rights Act and the EEOC.. 5/10
    2. State Fair Employment Practices Statutes 5/11
    3. Common law torts 5/11

E. Objective Four: Reforming the Company 5/12
    1. The Civil Rights Act and the EEOC.. 5/13
    2. State Fair Employment Practices Statutes 5/13
    3. Common law torts 5/14

F. Special Scenario: The Not-So-Rosy Case of Ms. Riveter...................................... 5/14

There are three broad legal protections or remedies that ensure a woman's right to be free from sexual harassment in the workplace:

1. The U.S. Civil Rights Act administered by the U.S. Equal Employment Opportunities Commission (EEOC)

2. State fair employment practices (FEP) statutes, and

3. Lawsuits under common law tort principles.

Although each of these is discussed individually in later chapters, this chapter compares their effectiveness in different situations. Here, we look at how a harassed employee can use the remedies to stop the harassment, recover lost wages and other job-connected losses, obtain compensation for personal injuries and make structural reforms within the company.

The example in Section F describes in detail how all the legal remedies may be applied in an actual sexual harassment case.

A. Legal Remedies: An Overview

Here is a brief description of the three legal remedies generally available to employees.

1. The U.S. Civil Rights Act and the EEOC

Title VII of the U.S. Civil Rights Act—often shortened to Title VII—prohibits discrimination and sexual harassment in employment. It applies to most employers throughout the United States who employ 15 or more employees. This federal statute is administered by the U.S. Equal Employment Opportunities Commission (EEOC).

The EEOC investigates employee harassment and discrimination complaints by taking statements from the company and any witnesses, examining documents and records and using its subpoena power to compel the employer and others to turn over evidence they are reluctant to disclose. The EEOC usually tries to enforce a harassed employee's rights under the Civil Rights Act by negotiating with the employer in a process called "conciliation." The agency can also file a lawsuit on behalf of the employee to enforce her rights if negotiation fails. However, in the vast majority of cases, the EEOC simply issues a "right-to-sue" letter to the employee allowing her to file a lawsuit to enforce her rights under the Civil Rights Act.

If the employee wins her case in court, the Civil Rights Act provides the following possible relief:

> REINSTATEMENT AND PROMOTION. *The court can order the company to rehire the employee and promote her to the job to which she was entitled.*

> BACK PAY AND BENEFITS. *An award of any salary and benefits the employee lost as a result of being fired or forced to quit, demoted or passed over for advancement.*

> MONEY DAMAGES (LIMITED AMOUNT). *An award of money for personal injuries, such as stress-related problems, caused by the harassment. The amount is limited to out-of-pocket losses, such as medical expenses and other damages up to a limit of between $50,000 and $300,000—depending on the number of people employed.*

> INJUNCTIVE RELIEF. *A court order directing the company to change its policies to prevent similar harassment in the future.*

> ATTORNEY'S FEES. *An amount awarded by the court to pay for the employee's attorney's fees—or at least a portion of them.*

(See Chapter 6 for a full discussion of the U.S. Civil Rights Act and EEOC procedures.)

2. State Fair Employment Practices Statutes

Employees in most states also have rights under state fair employment practices (FEP) statutes. FEP statutes generally prohibit sexual harassment committed against a woman employed in that state, but not every state has an effective FEP law. A few states, such as Alabama and Arkansas, have no FEP statutes at all. However, most states have FEP statutes that cover most workers, including those employed by smaller companies that might not be covered under the 15-employee minimum of the U.S. Civil Rights Act.

Most states have adopted a definition of sexual harassment that is similar to the definition used by the EEOC. (See Chapter 2, Section C.1.) Most states have also created agencies similar to the EEOC to investigate and settle employees' claims, and a few local governments have such agencies as well. These federal and state agencies use similar techniques for investigating claims, sometimes doing the work for each other under work-sharing agreements—and allowing an employee to file a claim simultaneously under both the Civil Rights Act and state FEP law under a dual-filing arrangement.

There are important differences, however, in the procedures and remedies offered to harassed employees under the various state FEP laws. The most important differences have to do with allowing employees to recover money damages for personal injuries suffered as a result of the harassment. (See Chapter 7 for a discussion of state FEP laws generally and a state-by-state list of such laws.)

3. Common law torts

Common law tort lawsuits, such as intentional infliction of emotional distress and assault and battery, provide a remedy in certain types of sexual harassment cases that is totally independent of any of the statutes or governmental agencies. The common denominator in tort cases is money; these actions allow a harassed employee to be compensated for her personal injuries. (See Chapter 8 for a detailed discussion of torts commonly brought in sexual harassment situations.)

The facts of a sexual harassment case can often be fitted into one or more recognized categories of torts. For example, the same facts needed to prove a sexual harassment claim might also be sufficient in some cases to prove a claim for intentional infliction of emotional distress or assault and battery. Not every sexual harassment claim fits a common law tort theory. But if a tort lawsuit is successful, a woman may recover substantial monetary damages for the sexual harassment she has suffered.

4. Linking the harassment with a remedy

An employee who has been sexually harassed may need one or all of the legal remedies described to accomplish one of four common objectives in taking action against sexual harassment:

1. Stopping the harassment

2. Recovering lost wages and other job-connected losses

3. Obtaining compensation for personal injuries, and

4. Making structural reforms within the company.

We have separated these objectives for analysis only. In most real-life situations, an employee will have a combination of goals, such as getting her job back and obtaining compensation for her injuries.

B. Objective One: Stopping the Harassment

Your main goal may be to simply end the harassment before it gets worse. Frequently, your best course of action is to use a direct approach and confront the harasser yourself. (See Chapter 3, Section E.) In other cases, a good company complaint procedure can be used for this purpose. (See Chapter 4, Section C.) But direct action is not appropriate in all cases and not all companies have effective complaint procedures.

1. The Civil Rights Act and the EEOC

Filing a complaint with the EEOC can be helpful if your principal aim is to stop the ongoing acts of harassment.

EEOC procedures allow you to file a complaint without disclosing your name, and the EEOC will not reveal your identity without your consent. (See Chapter 6, Section G.) The EEOC encourages employers to settle problems from within, if possible.

An EEOC investigation may uncover facts that the company management did not know, such as harassing incidents against other employees. As the

EEOC develops such information, it may induce the employer to settle the case and adopt policies to prevent further harassment.

An EEOC investigation may induce an otherwise lethargic management to correct some long-standing abuses. But it can also create more friction if the company management bristles at the idea of a government investigation. For that reason, it is sometimes better to use a good company complaint procedure, if one is available, than to look first to the EEOC for help.

SEXUAL HARASSMENT ON THE JOB IS NOT A PROBLEM FOR THE VIRTUOUS WOMAN, EXCEPT IN THE RAREST OF CASES. WHEN A WOMAN WALKS ACROSS THE ROOM, SHE SPEAKS WITH A UNIVERSAL BODY LANGUAGE THAT MOST MEN INTUITIVELY UNDERSTAND.
—ANTI-FEMINIST PHYLLIS SCHLAFLY, TESTIFYING AT 1981 LABOR COMMISSION HEARINGS ON THE EEOC SEXUAL HARASSMENT GUIDELINES

2. State Fair Employment Practices Statutes

Most FEP agencies have the same power as the EEOC to seek a court order to stop harassment within a company, but the normal practice within both agencies is to attempt to settle the problem through negotiations or conciliation.

WHERE SHOULD YOU FILE?

Since the investigative powers of state FEP agencies and the EEOC are similar, choosing the best place to file often boils down to practical considerations. Which agency—state or federal—has the better staffing, smaller case loads, or bigger budget in your community? Sometimes women's groups and knowledge-able attorneys can give you a few tips.

There are two other points to keep in mind in choosing between a state FEP agency or the EEOC:

Eligibility. The Civil Rights Act and the EEOC only apply to businesses with 15 or more employees. (See Chapter 6 for a discussion of how employees are counted for this purpose). Many state FEP statutes protect employees who work for smaller employers.

Confidentiality. The EEOC will maintain the confidentiality of your identity during the investigation if you request it. A few state FEP agencies will also keep the employee's identity confidential, but most do not offer this protection. (See Chapter 7 for a state-by-state list of eligibility requirements and confidentiality policies of state FEP agencies.)

3. Common law torts

A common law tort action is not an appropriate remedy if your only goal is to stop the harassment. The greatest strength of tort lawsuits is that they allow you to recover money damages for injuries. But the downside of this is that there is no administrative mechanism to preserve confidentiality, protect against retaliation, seek conciliation or encourage the company to make changes. Also, consider that filing a lawsuit is usually an inflammatory act— likely to jeopardize your job status and aggravate your working relationship with your employer.

C. Objective Two: Recovering Wages and Other Losses

You may suffer a number of losses if you are fired, demoted, reassigned or otherwise penalized. The direct losses can include loss of wages, pension contributions, medical benefits, regular overtime pay, regular bonuses, back pay, shift differential pay, vacation pay and participation in any company profit-sharing plan. You may also need legal help to recover your job, promotion or any other favorable work status lost because of the sexual harassment.

1. The Civil Rights Act and the EEOC

The EEOC can be helpful in recovering your lost wages and other job-connected benefits. If the EEOC finds merit in your claim, it will attempt to negotiate a settlement that might include reinstatement if you have been wrongfully terminated, as well as any lost promotions, wages and other job-connected benefits. If the EEOC cannot negotiate a settlement of your claim on your behalf, it can take the case to court. But more likely, it will issue you a right-to-sue letter, enabling you to file a lawsuit on your own. If you win that lawsuit, you may also be awarded attorney's fees to help defray your legal expenses.

2. State Fair Employment Practices Statutes

As with the EEOC, there are many administrative steps within a typical state FEP agency to encourage settlement. Most state FEP agencies can take a sexual harassment claim to court, but you must usually take that action on your own, with the help of an attorney.

In some states, including New York and New Jersey, the FEP agency has the additional power to conduct an administrative hearing and issue an order granting you money for job-connected losses. It may also order reinstatement, reassignment or other relief. (See Section D.)

3. Common law torts

A common law tort action is a good remedy for going after lost wages and other job-connected losses in some limited situations, but a poor remedy in many others.

A common law tort suit is usually only appropriate if you want to recover money damages and are not interested in continuing to work for the company. In a tort lawsuit, the court cannot order that you be reinstated, promoted to a higher paying job or protect you from being retaliated against or fired.

The common law tort remedy that may work best for recovering lost wages is wrongful discharge—which is an action against being fired unlawfully. However, this tort remedy has not been accepted in several states, and in many other states it is unclear whether it protects against sexual harassment. (See Chapter 8, Section B.6.) If a court is willing to consider your claim for wrongful discharge, it may be to your advantage because you may then be entitled to substantial punitive damages—that is, money awarded to you to punish the wrongdoer.

D. Objective Three: Compensation for Personal Injuries

The types of injuries and illnesses that can arise out of a sexual harassment situation are many and varied. Sometimes, physical injuries result directly from violent harassment. There are also mental and emotional injuries. Sometimes these grow out of work performance stress, but they can also be the result of sexual trauma, fear of sexual assault or any other medically diagnosable injury.

If you have suffered severe injuries from sexual harassment, your objective may be to recover compensatory damages and, if possible, to recover punitive damages as well.

Compensatory damages are "open-ended" in the sense that the money necessary to compensate you for your injuries cannot be predicted in advance. The illness or injury that you may develop—as well as the cost of treating it— may vary greatly from what another employee might experience. What you will be seeking, therefore, is compensation for the actual amount of your injuries.

> **I** AM ONLY SPEAKING FROM WHAT I EXPERIENCED. I RESENT THE
> IDEA THAT PEOPLE WOULD BLAME THE MESSENGER FOR THE
> MESSAGE RATHER THAN LOOKING AT THE CONTENT OF THE MESSAGE
> ITSELF.—PROFESSOR ANITA HILL, SHORTLY AFTER TESTIFYING
> BEFORE THE SENATE COMMITTEEE INVESTIGATING HER ALLEGATIONS
> THAT CLARENCE THOMAS SEXUALLY HARASSED HER

You may also seek punitive damages, which is an additional amount of money that can be awarded if the harassment has been particularly outrageous. As the name suggests, punitive damages are awarded to punish the harasser and discourage future harassment. Punitive damages are only awarded if a judge or jury feels a sense of moral outrage after having heard all the evidence. That's often hard to predict.

1. The Civil Rights Act and the EEOC

The Civil Rights Act allows a sexually harassed woman to recover compensatory and punitive damages for her injuries, but the amount is limited.

You can recover the actual amount spent for out-of-pocket expenses, such as doctor and medical bills. But the total of any other compensatory and punitive damages that you can recover is limited to an amount based on the number of employees in the company:

$50,000 if there are 15 to 100 employees

$100,000 if there are 101 to 200 employees

$200,000 if there are 201 to 500 employees, and

$300,000 if there are 501 or more employees.

If the company has fewer than 15 employees, no damages can be awarded because the Civil Rights Act will not apply.

These limitations have no relationship, of course, to the severity of your injuries; your injuries are the same no matter how many people your company employs. These dollar limitations seriously limit the usefulness of the Civil Rights Act for recovering monetary damages, particularly for employees of small companies.

2. State Fair Employment Practices Statutes

Some state FEP laws provide very good remedies for the recovery of damages for personal injuries, while others provide no remedy at all. The effectiveness of FEP laws depends upon the particular nuances of the laws where the harassment occurred.

FEP statutes in several states allow employees to collect substantial monetary damages for personal injuries—most often for their actual amount without any of the limitations contained in the Civil Rights Act. If you work in such a state and have suffered substantial personal injuries, consider pursuing your claim under the state FEP law. It is likely to be your most effective remedy.

However, if you work in a state in which the FEP statute does not allow compensation for personal injuries, you are clearly better off pursuing your sexual harassment claim for personal injuries under the U.S. Civil Rights Act; it at least allows the right to recover limited money damages.

3. Common law torts

Common law tort cases may be one of the best remedies if your objective is to recover for personal injuries, because they usually allow unlimited money damages.

However, it's often difficult to find a tort action that fits the facts of your case. Also, not all common law tort theories are recognized or interpreted the same way in every state. (See Chapter 8 for a detailed discussion of tort actions.)

But an advantage to a common law tort lawsuit is that it can be filed immediately in many situations. In a strong case where you and your attorney are clear on the merits and the facts, there is no need to file anything with the EEOC or a state FEP agency, or to wait around for a right-to-sue letter before filing the common law action.

Cases involving serious personal injuries are much less likely to require the buffer of an EEOC or state FEP investigation. Earlier we focused on objectives such as stopping harassment or getting your job back, and we indicated that in those situations it is important to have a governmental agency that can investigate your claim, protect you from retaliatory firing and try to settle the matter. But by the time you have decided to file a tort lawsuit, you have probably long since left your job and are prepared for an all-out legal battle to recover for your injuries.

E. Objective Four: Reforming the Company

Sometimes, the principal goal of you and a group of your co-workers is to force the company to make largescale reforms to end sexual harassment and change the way that it treats women employees.

It usually takes a lot of money to reach this goal—and these cases are only undertaken after careful planning and with strong support from a workers' rights or similar organization. In one such frequently mentioned case, a woman shipyard worker named Robinson sued the Jacksonville Shipyards in Florida with the assistance of the NOW Legal Defense & Education Fund, claiming that the workplace was pervaded by pornography and misogynist humor.[1] The main thrust of the *Robinson* case was to obtain a court order forcing the company to adopt and implement an effective sexual harassment policy and complaint procedure.

---

[1] *Robinson v. Jacksonville Shipyards, Inc.*, 760 F. Supp. 1486 (M.D. Fla. 1991).

1. The Civil Rights Act and the EEOC

If the EEOC wants to challenge broad patterns of illegal conduct within a particular company or industry, it can expand the scope of a case on its own to investigate sexual harassment suffered by other employees. It can also seek a court order that will force the company to correct the overall harassment problems within the workplace.

This, then, is the larger leadership role that the EEOC is supposed to play—taking the initiative in important cases and dealing with sexual harassment issues of general importance to large groups of employees. But the agency only performs at this level when it has proper funding and strong leadership—something that it hasn't enjoyed much in recent years.

If you have an important case and the EEOC does not act on it, you may be able to work with public interest groups to bring the case to court. After receiving a right-to-sue letter, you can file a lawsuit under the Civil Rights Act to challenge a pattern of sexual harassment within the company and seek a strong court order that will help all the women employees in the company. That is what happened in the *Robinson* case: Based on the harassment suffered by one employee, the court issued an order directing the company to adopt and implement a specific, detailed sexual harassment policy and complaint procedure for all employees working there.

2. State Fair Employment Practices Statutes

Most state FEP agencies have powers similar to those of the EEOC to seek an end to patterns of sexual harassment and make broad reforms within a company.

Ideally, the FEP agency would pursue such a case with its own resources after it has received a complaint from a harassed employee, but problems of caseload, budgets and institutional inertia keep state FEP agencies, just like the EEOC, from pursuing many such cases on their own.

3. Common law torts

In a tort case, the only relief that the court can award is money damages for injuries suffered. The court has no authority to order a company to stop harassment, to adopt a sexual harassment policy, to implement a complaint procedure or to do anything else.

Despite that, some lawyers will argue that a tort case is still the best way to get a company to change its practices. Their argument is that nothing catches a company's attention like the negative publicity of a big tort case and the prospect of a fat money judgment against it. The company will make quick changes, so the argument goes, if it is faced with the prospect of digging deep into its pocket again to pay off possible future plaintiffs.

THE PROBLEM OF SEXUAL HARASSMENT, LIKE OTHER PROBLEMS OF GENDER AND INEQUALITY, IS THE LACK OF PUBLIC RECOGNITION THAT IT IS A PROBLEM.—DEBORAH RHODE, PROFESSOR OF LAW, STANFORD UNIVERSITY

F. Special Scenario: The Not-So-Rosy Case of Ms. Riveter

Often, a harassed employee wants to pursue more than one of the remedies that are available. The example here illustrates how to do just that.

To a certain extent, we are jumping ahead here, mentioning details about legal procedures we will be discussing more thoroughly in the next three chapters. But at this point, the details are not important: We are simply presenting a scenario of a sexual harassment case to give you an idea of how these remedies interact.

The factual scenario we are using, of course, is just one out of many sexual harassment situations. It may seem grimmer or more intractable than any you face, but it is unfortunately not rare. We do not profess to present the one right solution to this problem, but rather one of many possible solutions. Many harassed women and their attorneys would deal with the problem differently.

■ ■ ■

The Not-So-Rosy Case of Ms. Riveter

1. The new job

Rose Riveter is a single mother with two young children. She takes a job as an assistant truck dispatcher for Minnesota Builders, a large, non-union construction firm in Minneapolis. She is one of only three women working in a plant of about 85 men. The dispatcher she replaced was a man, as are all the other dispatchers. On her first day there, one of the other women employees, a file clerk, warns her to watch out for some of the men.

During her first week, Roy Harlow, one of the truck drivers, makes sexual comments to her each time he comes into the office. One time he talks about her breasts. Another time he tells her that she has "nice pouty lips" and that "he could put them to good use."

Riveter tells Harlow she doesn't appreciate his comments. He then leers at her and says: "Women like you don't know what the hell they like, 'til someone puts it to 'em." The next time he comes into the office, he asks her to get something off a bottom shelf, and as she bends over he says: "Just as I thought—that's pretty nice, too."

After the last incident, all within her first week on the job, Riveter complains to her supervisor. He says: "You know, that's the way guys are sometimes. I'll see what I can do."

Two days later, Harlow comes up to her desk and says: "What the hell are you trying to do, get me in trouble?" An hour later she finds an anonymous, typewritten note on her desk that reads: "Are you really dumb enough to think that anyone's after that body of yours? I guess those lips are only good for talking."

There is a notice about a Complaint Committee posted on the company bulletin board, and Riveter goes to that office and writes out a short statement about what happened. She's told that one of the staff members will look into the matter.

Analysis

Let's look at Riveter's situation so far—and what her options are for changing it.

The legal definition of sexual harassment. This is clearly a sexual harassment situation in a legal sense. Each of the four factors discussed in Chapter 2 are present: Harlow is obviously engaged in a form of unwelcome sexual conduct, and there is little doubt that a reasonable woman would find it offensive. All of this happened within one week, and the file clerk's warning suggests that it's happened before. Therefore, it seems likely that the threshold level for severe or pervasive harassment has been reached as well.

Confronting the harasser. It seems unlikely that Harlow will yield to any reasonable discussion about the problem as discussed in Chapter 3. His hostile response to Riveter when she asked him to stop his obnoxious comments pretty much cuts off communication, and he continues to escalate such conduct even after her clear indication the comments were unwanted.

Using the company complaint procedure. Riveter has taken the necessary steps to use the company complaint procedure, and that seems like a good thing to do. This is the kind of problem that should ordinarily be resolved under an effective complaint procedure. (See Chapter 4.)

Putting the company on notice. Riveter has protected her legal rights by both reporting the incidents to her supervisor, and making a report to the company complaint committee. She is now assured that the company knows of the harassment. If the company has notice and fails to do anything to correct the situation, it can be held responsible for the consequences of any future sexual harassment.

2. Her word against his

During her second week on the job, two other truck drivers start referring to Riveter as "Lips" around the office. When she asks them where they got that name, they just laugh. In the same week, she receives several anonymous telephone calls in which the caller makes pornographic remarks about her body. A picture of a naked woman is left on her desk anonymously. There's an arrow pointing to the crotch, and in block lettering it says: "See the difference? Here's what a real woman looks like." After she receives this, she breaks down crying at her desk and then leaves the office for about an hour to regain her composure.

Riveter returns to the office of the Complaint Committee, which tells her that they looked into the matter and that there was nothing they could do. According to the committee, Harlow denies everything. He's a good employee, she is told, and he has worked there 15 years. So it's just his word against hers.

Analysis

The complaint procedure in this company has turned out to be useless. Not only has it done nothing to help Riveter, but the problem has become greater and other employees are now engaged in the harassment.

3. Retaliation and getting help

In her third week on the job, Riveter finds more notes left on her desk. One includes a naked photo of a woman taped onto a drawing of a dartboard. The picture has her name next to it. Riveter is so upset, she becomes nauseated and starts to shake. Later, when she files a stack of papers, she puts them in the wrong file—a fact she doesn't discover until several days later when her boss yells at her.

Riveter feels so ill that she takes the rest of the day off as well as the next day. On the day she is home, she gets an anonymous phone call from a male caller who laughs and asks her if she is enjoying all of her leisure time.

On Friday, she returns to work and is told by her supervisor that she will be reassigned to a lower-paying secretary job in a small branch office in an undesirable location. The reason he gives is that her work performance is poor and the company needs better attendance in the dispatcher's job.

A friend advises Riveter to call some government agency for help. She locates the Minneapolis office of the U.S. Equal Employment Opportunities Commission and files a complaint in that office. A few days later, she gets a letter from the Minnesota Department of Human Rights in St. Paul, stating that her complaint has also been received by that office.

Analysis

By this point, Riveter has suffered substantial injuries.

Lost wages and other job-connected losses. Riveter is now threatened with serious job-connected losses—the most important of which is her impending demotion to a secretarial job in another location. This appears to be in retaliation for reporting the sexual harassment. The specific losses are: the demotion, the forced reassignment, the loss of pay and the costs of relocation.

Personal injuries. Riveter is also starting to suffer personal injuries—nausea and shaking that are beginning to affect her job performance. She's also lost a day and a half of work. If she loses pay for that time off—quite likely since she's a new employee—that could either be considered a job-connected loss or a personal injury loss.

Filing a claim with the EEOC. Riveter files a claim with the EEOC and then gets a letter from the Minnesota FEP agency, saying that the claim is filed there as well. This means that the claim has been dual-filed with both agencies. Riveter thought about having someone else file the complaint for her to keep her identity a secret, but she decided not to bother since the company is likely to guess her identity because of her prior complaints and the few women who work there.

4. Confrontation and investigation

The day after she files the complaint, Riveter is told by two drivers that another employee, Harris, wants to see her in the storeroom. She finds Harris standing there alone with his pants unzipped, exposing himself.

She turns around to go back out of the room and finds Harlow and the two other truck drivers blocking the hallway and laughing at her. They ask her if she "saw anything she liked." She pushes past them to get out of the building, afraid. She tries to move faster to get out of their way, and hits her knee against a desk. Her knee buckles as she falls down. She is pain for several days, and takes time off.

The EEOC investigators tell her that they have had other complaints against Minnesota Builders. They interviewed some of the other women employees, both past and present, and found that three of them had been subjected to similar behavior. One woman had also been cornered in the storeroom. The EEOC subpoenas the company personnel records and finds out that the company also has a report on file about a prior sexual harassment incident involving Harlow and Harris.

The EEOC says that the only thing the company is willing to do is to transfer her to another dispatcher job away from Harlow and Harris. But they'll only do that if she drops the rest of her claim. The EEOC doesn't know whether any further conciliation efforts will be successful, and the agency has not yet decided whether it can take the case to court.

Analysis

The EEOC investigation has turned up some important information: other complaints in the EEOC files, a previous harassment incident in the company files and three other witnesses who have suffered similar harassment. (See Chapter 6, Section J.)

But the company isn't willing to pay anything for Riveter's injuries, and the EEOC isn't sure that it can take the case to court. Any further action by the EEOC is likely to take many more months—in fact, we've speeded up the time it takes for a normal investigation for purpose of this scenario.

> **B**ULLIES AND CREEPS ARE NOT ALWAYS BORN; MANY OF THEM ARE
> MADE. AND IF WE CAN STOP THAT PROCESS WE WILL HAVE HELPED
> OURSELVES ENORMOUSLY. —NANCY MCCARTHY IN A LETTER TO THE
> EDITOR, *THE WALL STREET JOURNAL*, 11/6/91

5. The last straw

Riveter is still suffering from nausea and shaking, as well as loss of sleep. She can only work intermittently. The pain medication she takes for her sore knee has increased the nausea and caused fainting spells. She consults an orthopedist who tells her that she has torn cartilage that will require surgery. He also makes an appointment for her with a psychologist to see if she has any emotional or mental disorders that might be causing her problems.

She returns home from the doctor's office, and her nine year-old son is waiting at the door. "What's a whore?" he asks, handing her an unsigned note that he says he found under the door. The note says: "Why the hell don't you just leave? We don't need whores like you around."

Riveter starts shaking uncontrollably and checks herself into the emergency room at the county hospital that evening. She is hospitalized for two weeks.

When she gets out of the hospital, Riveter contacts a women's support group that urges her to fight back and do what she can to make Minnesota Builders a safer place for women to work. They refer her to an attorney experienced in handling sexual harassment cases, who listens to Riveter's account and agrees to take the case on a contingent fee basis. (See Chapter 9, Section A.4.) The attorney advises Riveter to notify the EEOC immediately so that she can amend her claim or file a new one to reflect the latest events. Her attorney also asks the EEOC to issue her client a right-to-sue letter as soon as possible so that she can proceed to court with her client's lawsuit.

Analysis

The case has reached a critical point where several things start to come together.

Hiring an attorney. Riveter decided to hire her own attorney, who agreed to take the case on a contingent fee basis. This step is critical. Without the attorney's willingness to take the case for a contingent fee, Riveter would never have been able to afford such legal services.

Filing a lawsuit. The attorney advises Riveter to file a lawsuit and not wait for further action by the EEOC. The attorney says it is unlikely that the EEOC will decide to take the case to court itself on her behalf, and the injuries she has suffered cannot be redressed completely by a lawsuit under the U.S. Civil Rights Act. The attorney has in mind a strategy that includes filing several types of legal claims, but Riveter will be able to use the evidence that the EEOC has turned up during its investigation.

No administrative hearing. Riveter could have her case heard in an administrative hearing within the Minnesota Department of Human Rights, the Minnesota FEP agency. Since that agency can award her damages for her injuries, that wouldn't be a bad idea in many situations. (See Chapter 7 for a state-by-state list of FEP agencies empowered to award damages for personal injuries.)

But the Minnesota FEP agency doesn't have the power to award punitive damages. Riveter's attorney feels that her client has a chance in this case for a large recovery for both compensatory and punitive damages once she presents all the facts to a judge and jury about Riveter's injuries and the outrageous conduct of the company and its employees.

Speeding up the right to sue. Riveter's attorney is anxious to file her case in court as soon as possible. Even after a case is filed, there will be a considerable delay in bringing it to trial as the court puts it on its crowded trial calendar, so there is no reason to wait. Riveter and her attorney want to include a claim under the U.S. Civil Rights Act, even though it probably won't be the principal focus of the case. For this she needs a right-to-sue letter from the EEOC.

Riveter asks that agency to issue a right-to-sue letter immediately. Once that request is made, the EEOC is obliged to issue the letter within 180 days from the date the claim was originally filed. (See Chapter 6, Section L.2.) She does not have to ask the Minnesota Department of Human Rights to issue a right-to-sue letter, because there is no such requirement under the Minnesota FEP law.

Personal injuries. It's time to take another look at Riveter's personal injuries, which have gotten worse since we looked at them last.

- *Stomach illness and psychological problems:* She doesn't have a complete diagnosis of the problems, so we don't know how serious they are. At the trial, Riveter's attorney is planning to put a doctor on the stand who will testify that the injuries were stress-related and resulted from the sexual harassment.

- *Knee problem:* Riveter will testify that she fell because she was scared and trying to get away from the co-workers who had cornered her. The co-workers may try to argue that they couldn't foresee that she would fall down and injure her knee, so they shouldn't be liable for the injury. But that kind of argument usually doesn't work. The basic rule here is that the defendants—the co-workers, in this case—are liable for whatever happened as a result of their conduct, whether anyone could have foreseen it or not.

- *Reaction to the medication:* Riveter will also claim she was injured by the drug reaction and should be compensated for that. The defendants may try to argue that her stomach problem wouldn't be as bad as it is, if she didn't have a bad reaction to the pain medication. That kind of argument usually doesn't work either. Once again, the basic rule is that the defendants are liable for whatever happened as a result of their conduct even if some later event, like a drug reaction, made the situation worse.

Compensatory damages. At trial, Riveter's attorney will ask the jury to award a large amount of compensatory damages, which will include:

- loss of wages for days she was out ill

- loss of future employment if she's not yet ready to return to work

- cost of doctors, hospitals, medicine, therapy and other out-of-pocket expenses

- costs of home care for Riveter, if necessary, and the cost of taking care of her children while she is hospitalized or incapacitated

- If her leg is permanently impaired, an amount to cover future loss of income and enjoyment of life, and

- compensation for her pain and suffering.

Punitive damages. Punitive damages can be awarded at the discretion of the judge or jury if the defendants' conduct has been particularly outrageous. Riveter's attorney is getting ready to argue that:

- the acts of Harlow and Harris were particularly vicious and outrageous, and

- Minnesota Builders showed a reckless disregard for Riveter's safety and well-being by failing to discipline its employees or do anything to protect her safety.

6. Riveter strikes back

Riveter's attorney files a lawsuit against Harlow, Harris and Minnesota Builders that joins together several of the legal claims her client may have. They include:

a. sexual harassment under the Minnesota FEP law

b. sexual harassment under the Civil Rights Act

c. assault, a common law tort

d. intentional infliction of emotional distress, a common law tort

e. reinstatement to the job under the Civil Rights Act and FEP law

f. a request for injunctive relief under the Civil Rights Act and FEP law

g. a request for attorney's fees under the Civil Rights Act and FEP law.

Analysis

Attorneys filing lawsuits often include claims that seem to duplicate each other out of an excess of caution. In Riveter's case, there is a purpose behind each of the these claims:

MEN HAVE NOT UNDERSTOOD THE POWER THEY HAVE HAD OVER WOMEN IN THE WORKPLACE, AND WOMEN HAVE NOT REALIZED HOW MUCH THEY HAVE HAD TO RELINQUISH IN ORDER TO STAY ON THE JOB.—GALEN ELLIS, DIRECTOR OF THE CENTER FOR WORKING LIFE, A NONPROFIT ORGANIZATION THAT HELPS WORKERS COPE WITH HARASSMENT

a. The Minnesota FEP law

The Minnesota Human Rights Act, the state's FEP statute, seems to allow Riveter to recover compensatory damages for her injuries—including mental anguish, without any limitation as to the amount. Her attorney is uncertain, however, about whether she can recover for the knee injury because she hasn't found any court decision among sexual harassment cases that involved a physical injury of that type.

There is one limitation that is unique to the Minnesota FEP law that her attorney doesn't like: Punitive damages are limited to $8,500. She knows she can get a jury to go for a lot more than that if there is no restriction on the amount.

But there is something about the Minnesota law that Riveter's attorney really likes: The court is authorized to triple the actual damages. That functions as a form of punitive damages. Both of these provisions are unique to Minnesota law, but other states have their own unique provisions. (See Chapter 7 for a state-by-state listing.)

b. The Civil Rights Act

The U.S. Civil Rights Act also provides compensatory damages for Riveter's injuries, but her attorney still has the nagging worry about whether a knee injury is covered. The main problem with this remedy, however, is that the total amount of compensatory and punitive damages is limited to an amount between $50,000 and $300,000 based upon the number of employees in the company.

Riveter's attorney will try to allocate the damage claims between the Civil Rights Act and FEP statutes to get the highest possible money award for Riveter. She will argue that:

- the compensatory damages awarded to Riveter should all be allocated to the Minnesota FEP statute (where there's no limitation), and

- the punitive damages awarded to Riveter should all be allocated to the U.S. Civil Rights Act where the limit on damages is between $50,000 and $300,000 (depending on the number of employees of the company) instead of to the Minnesota FEP law where there is a limit of $8,500 on punitive damages.

That trick of allocation might get Riveter close to $300,000 more than she would otherwise get. The 1991 amendments to the Civil Rights Act have never been tested in court, so no one knows if such an allocation will work.

c. Assault

If Riveter's attorney can prove Minnesota Builder's employees committed the common law tort of assault, she can get around the problem of limitations on damages under the Minnesota FEP law and the U.S. Civil Rights Act. There are no arbitrary limits to monetary damages in a common law tort action of this nature, so the jury is free within broad limits to award the appropriate amount of compensatory and punitive damages.

The difficulty with this claim, however, is to prove that an assault actually occurred. The only time Riveter had physical contact with her harassers is when she pushed past them in the hallway. No doubt she was afraid they would grab her, and that is why she stumbled and hurt her knee. But to prove an assault, she has to prove that they intended to grab her. It is not clear at this point whether she can prove this. (See Chapter 8, Section B.1 for a discussion of assault.)

The problem is this: A sexual harassment claim under the FEP law or Civil Rights Act is easier to prove under these facts than assault, but an assault claim gives a clearer chance for an unlimited damage award. In this situation, an attorney would likely file all possible claims and hope to slide by the problems at the time of trial.

d. Intentional infliction of emotional distress

There are similar advantages and disadvantages to the other common law tort theory, intentional infliction of emotional distress. If this tort is proven, there is a right to full compensatory and punitive damages. But the problem is proving it. A claim for intentional infliction of mental distress generally requires proof of a great degree of outrageousness. (See Chapter 8, Section B.2.) Conduct may be severe enough to violate the prohibition against sexual harassment and still not amount to what the law would consider an intentional infliction of emotional distress.

Riveter's attorney will push this claim hard, but she still has two statutory claims for sexual harassment under the Civil Rights Act and under the Minnesota FEP law to fall back on.

e. Reinstatement to the job

Riveter says she wants her dispatcher job back, so there's no reason not to ask for it in the complaint. If she has changed her mind when the case comes to trial, she can always drop it at that point.

f. Request for injunctive relief

In the ordinary lawsuit to recover damages for personal injuries, a claim for injunctive relief will either be dropped or not pushed very hard. The employee is usually seeking only damages for injuries and has no intention of going back to work at that particular company.

But there is no reason that an employee like Riveter cannot try to obtain a court order that will force the company to correct certain sexual harassment abuses if that is what she wants to do. In this case, she has been persuaded by the women's group that assisted her that she should at least consider using her lawsuit to force certain reforms upon Minnesota Builders.

The main problem with including this type of reformist claim is that it upsets the legal fee arrangements. Riveter's attorney is pursuing the claim for damages on a contingent fee contract, because if she wins she will get a percentage of the money damages as legal fees. A claim for injunctive relief cannot be handled that way, because even if her attorney is successful in obtaining a court order there is no money award from which she can deduct her fees.

As a practical matter, therefore, this type of claim would either be filed separately from the personal injury claim—and the attorney paid on an hourly basis or similar retainer—or some sort of special arrangement would be made to fund the injunctive relief part of the employee's claim separately from the personal injury claim. In this case, Riveter's arrangement with her support group is that she will only pursue this type of relief if the group can come up with the money to pay for the legal fees connected with it.

g. Request for attorney's fees

The court is authorized to award an amount of attorney's fees to be added to the judgment if Riveter wins the case. Theoretically, the attorney's fees should only be awarded on the Civil Rights Act claims and the FEP claims, and they should not be awarded for the work done on the two common law torts. As a practical matter, however, it is very difficult to divide up an attorney's time with precision when these type of overlapping legal theories are litigated.

REFORMS ARE MADE, IMPORTANT ONES; BUT THE STATUS OF WOMEN RELATIVE TO MEN DOES NOT CHANGE. WOMEN ARE STILL LESS SIGNIFICANT, HAVE LESS PRIVACY, LESS INTEGRITY, LESS SELF-DETERMINATION. THIS MEANS THAT WOMEN HAVE LESS FREEDOM.—FROM *INTERCOURSE*, BY ANDREA DWORKIN (MACMILLAN, 1987)

6

The EEOC and the U.S. Civil Rights Act

A. When To Use the Civil Rights Act 6/3

B. Coverage and Remedies.. 6/4
    1. Employees who are covered... 6/4
    2. Remedies available 6/4
    3. Filing a claim is a prerequisite.. 6/5

C. The Importance of Counting Employees 6/5
    1. The 15-employee minimum requirement... 6/6
    2. The limitation on damages.. 6/6

D. How To Count Employees... 6/7
    1. The counting period.. 6/8
    2. Which employees are counted 6/9

E. Independent Contractors.. 6/12
    1. True status of employee.. 6/12
    2. The status of other employees.. 6/13

F. Where To File an EEOC Claim 6/14
    1. File at an EEOC office 6/14
    2. Dual-filing 6/14

G. How To File a Claim 6/16
    1. Filing in person or by mail 6/16
    2. Keeping your identity confidential 6/16

H. Time Limits for Filing a Claim... 6/18
    1. Within 180 or 300 days 6/18
    2. Claim must be actually filed.. 6/18
    3. Company procedure does not extend time 6/18
    4. Determining the date of the harassment................................ 6/19
    5. Exceptions for late claims 6/19
    6. Restructuring the claim to stress later events........................ 6/20

I. Contents of the Sexual Harassment Claim 6/21
    1. Name and address of the employee....................................... 6/23
    2. Name and address of the person charged 6/25
    3. The approximate number of employees................................ 6/26
    4. A statement of the facts.. 6/27
    5. Tips for writing an effective EEOC claim.............................. 6/29

J. EEOC Investigation of the Claim 6/30
    1. Investigative procedures... 6/30
    2. Subpoena power 6/31

K. EEOC Action After Completing the Investigation............................ 6/32
    1. Conciliation by the EEOC... 6/32
    2. A finding of no cause by the EEOC 6/33

L. Lawsuit By the EEOC or By the Employee...................................... 6/33
    1. Lawsuit by the EEOC... 6/34
    2. When the right-to-sue letter is issued................................... 6/34
    3. Filing a lawsuit under the Civil Rights Act............................ 6/36

M. EEOC District Offices 6/37

Chapter 5 compared the different legal remedies for sexual harassment—and discussed the most appropriate legal paths for sexually harassed employees. This chapter takes a closer look at one of the laws prohibiting harassment, the Civil Rights Act, which is also called Title VII. We also explain how the Equal Employment Opportunities Commission (EEOC) enforces the Act.

WHEN YOU DON'T NEED TO READ THIS CHAPTER

This chapter is intended for those who are seriously considering filing a claim with the EEOC under the U.S. Civil Rights Act—or for those who are considering filing a claim under their state fair employment practices law and want to know more about the administrative procedures which are similar for both federal and state agencies.

If you do not wish to file charges, but instead want to try informally to stop the harassment, see Chapter 3.

A. When To Use the Civil Rights Act

There are several reasons to file a claim with the EEOC under the U.S. Civil Rights Act.

- It provides a system of investigating and settling sexual harassment claims that is comparable too, and in some cases better than, similar systems provided by the various state fair employment practices (FEP) agencies.

- Because of dual-filing agreements between the EEOC and most state agencies, filing a claim with the EEOC will ordinarily protect your rights under both the Civil Rights Act and the particular state FEP law. (See Section F.2.)

- The Civil Rights Act provides a limited amount of money damages for personal injuries, based on the number of employees in the company. In this respect, it is better than many state FEP laws but not as good as others. (See Chapter 7.)

B. Coverage and Remedies

There are some limitations as to which employees are covered and what remedies are offered under the Civil Rights Act.

1. Employees who are covered

The Civil Rights Act extends protection against sexual harassment to employees of all public and private employers in the United States, including U.S. citizens working for a U.S. company in a foreign country. The Act also applies to labor unions, both to the workers they employ and to their members.

However, there is one major exception: The Civil Rights Act does not apply to any company that has fewer than 15 employees. (This 15-employee minimum is discussed in detail in Section C.1.)

2. Remedies available

Remedies that the courts or the EEOC can provide under the Civil Rights Act to a sexually harassed employee include:

Reinstatement and promotion. A court can order the employee rehired, promoted or reassigned to whatever job she lost because of sexual harassment.

Wages and job-connected losses. A court can award any salary and benefits the employee lost as a result of being fired, demoted or forced to quit because of sexual harassment. This can include loss of wages, pension contributions, medical benefits, overtime pay, bonuses, back pay, shift differential pay, vacation pay and participation in a company profit-sharing plan.

Money damages (limited amount). A court can award damages to compensate for personal injuries. This can include money to cover the actual amount of out-of-pocket losses, such as medical expenses. It can also include other compensatory and punitive damages, but the amount of such damages is limited to between $50,000 and $300,000—depending on the number of people employed by the business. (See Section C.1.)

Injunctive relief. A court can direct the company to change its policies to stop sexual harassment and to prevent similar incidents in the future.

Attorney's fees. If the employee wins her case, a court can order the company to pay part of her attorney's fees.

3. Filing a claim is a prerequisite

You must file a claim with the EEOC to use the U.S. Civil Rights Act. Even if you or your attorney would prefer to skip the EEOC investigation and proceed directly to court, you must first file a claim with the agency and obtain a right-to-sue letter. (See Section L.)

IF YOU WORK AT A LARGE COMPANY

If you work for a large company with well over 500 full-time employees, skip the next three sections and go directly to Section F.

C. The Importance of Counting Employees

If you want to use the U.S. Civil Rights Act, you must know how many people work for your employer. This number is important for two reasons:

1. The Civil Rights Act only applies to companies with 15 or more employees, and

2. The amount of money damages you can recover is based on the total number of employees in the company.

1. The 15-employee minimum requirement

The 15-employee minimum can have very harsh results: If your company has fewer than 15 employees, the Civil Rights Act does not protect you. This means that the EEOC will not accept your case, will not investigate or negotiate your claim—and you can't sue your employer for damages under the Civil Rights Act.

The reason for this rule is not entirely clear, but Congress apparently felt that it should confine its legislative efforts to larger businesses and leave it to the states to prevent discrimination by smaller employers. If this is what Congress had in mind, it hasn't worked. Many state FEP laws also have a 15-employee minimum rule. And even among the state FEP laws with a smaller minimum requirement, several provide less effective remedies than the Civil Right Act. (See Chapter 7 for a state-by-state listing, including required number of employees.)

Workers in small firms should carefully read the next section to be sure they are counting correctly. But, sadly, there will be some employees who will conclude that no amount of creative counting will bring them under the protection of the federal or state sexual harassment laws. Their only hope for legal redress will stem from the common law tort remedies. (See Chapter 8.)

2. The limitation on damages

The number of employees also determines what limit on money damages will be placed on your claim. Prior to November 1991, there was no need to count employees for this purpose, because there was no right to money damages at all. Then Congress amended the Civil Rights Act, giving an employee the right to sue for compensatory and punitive damages, limited to:

$50,000 if the employer has 15 to 100 employees,

$100,000 if the employer has 101 to 200 employees,

$200,000 if the employer has 201 to 500 employees, and

$300,000 if the employer has 501 or more.

These limits are, of course, purely arbitrary; they have nothing do with the actual damages a harassed employee may have suffered. The reason they are in the law at all is strictly political. (See Chapter 1, Section D.)

The money restrictions do not apply to back wages, nor do they apply to out-of-pocket losses, such as doctor's bills. But they do set an upper limit on the combined total of all other compensatory and punitive damages, regardless of your injuries.

Example: Etta Stone works for a company that has 150 employees. She files a sexual harassment lawsuit against the company under the Civil Rights Act and convinces the jury that she has suffered severe injuries. The jury awards Etta $15,000 for her medical expenses, $150,000 for her pain and suffering and $200,000 in punitive damages.

However, the judge reduces her award based upon the limitations in the statute: Etta gets the $15,000 in out-of-pocket expenses, but the other $350,000 in damages is reduced to $100,000. The judge reduces the damage award because the number of employees where Etta works (150) places her in a category in which the maximum allowable damages under the Civil Rights Act is $100,000.

D. How To Count Employees

Any time a law sets arbitrary limits, you can expect problems. By setting a 15-employee minimum and damage limitations based on the number of employees in the company, Congress served up a plate with more than a few worms on it.

Counting the number of employees in your company is more complicated than it sounds. Here are a few tips on adding up these numbers.

1. The counting period

The Civil Rights Act states that the required number of employees—whether 15, 201 or 501—must be employed "in each of 20 or more calendar weeks in the current or preceding calendar year." There are ways you can use that language to your advantage.

a. Count in weeks

The number of employees is measured in weeks, not days. This means that if the necessary number of employees works for the company over a period of a week, the company is covered even though the number working on any given day may be smaller.

> **Example:** A clothing store is open seven days a week and maintains a staff of 75 employees each workday. Since no employee works more than five days each week, it has a total of 105 employees that it uses each week to field a daily staff of 75. The store fits in the $100,000 damage-limitation bracket (101 to 200 employees) rather than the $50,000 bracket (15 to 100 employees).

b. Weeks need not be consecutive

There is no requirement in the statute that the "20 or more calendar weeks" be consecutive, as long as the 20 weeks fall within the "current or preceding calendar year." The courts are not entirely clear on this point, but it appears that any 20 weeks within that period will do.

> **Example:** A fruit canning company has on staff 535 employees each week between September 1, 1991, and November 15, 1991, and again between September 1, 1992, and November 15, 1992. Between those two peak periods, the number of employees working each week drops to 87. On November 10, 1992, an employee is sexually harassed. The limit for her claim should be $300,000 (more than 500 employees), because the company employed more than 500 employees for two ten-week periods during 1991-1992.

c. Count need not be during peak employment

The language of the statute doesn't require that the sexual harassment have occurred during one of the "20 or more calendar" weeks in which the company has the required number of employees.

> **Example:** Marika Lim goes to work for a new real estate development firm on February 1, 1992. At the time the company only has ten employees. On February 10, 1992, her supervisor gives Marika a ride home, and while they are in the car he tries to talk her into having oral sex with him. When he won't back off, she has to force her way out of the car. Marika is under a doctor's care for several weeks, and she is fired on March 15, 1992. By June 1, 1992 the firm, which bought out another business, is up to 210 employees and stays at that level until the end of the year.
>
> Here, the company was below the 15-employee minimum at the time the incident occurred. But it later exceeded that minimum for more than 20 weeks during the same calendar year, so the case is covered under the Civil Rights Act. The case also fits within the $200,000 damage limitation bracket because the company had between 201 and 500 employees for more than 20 weeks during that year.

2. Which employees are counted

There can also be problems in determining which employees are counted for purposes of the 15-employee minimum and the damage restrictions. The harassed employee will want to count as many as possible, but the employer will want to keep the employee count down.

> DON'T BUY INTO THIS CRAP THAT MEN ARE SAYING, "YOU CAN'T EVEN SAY HELLO IN THE OFFICE ANYMORE WITHOUT BEING ACCUSED OF BEING A HARASSER."—BARBARA OTTO, 9TO5 SPOKESPERSON

a. Part-time employees

An employee who regularly works 20 hours per week or more should definitely be counted. The status of part-time employees who work less than 20 hours per week is less clear, but some courts have indicated they should also be counted. If your company has more than a handful of part-time employees who work less than 20 hours per week, argue that part-time employees are the norm within your company and that it would therefore defeat the purpose of the Civil Rights Act to exclude them. A court is least likely to count employees who are hired merely as temporary replacements for regular employees.

Part-time employees are entitled to the protection of the U.S. Civil Rights Act, whether or not they are counted for any of these purposes. In other words, the counting rules are only important in determining whether the company is large enough to meet the 15-employee minimum or in determining the damage limitation. Once it is determined that the Act applies to a company, all employees are covered—no matter how few hours per week they work.

> **Example:** A college student, Leah Fong, works ten hours each week as a stock clerk in a hardware store as a replacement for a regular employee who is on a month-long vacation. She and Michelle Sexton, one of the regular employees of the store, are sexually assaulted by the manager in the back room of the store.
>
> The EEOC investigator determines that the store is covered under the statute based on the fact that there are 15 full-time employees in the store. In making this calculation, she counts Sexton, the regular employee, but she does not count Fong, the substitute employee. But having now established that the Civil Rights Act applies, the EEOC accepts the sexual harassment claims filed by both employees.

b. Employees at other worksites

All employees of the company should be counted, no matter where they work. The count is not limited to the number at the worksite, in the particular division or even at the plant or building in which the harassed employee worked. In estimating the total number of employees in a relatively small company, remember that there may be additional employees who work at home or away from the worksite who should also be counted.

c. Employees of related companies

If the company where the sexual harassment occurs is one of a number of related companies that have some common ownership or linkage—for example, parent-subsidiary or franchisor-franchisee—the question frequently arises whether the employees of those related companies should be counted.

This question is answered on a case-by-case basis. According to the EEOC, its investigators will evaluate the "interrelationship of operations, common management, centralized control of labor relations, common ownership, and power of control over employees." If the companies are found to be integrated enterprises, all of the employees will be counted.

In some cases, it may be very important for a harassed employee who works for a small company to show that it is closely connected with a large, nationwide business.

THE PROBLEM IS THAT WE DON'T HAVE ENOUGH MEN (FIVE MEN, 40 WOMEN ON THE EDITORIAL STAFF) TO GO AROUND FOR THE HARASSING.—HELEN GURLEY BROWN, EDITOR IN CHIEF OF *COSMOPOLITAN* MAGAZINE, WHEN ASKED WHETHER THERE WAS ANY SEXUAL HARASSMENT IN HER OFFICE

Example: Tamina Darwin is sexually accosted by the manager and his supervisor at the ice cream store where she works. As far as she knows, there are only 12 employees of the store who work in shifts of six at a time. The ice cream shop is part of a heavily advertised, nationwide chain. The manager claims to be president of the corporation that owns the store, but he also appears to report directly to the supervisor who works for the nationwide franchisor.

If the individual ice cream shop is considered the "company," then there are not enough employees to meet the 15-employee minimum required by the Civil Rights Act. However, the store is part of a chain that advertises all of its stores nationwide. The store is also directly supervised by someone from the parent company—in fact, he participated in the sexual harassment. Although the manager is the president of the company, he does not act as if he or that company really owns the ice cream store.

These and other facts may be enough to show that the parent company had substantial ownership or control of the ice cream shop and would be considered one integrated business. If so, this would mean that there would be more than enough employees to put the business over the 15-employee minimum—and that a count of all the employees in the nationwide chain would be necessary to determine which damage limitation should apply.

E. Independent Contractors

The Civil Rights Act only prohibits discrimination and sexual harassment against employees. So if you have been classified as an independent contractor by your employer, you may have trouble using the Act.

1. True status of employee

Often a worker is required to sign a document stating that she is an independent contractor, when in fact she is treated as an employee. However, courts enforcing the Civil Rights Act may look through the label of "independent contractor" to protect you from sexual harassment.

Generally, you will be considered an employee for purposes of the Civil Rights Act if you do not have true independent control over how you do your work. The control must be real, not in name only. To be a true independent contractor, you must control not just the end product of the work, but also the details and means by which that result is accomplished.

2. The status of other employees

Your case can also be harmed if other employees are characterized as independent contractors. If a significant number of employees are classified as independent contractors, then they are not counted as employees for purposes of the Civil Rights Act. In a small company, you may find yourself not only trying to refute the argument that you are an independent contractor, but also arguing that your co-workers are not independent contractors, either.

HARASSMENT COMPLAINTS ON THE RISE

In 1981, a total of 3,661 complaints of sexual harassment were filed with the federal Equal Employment Opportunity Commission. By 1990, the number of complaints had climbed to 5,694—an increase EEOC officials attributed to the Supreme Court's unanimous recognition in 1986 that "without question," sexual harassment is a form of sex discrimination and that hostile environment as well as sex-for jobs harassment violates the Civil Rights Act (*Meritor Sav. Bank v. Vinson*, 477 U.S. 57 (1986)).

The number of EEOC harassment complaints is again expected to mount dramatically in the wake of 1991's public and publicized hearings in which U.S. Supreme Court nominee Clarence Thomas was alleged to have sexually harassed former co-worker Anita Hill while at the EEOC.

According to an EEOC spokesperson, quarterly tallies of the number of complaints filed show that 728 were filed during the first quarter of 1991—and 1,244 complaints were filed during the first quarter of 1992, just after the hearings.

F. Where To File an EEOC Claim

Filing a claim with the EEOC is relatively simple. You can do it alone—or with the assistance of an attorney or other advisor.

1. File at an EEOC office

A sexual harassment or discrimination claim can be filed at any EEOC office. There is no charge for filing.

There are EEOC offices throughout the United States. (See the end of this chapter for the addresses and telephone numbers.) Normally, it is best to file the complaint in the office nearest to you or your place of employment, but you can legally file it in any office.

2. Dual-filing

You also have the option in most states of filing your claim in the offices of a state FEP agency or sometimes a local FEP agency. The EEOC maintains "dual-filing" agreements with most state FEP agencies, as well as several local FEP agencies.

Dual-filing means that a claim filed in the state or local office is automatically filed at the same time with the EEOC office in the area. The reverse is true as well: Any claim filed with an EEOC office is automatically filed with an FEP office of the state where the employee works, if there is a dual-filing agreement. (See Chapter 5, Section F for an example of how dual-filing works.)

Even if a claim is dual-filed, there is usually only one investigation. Ordinarily the agency in which the claim is first filed does the actual work of investigation, but sometimes the two agencies also have a work-sharing agreement that allows them to shift the work of investigation back and forth.

Dual-filing can be important, because it allows you to get the benefit of both the Civil Rights Act and the state FEP law. This is particularly important if you have not hired an attorney. If you are unsure whether state or federal law offers the best protection, you can dual-file with both agencies and decide later which avenue to pursue after receiving legal advice.

If you file a claim with the state FEP agency or with the EEOC, ask if it will be dual-filed with the other agency. The EEOC does not have these agreements with every state FEP agency, and the agreements are subject to change without notice. If your claim has been dual-filed, you should receive a letter within a week or so confirming that fact. If you don't receive a letter, check with the other agency to confirm that it has been filed.

If for any reason the two agencies do not dual-file the claim, do it yourself. Tell the second agency that you already have a claim on file with the other agency and that you are only filing this second claim to protect your rights under both federal and state law.

EXPECT THE UNEXPECTED WITH EEOC PROCEDURES

For the most part, the EEOC does what it is supposed to do, but you shouldn't expect every case to proceed exactly as described in this chapter. EEOC offices differ in caseloads, local procedures and the quality of their personnel. Investigations are usually slow, sometimes taking as long as three years or more. The EEOC takes only a small portion of its cases to court—as few as 1% of those that are filed with it. These and other factors can have an impact on how a case is actually handled.

Some things to keep in mind:

Stay alert. Don't assume that the EEOC will do everything and that you don't have to monitor what is going on. Check periodically with the EEOC to find out to what is happening with your case.

Be assertive. If some EEOC action—or, more likely, inaction—is causing you serious problems, call that to the attention of the people handling your case.

Keep your options open. Filing a claim with the EEOC does not prevent you from taking other action to deal with your case. You still have a right to use a company complaint procedure or try to solve the problem on your own. You also have the right hire an attorney to file a lawsuit, if that is appropriate for your situation.

G. How To File a Claim

An EEOC claim can either be filed in your own name or by someone else acting for you to keep your identity confidential.

1. Filing in person or by mail

A sexual harassment claim can be filed in person or by mail at any office of the EEOC. It must be in writing to be valid. Certified mail is not necessary, but if you're filing a claim close to the deadline (see Section H), you should use certified mail with a return receipt or some other method that proves the date of delivery.

If you have the time and are able to do so, file the claim in person. Not only can you be sure that it has been received, but you can also become acquainted with some of the staff and pick up information on local office procedures. The claim does not have to be filed on any particular form to be valid, but if you file it in person, you can file it on the EEOC's specially-designed charge form.

If the particular EEOC or state FEP office requires you to make an appointment before coming in to file a complaint, be careful about the timing. You must file your claim within a certain time period (see Section H), and you have to be sure that the date set for your appointment is within the required time. Merely calling for an appointment within the required time is not enough to comply with the filing deadline.

2. Keeping your identity confidential

EEOC procedures permit another person or organization to file the claim on your behalf to keep your identity secret. This can be done by an attorney, a union, an employment rights group or any other person acting on your behalf.

This confidentiality rule has two purposes:

* to protect you from retaliation while the investigation is proceeding, and

- to encourage employees to file charges promptly after the sexual harassment has occurred.

Anyone filing on your behalf must do it in the same form and within the same time limits as you would if you were doing it yourself. The person or agency actually filing the claim must provide the EEOC with your name, address and phone number in a separate document so that EEOC personnel can contact you and verify that you authorized filing the charge. If at that point you continue to request that your identity remain confidential, the EEOC must honor your request.

Most state FEP laws do not have this type of confidentiality procedure. If you want to file confidentially at a state office, check first to be sure that the agency will protect your identity to the same extent as the EEOC. It is also a good idea to make sure that the confidentiality of your identity will be preserved when the EEOC dual-files your claim with the state FEP agency.

BEWARE OF RETALIATION

Although the EEOC may keep your identity confidential, there is nothing to prevent company management from figuring out your identity from the specific charges in the sexual harassment claim. If you are the only mailroom supervisor in the company and your complaint relates to harassment in the mailroom, it won't take long for the company to determine who is bringing the complaint. In this situation all you can do is watch for acts of retaliation and ask the EEOC to take protective action on your behalf if necessary.

Many EEOC investigations proceed to the point where conciliation or some other specific remedy for the employee is discussed, and it is usually impossible to resolve the case without telling the employer your name. Usually when settlement is in the offing, confidentiality of your identity may not be so critical. But if you are still concerned about possible retaliation by your employer, ask the EEOC staff if it will go to court, if necessary, to prevent the employer from retaliating against you.

H. Time Limits for Filing a Claim

Despite the fact that the EEOC is a nationwide agency, there is no uniform rule about the time limit in which a claim must be filed.

1. Within 180 or 300 days

The EEOC has two different time limits, called "statutes of limitation" in legal jargon, for filing sexual harassment claims. In some states, it's 180 days from the date of the sexual harassment incident; in others, it's 300 days from the incident. The EEOC tends to allow a longer filing limit in states that have longer time limits under their own FEP law, and to use shorter time limits in other states.

There is no penalty for filing early, but there are serious problems if you file late. Therefore, you should assume that the time limit for filing a claim is 180 days from the date of the harassment unless you are clearly told, preferably in writing, by the EEOC or state FEP agency that you have a longer time.

2. Claim must be actually filed

The written sexual harassment claim must be actually filed within the 180 period—or 300 days, if that applies. Talking on the phone with the EEOC personnel or setting up an appointment within the time period is not sufficient. The written claim must be on file.

3. Company procedure does not extend time

The time for filing with the EEOC is not extended if you attempt to resolve your claim through a company complaint procedure. However, under some state FEP laws, the time you spend using a company complaint procedure extends the time you have to file.

If you are engaged in a lengthy negotiation procedure with your employer over your claim but don't want to give up any of your other rights, file your claim within the 180 days and ask the EEOC to defer action until negotiations are finished.

4. Determining the date of the harassment

The 180-day period for filing the complaint begins on the day the act of sexual harassment actually occurs. But even though the events of the harassment may be etched in your mind, it is sometimes difficult to determine as a legal matter what incident triggers the 180-day period. The safest course is to file your claim within 180 days of the earliest harassment incident.

> **Example:** Sondra Felipo has been bothered by a co-worker who has pestered her for dates and made sexual innuendos to her. On November 1st, a friend tells her that one month earlier, the same man sent a photo of a woman to another male worker. The woman in the photo was naked with an arrow pointing toward her crotch. Attached was a note that read: "Looks just like Sondra Felipo to me." Sondra complained of this incident to her supervisor. It turns out that the co-worker is a friend of her supervisor, and on December 1st, Sondra is fired.
>
> The date of the incident that would begin the 180-day filing period may be December 1st when the most significant injury occurred to Sondra—the loss of her job. However, it could also be argued that the time period began on November 1st when she discovered the most serious act of harassment—the pornographic photo. Or it could be October 1st, when the actual incident occurred. The safest course for Sondra is to file her claim promptly. As long as she is within 180 days of the October 1st incident, there is no need for her to pinpoint the exact date of the harassment.

5. Exceptions for late claims

If you miss the deadline for filing a claim, the EEOC or the courts will allow you to file late in a few extenuating circumstances. Here are some of them:

a. Being misled about the facts

If you can show that you were misled about the real reason behind certain important events, you may be able to convince the EEOC to accept a late claim if you file promptly after discovering the facts.

> **Example:** Roberta Farrell is sexually accosted in the lunchroom by a co-worker—and she calls company security to get him away from her. Two weeks later, Roberta's supervisor tells her that she is being laid off because the company has to cut back on her department. One year later, she learns that there was no cutback in her department and that the supervisor who fired her is the brother-in-law of the co-worker who accosted her. In this case, the EEOC would likely allow Roberta to file a claim for sexual harassment if she did so promptly after learning the truth.

b. Being misled about the law

If you complain about a sexual harassment incident to your employer and the employer misleads you about your rights, then the EEOC filing date may be extended. A common example of this would be if your employer tells you that you can protect your rights by participating in a lengthy complaint procedure—and then fails to tell you when the time is running out for you to file your claim with the EEOC.

c. Hardship

If you have a legitimate reason why you were unable to file the charge with the EEOC within the proper time period, the agency may extend the filing deadline. If, for example, you had a lengthy illness, file the charge with the EEOC and give a plausible and detailed explanation as to why you should be granted an exception.

6. Restructuring the claim to stress later events

Even if an incident is barred by the 180-day or 300-day filing rule, there may be a later incident that is within the filing period. In this situation, you may not be able to recover damages for the earlier incident, but the later incident may be strong enough to sustain a damage award, particularly if there is strong evidence that the sexual harassment was part of a long pattern of behavior.

In this situation, you should file a claim based on the incidents that occurred within the filing period. But be prepared to point out to EEOC investigators how the things that occurred earlier had an impact on your injuries.

Example: Patrice Gabel received a series of six bizarre letters over a period of three years from one of her co-workers, expressing in strong terms his desire to go out with her. Patrice considers his behavior at work for the few weeks or so after each letter to be threatening and weird. During that period, he also phoned her at home and parked in front of her house. Patrice reported each of the the incidents to her supervisors, but they did nothing about it. Finally, after the last incident, Patrice sought psychiatric care. Within 180 days after the last incident, she filed a claim with the EEOC.

Patrice's EEOC claim was within 180 days of the last incident, but the earlier incidents would technically not be covered because they are beyond the 180-day period. However, the courts and the EEOC would probably allow evidence of the earlier incidents to be considered to show a pattern of conduct. Also, she could probably show that her need for psychiatric care, although triggered by the latest incident, was built up over a period of time. In other words, her injuries are current, but they are aggravated by what had happened before.

I. Contents of the Sexual Harassment Claim

A sexual harassment claim does not have to be filed on a government form. Any written document containing the necessary information will do. According to the EEOC regulations, a claim need only identify the parties and generally describe the harassment.

However, if you file a claim containing only the bare minimum of information, the EEOC will later ask for further information. So to save time, include all the important information from the start. EEOC regulations also ask that you state in your claim whether or not you have already filed a claim about the same sexual harassment incident with any other governmental agency.

According to EEOC regulations, the claim should include:

1. *The full name, address and telephone number of the person making the charge, or that of the person or organization filing a confidential complaint*

2. *The full name and address of the person charged with harassment, if known*

3. *A clear and concise statement of the facts, including pertinent dates when the alleged unlawful employment practices occurred, and*

4. *If known, the approximate number of employees of the employer or the approximate number of members of the labor organization, as the case may be.*

This information seems relatively straightforward, but you should be careful in writing up your charge. In fact, this may be a good time to get legal advice from an employee's organization or women's group. Many of them will be willing to review your claim with you before you file it. (See the Appendix for contact details.)

Here are some points to remember in answering each question.

S EXUAL HARASSMENT IS A SUBTLE RAPE, AND RAPE IS MORE ABOUT FEAR THAN SEX. —JOHN GOTTMAN, PSYCHOLOGIST AT THE UNIVERSITY OF WASHINGTON

1. Name and address of the employee

In most cases, you will simply write down your own name, address and telephone number.

SAMPLE LETTER

April 1, 199X

Equal Employment Opportunities Commission
Federal Building, Room 178
110 South Fourth Street
Minneapolis, MN 55401

Dear Madame or Sir:

I am writing to you to file a charge of sexual harassment against my employer under Title VII of the U.S. Civil Rights Act.

I have not filed a previous complaint with any government agency.

My name, address and telephone number are:

Ms. Rose Riveter
4321 South Spring Street
Minneapolis, MN 55401
612/123-4567

If someone else is filing the claim on your behalf so that your identity will remain confidential, a little more paperwork is required. Do not include your name on the claim letter. Instead, write in the name, address and telephone number of the person or organization filing the claim for you. This person or organization should also include a separate letter or document that states your name, address and telephone number with an indication that the claim is being filed on your behalf.

The claim or charging letter will at some point be shown to your employer and the individuals charged with the harassment. However, the cover letter, which includes your name, should remain in the EEOC files and not be shown to anyone.

SAMPLE COVER LETTER REQUESTING CONFIDENTIALITY

April 1, 199X

Equal Employment Opportunities Commission
Federal Building, Room 178
110 South Fourth Street
Minneapolis, MN 55401

Dear Madame or Sir:

Enclosed is a charge of sexual harassment against
Minnesota Builders that this organization is filing on
behalf of Ms. Rose Riveter, an employee of that company.

We are filing this charge on behalf of Ms. Riveter because
she wishes her identity to remain confidential pursuant to
29 C.F.R. 1601.7.

We request that this letter remain confidential and that
the information in it not be provided to any
representative of the people or organizations named in the
charge.

Ms. Riveter's address and telephone number are:

4321 South Spring Street
Minneapolis, MN 55401
612/123-4567

Sincerely yours,

Thelma Barrett
Minneapolis Women's Advocates
3214 Well Street
Minneapolis, MN 55401
612/765-4321

SAMPLE LETTER WITH CONFIDENTIAL CLAIM

```
April 1, 199X

Equal Employment Opportunities Commission
Federal Building, Room 178
110 South Fourth Street
Minneapolis, MN  55401

Dear Madame or Sir:

We are writing to you to file a charge of sexual
harassment against an employer under Title VII of the U.S.
Civil Rights Act.

We are filing this complaint on behalf of the employee to
maintain the confidentiality of her identity pursuant to
29 C.F.R. 1601.7. We have sent you a separate letter
giving her name, address and telephone number.

We have not previously filed a complaint in this matter
with any other government agency.

Our name, address and telephone number are:

Minneapolis Women's Advocates
3214 Well Street
Minneapolis, MN  55401
612/765-4321
```

2. Name and address of the person charged

When naming those charged in your claim, you should ordinarily include at least two names:

- the name of the person or people who sexually harassed you, and
- the name of your employer. If your employer is a franchisee, subsidiary or affiliate of some other company, or if you're not sure of the proper name of the company, list all the names you know.

Both the harasser and the employer should be named, because you will ordinarily want to establish that both are responsible for the sexual harassment and should be held liable for it.

Name any parent or affiliated companies as well. There are several reasons for doing this. You may want to establish that a parent company is liable for the harassment, because the subsidiary or affiliated company you work for may be unable to pay off any judgment for damages. There may also be some uncertainty about whether you and the harasser are technically employed by the same company, and you will want to show that all of the affiliated companies should be held liable. Also, you should be sure that all the employees in the affiliated and parent companies are counted together to bring your case into a higher damage limitation bracket. (See Section C.1.)

SAMPLE

The name and address of the businesses and person against whom the charge is made are:

Minnesota Builders
8976 Industrial Parkway
Minneapolis, MN 55401

Minnesota Construction Associates
(an affiliated company at the same address)

Roy Harlow
(address unknown, but he works at Minnesota Builders)

---

3. The approximate number of employees

The EEOC requests that you give the approximate number of employees for two reasons:

- to determine whether the company meets the 15-employee minimum under the Civil Rights Act, and

- to determine the appropriate damage limitation for your claim based upon the number of employees in the company.

It is unlikely that the EEOC will make a determination about the size of the company based on your estimate alone. But avoid making a low estimate of the number of employees whenever possible. If you estimate the number of employees at 500 or less, that could limit your potential damages to something less the $300,000 maximum allowed against larger companies. It is never advisable to state a number of employees that is less than 15.

Since you're unlikely to be in a position to know the precise number of employees, state an approximate amount with an open upper limit, such as: at least 500 to the best of my knowledge. If you have no idea of the number of employees, simply state that you don't know.

SAMPLE

I don't know the total number of employees at all of the offices of Minnesota Builders, but I believe that there are more than 500 employees.

---

4. A statement of the facts

You must include a brief statement of what happened to you in your claim to the EEOC. It should be written in plain English, rather than legalese, and the precise form is not important. You technically only have to include enough information to allow the EEOC to begin its own investigation, but it's best to include enough information to impress the agency with the seriousness of your sexual harassment claim.

If someone else is filing a claim on your behalf to protect your confidentiality, be sure the facts are stated so that they do not inadvertently reveal your identity. Sometimes the only way to do this is to make a statement of facts that is somewhat incomplete. If you are faced with this problem, explain the situation to someone at the EEOC and ask what information it will allow you to leave out of your claim letter.

SAMPLE STATEMENT OF THE FACTS

A statement of the facts is as follows:

On March 2, 199X, I started work as an assistant truck dispatcher for Minnesota Builders in Minneapolis. I was the only woman employee in my office.

During the first week I was there, one of the truck drivers, Roy Harlow, came into my office several times and made rude, sexual comments about my breasts, my lips and my buttocks. I told him to stop, but he continued.

On Friday, March 6th, I complained to my supervisor, but right after that, Mr. Harlow made a very hostile statement to me, which indicated that he had heard about my complaint but was still going to keep harassing me.

The next week, some of the other truck drivers began calling me by a derogatory nickname first used by Mr. Harlow. I don't know all of their names, but one of them is named John Harris. Also I received several anonymous phone calls and a note left on my desk with a pornographic picture. There was a very disparaging comment about me next to it. This happened on March 12th.

On March 13th, I filed a complaint with the company grievance committee, but they told me later they couldn't do anything about it. The following week on March 19th, someone left a photo on my desk of a naked woman on a dartboard.

The tension from all of this has left me ill, and I've found it hard to concentrate on my job. I've had nausea and a shaking problem I can't control. I had to take some time off from work, and while I was home I received an anonymous call from someone mocking me for taking time off.

When I got back to work on March 20th, my supervisor told
me that I was being demoted and assigned to another office
because he said my work wasn't adequate and I took too
much time off. However, my work was fine when I wasn't
being harassed by Mr. Harlow and whoever else is involved.
I think his real reason for demoting me was that I had
reported that I was being harassed.

Sincerely,

Rose Riveter

5. Tips for writing an effective EEOC claim

While charges to be filed with the EEOC can be informal, there are a few tips
you can follow to be sure your claim is as effective as possible.

Give the important facts, including attitudes. Include everything that might be
important. This includes facts about the events: "After I wouldn't go out with
him, he gave the promotion to a less experienced person." It may also include
facts about the attitudes of the harasser or management: "He always made a
lot of disparaging comments about women," or "He got hostile towards me
when I rejected his advances."

Don't worry about legal theories. You don't have to know what legal theory
applies to your case or to use technical legal language. Take, for example, a
48-year-old black woman who rejected her supervisor's advances and was
then passed over for a promotion. She may not know what his exact motivation was, but she should state the facts clearly so that the EEOC can investigate: "I am a 48-year-old black woman and I was passed over for promotion
under the following circumstances... "

The EEOC may ultimately decide that she was discriminated against because of her sex, her race, her age, her refusal of his sexual advances or some
combination of the four.

Don't exaggerate or understate your case. Avoid exaggerations and sweeping generalities in the charge you file with the EEOC, but don't be falsely modest or apologetic. Simply state the facts favorable to your position and avoid mentioning any doubts you may have.

If you state in your charge: "I felt that he was making a sexual advance to me," stop the sentence at that point. If you add an apology, such as: "maybe I was overreacting" or "maybe someone else wouldn't have taken it that way," you're only weakening your case. State your side of things, and leave it to the employer to argue against you.

Watch the dates. You must include the dates on which you were harassed, so be sure that the dates fit within the limits for the filing deadlines discussed earlier. (See Section H.) Always include the most recent or on-going acts of sexual harassment that fall within the proper time limits. If you describe only an act of sexual harassment that occurred a year or so ago, the EEOC may decide that you filed your claim too late.

Be brief. You need to cover all of the pertinent facts, but you don't have to go into elaborate detail with any one of them. The EEOC will interview you and investigate the claim thoroughly later.

J. EEOC Investigation of the Claim

Once the claim is filed, the EEOC follows its own routine in investigating the complaint and trying to resolve it. There is little you can do to speed up the process except to be prompt and thorough in responding to EEOC requests for information. Investigations take anywhere from several months to several years.

1. Investigative procedures

The EEOC has a number of different investigation techniques.

The first thing the EEOC does is notify the employer and other people charged within 10 days after the sexual harassment claim is filed. This is normally done by sending it a copy of the claim or charge filed by the employee. The employer and the others charged with harassment then have the right to file their own version of what happened.

The EEOC will accept any additional evidence or statements from friendly witnesses that either side wishes to present. The EEOC also gathers information by interviewing potential witnesses, so it is important to tell the EEOC what witnesses you would like its investigators to talk to.

You have a right to see any information the EEOC obtains through its investigation. You can use that information later in court if your case gets that far. It is important, therefore, to work with the EEOC to make the investigation as thorough as possible.

If the EEOC needs more information, it may ask you to make a more detailed statement. It may also request a fact-finding conference, at which you and your employer will sit down with EEOC investigators to figure out what facts you agree on—and what facts you don't agree on.

The EEOC can go to court while the investigation is going on to seek a court order, if necessary, to prevent your situation from getting worse. This is not something that the EEOC does very often. If you are faced with retaliation or some other threat from your employer during the course of the EEOC investigation, tell the agency and ask it to seek a court order, if necessary, to stop your employer from retaliating against you.

2. Subpoena power

The EEOC can also issue subpoenas to gather information. A subpoena is a court order that forces a witness to answer questions, to produce documents or give other information.

The EEOC can use this power to force an employer or any other witness to answer questions, disclose records or other evidence that might have a bearing on the case. Frequently, the crucial evidence that will make or break your case will be in the company files and the employer probably wouldn't give it to you without a subpoena. This could include performance reports, investigative reports of harassment incidents, personnel or hiring policies, or other documents.

Example: Lisa Goralsky files a claim with the EEOC, stating that she was fired from her job in a consulting firm because she complained about the sexual advances of a co-worker. The company files a response saying that Lisa was really fired because of poor job performance. At this point, Lisa remembers that a few months earlier, her supervisor had sent a letter to a prospective client, describing the consulting services they would perform, and praising her talents on the subject. She also remembers being told several months before that she had received a favorable job evaluation. She doesn't have a copy of either letter.

Although Lisa didn't have these crucial documents, by telling the EEOC investigators that they exist, she enabled the agency to subpoena documents from both her employer and the client company.

K. EEOC Action After Completing the Investigation

After the investigation is complete, the EEOC decides either to conciliate or dismiss the case.

1. Conciliation by the EEOC

If the EEOC decides there is reasonable cause to believe you were sexual harassed, it attempts to a negotiate a settlement informally.

Before trying to settle the case, the EEOC staff will normally meet with you to find out what to ask for. You may, for example, no longer want your job back but only be interested in recovering lost earnings and money damages resulting from the harassment. Once the EEOC knows how you want the case to be resolved, it attempts to get the employer to give you whatever you would get if you took the case to court and won. In other words, the agency has no authority to force you to accept anything other than your full legal rights by way of settlement.

If you agree, the EEOC ordinarily presents a proposal to the employer, requiring it to end its illegal practices and give you the agreed recovery in exchange for your agreement to waive your right to sue. If the employer agrees to this settlement, the EEOC must continue to monitor the case until it gets proof that your employer has fulfilled its obligations to you under the settlement. That ends the case.

If the employer rejects the settlement, then the EEOC will either file a lawsuit on your behalf or issue a right-to-sue letter that allows you to file your own lawsuit. (See Section L.2). All efforts at settlement are confidential, so none of the discussions or records from the conciliation process can be used later in court.

2. A finding of no cause by the EEOC

The EEOC will issue a "no cause" determination if it feels that your sexual harassment claim cannot be proven. If you receive a no cause letter from the EEOC, you have the right to appeal that decision. You can also treat the EEOC's no cause determination as the equivalent of a right-to-sue letter and take the case to court yourself.

If the EEOC dismisses your case or issues a no cause determination, consider carefully the reasons why it did so before taking the time and expense of pursuing the case further. Look at all the evidence, including any evidence the EEOC has uncovered. The EEOC can and does make mistakes, but ask yourself this question: Why am I any more likely to succeed in front of a judge or a jury than I have already done in front of the EEOC? Review your case with a women's support group or a knowledgeable friend and get their opinions.

Although the EEOC dismissal or no cause determination does not stop you from bringing your own lawsuit, your employer can use that evidence in a later trial to try to convince a judge or jury that you were not harassed.

L. Lawsuit By the EEOC or By the Employee

Either the EEOC itself or you and your attorney can bring a lawsuit if you have a right-to-sue letter.

1. Lawsuit by the EEOC

Once the EEOC has finished investigating and trying to settle the case, it can file a lawsuit itself based on the issues raised in your claim. However, this only happens in a tiny percentage of the cases that are filed with the EEOC.

If the EEOC files a lawsuit in your case, you can simply let it handle the entire matter and wait to see what happens. If you want your own attorney involved in the case, you can petition the court to make you an official party to the case. You and your attorney would then be formally involved in the entire decision-making process.

2. When the right-to-sue letter is issued

If the EEOC decides not to file a lawsuit itself, you can file a suit on your own. But you can't do so until the EEOC issues a right-to-sue letter.

Theoretically, the EEOC is required to complete its investigation within 180 days after the claim is filed, and is supposed to issue the right-to-sue letter at that point. But as a practical matter, the investigation usually takes a lot longer—sometimes three years or more. If left alone, the EEOC will not issue a right-to-sue letter until it feels that its investigation and conciliation efforts are complete. That may be several years down the line.

However, if the EEOC has not finished its investigation by 180 days after the claim filed, you can demand a right-to-sue letter. Also, upon request, the EEOC can issue a right-to-sue letter even before the 180 days are up if it determines that it probably will be unable to complete its investigation by the end of the 180-day period.

You ordinarily only have 90 days from the date you receive a right-to-sue letter to file a lawsuit, so it is very important that you receive it promptly. The right-to-sue letter is usually sent to you, so keep the EEOC informed of your current address to be sure you actually receive it.

There is a great deal of confusion about how the 90-day period should be measured. It is supposed to begin when you receive the letter. But while some courts have held that you must personally receive the letter to start the 90-day period, others have ruled that the period begins when it is received by a responsible person living at that address. If it is sent to your attorney, the 90 days runs from that date if it can be proven that you authorized the attorney to receive it for you.

To complicate matters further, some courts will assume that the 90 days begins five days after the letter was sent. Also, if you did not tell the EEOC of your current address, the 90 days will probably begin when the letter arrived at the last address you filed with the agency unless you have some very good reason for the miscommunication.

Failure to file the lawsuit within 90 days does not absolutely prevent you from bringing a lawsuit, because the court can allow you to proceed late if the delay was not your fault. However, you should not rely on the court's discretion. File your case well within the 90-day period to be sure you can bring a lawsuit.

WHEN TO DEMAND A RIGHT-TO-SUE LETTER

As mentioned, you can insist that the EEOC you a right-to-sue letter 180 days after you file your claim. This will allow you to proceed with your case quickly and avoid any further delay. But before doing so, there are two things you should consider.

- If the EEOC sends you a right-to-sue letter, it will ordinarily stop its investigation. From that point on, you are on your own, and whatever benefit you might have gotten from a further investigation is lost.

- Once you get the right-to-sue letter, you have a relatively short period of time to file your lawsuit. Ninety days may seem like a long time, but its not very long by a court's timetable. You will have to move quickly to get your case filed on time, so you should never ask the EEOC to issue a right-to-sue letter unless you have already retained an attorney who is ready to move on the case quickly.

---

3. Filing a lawsuit under the Civil Rights Act

Once the EEOC has issued a right-to-sue letter, you can then file a lawsuit in federal court—or, in some cases, in state court—to enforce your rights under the U.S. Civil Right Act.

T HIS FIRST SONG IS DEDICATED TO PROFESSOR ANITA HILL—MY NEW HERO.—SINGER/SONGWRITER BONNIE RAITT, LEADING OFF AN OCTOBER 12, 1991 CONCERT WITH THE SONG "[AIN'T GONNA BE YOUR] SUGAR MAMA [NO MORE]"

M. EEOC District Offices

As mentioned, there are EEOC offices throughout the United States. Normally, it is best to file a sexual harassment complaint at the office nearest to you or your place of employment. But if there is not one nearby or not one in your state, you can legally file it in any office.

ALABAMA

Birmingham District Office
1900 Third Avenue, North; Suite 101
Birmingham, AL 35203
(205) 731-0082

ARIZONA

Phoenix District Office
4520 North Central Avenue, Suite 300
Phoenix, AZ 85012-1848
(602) 640-5000

ARKANSAS

Little Rock Area Office
320 West Capitol Avenue, Suite 621
Little Rock, AR 72201
(501) 324-5060

CALIFORNIA

Fresno Local Office
1313 P Street, Suite 103
Fresno, CA 93721
(209) 487-5793

Los Angeles District Office
3660 Wilshire Boulevard, 5th Floor
Los Angeles, CA 90010
(213) 251-7278

Oakland Local Office
1333 Broadway, Room 430
Oakland, CA 94612
(510) 273-7588

San Diego Area Office
401 B Street, Suite 1550
San Diego, CA 92101
(619) 557-7235

San Francisco District Office
901 Market Street, Suite 390
San Francisco, CA 94103
(415) 744-6500

San Jose Local Office
96 North Third Street, Suite 200
San Jose, CA 95112
(408) 291-7352

COLORADO

Denver District Office
1845 Sherman Street, Room 201
Denver, CO 80203
(303) 866-1300

DISTRICT OF COLUMBIA

Washington Field Office
1801 L Street, NW, Suite 200
Washington, DC 20507
(202) 663-4264

FLORIDA

Miami District Office
1 Northeast First Street, 6th Floor
Miami, FL 33132
(305) 536-4491

Tampa Area Office
412 Madison Street
Tampa, FL 33601
(813) 272-5969

GEORGIA

Atlanta District Office
75 Piedmont Avenue, NE; Suite 1100
Atlanta, GA 30335
(404) 331-6093

Savannah Local Office
10 Whitaker Street, Suite B
Savannah, GA 31401
(912) 944-4234

HAWAII

Honolulu Local Office
677 Ala Moana Boulevard, Suite 404
Honolulu, HI 96813
(808) 541-3120

ILLINOIS

Chicago District Office
536 South Clark Street, 9th Floor
Chicago, IL 60605
(312) 353-2713

INDIANA

Indianapolis District Office
46 East Ohio Street, Room 419
Indianapolis, IN 46204
(317) 226-7212

KENTUCKY

Louisville Area Office
600 Dr. Martin Luther King Jr. Place
Room 268
Louisville, KY 40202
(502) 582-6082

LOUISIANA

New Orleans District Office
701 Loyola Avenue, Suite 600
New Orleans, LA 70113
(504) 589-2329

MARYLAND

Baltimore District Office
500 B Abel Wolman Municipal Building
Baltimore, MD 21202
(301) 396-5819

MASSACHUSETTS

Boston Area Office
1 Congress Street, 10th Floor
Boston, MA 02114
(617) 565-3200

MICHIGAN

Detroit District Office
477 Michigan Avenue, Room 1540
Detroit, MI 48226
(313) 226-7636

MINNESOTA

Minneapolis Local Office
220 Second Street South, Room 108
Minneapolis, MN 55401-2141
(612) 370-3330

MISSISSIPPI

Jackson Area Office
Cross Roads Building Complex
207 West Amite Street
Jackson, MS 39205-9996
(601) 965-4537

MISSOURI

Kansas City Area Office
911 Walnut Street, 10th Floor
Kansas City, MO 64106
(816) 426-5773

St. Louis District Office
625 North Euclid Street, 5th floor
St. Louis, MO 63108
(314) 425-6585

NEW JERSEY

Newark Area Office
60 Park Place
Newark, NJ 07102
(201) 645-6383

NEW MEXICO

Albuquerque Area Office
505 Marquette, NW; Suite 900
Albuquerque, NM 87102-2189
(505) 766-2061

NEW YORK

Buffalo Local Office
28 Church Street, Room 301
Buffalo, NY 14202
(716) 846-4441

New York District Office
90 Church Street, Room 1501
New York, NY 10007
(212) 264-7161

NORTH CAROLINA

Charlotte District Office
5500 Central Avenue
Charlotte, NC 28212
(704) 567-7100

Greensboro Local Office
324 West Market Street, Room B-27
Greensboro, NC 27401
(919) 333-5174

Raleigh Area Office
1309 Annapolis Drive, Suite 500
Raleigh, NC 27608
(919) 856-4064

OHIO

Cincinnati Area Office
The Ameritrust Building
525 Vine Street, Suite 810
Cincinnati, OH 45202
(513) 684-2851

Cleveland District Office
1375 Euclid Avenue, Room 600
Cleveland, OH 44115
(216) 522-2001

OKLAHOMA

Oklahoma City Area Office
531 Couch Drive
Oklahoma City, OK 73102
(405) 231-4911

PENNSYLVANIA

Philadelphia District Office
1421 Cherry Street, 10th Floor
Philadelphia, PA 19102
(215) 597-9350

Pittsburgh Area Office
1000 Liberty Avenue, Room 2038-A
Pittsburgh, PA 15222
(412) 644-3444

SOUTH CAROLINA

Greenville Local Office
15 South Main Street, Suite 530
Greenville, SC 29601
(803) 241-4400

TENNESSEE

Memphis District Office
1407 Union Avenue, Suite 621
Memphis, TN 38104
(901) 722-2617

Nashville Area Office
50 Vantage Way, Suite 202
Nashville, TN 37228
(615) 736-5820

TEXAS

Dallas District Office
8303 Elmbrook Drive
Dallas, TX 75247
(214) 767-7015

El Paso Area Office
The Commons Building C, Suite 103
4171 North Mesa Street
El Paso, TX 79902
(915) 534-6550

Houston District Office
1919 Smith Street, 7th Floor
Houston, TX 77002
(713) 653-3320

San Antonio District Office
5410 Fredericksburg Road, Suite 200
San Antonio, TX 78229
(512) 229-4810

VIRGINIA

Norfolk Area Office
252 Monticello Avenue, 1st Floor
Norfolk, VA 23510
(804) 441-3470

Richmond Area Office
3600 West Broad Street, Room 229
Richmond, VA 23230
(804) 771-2692

WASHINGTON

Seattle District Office
2815 Second Avenue, Suite 500
Seattle, WA 98121
(206) 553-0968

WISCONSIN

Milwaukee District Office
310 West Wisconsin Avenue, Suite 800
Milwaukee, WI 53203-2292
(414) 297-1111

7

State Fair Employment Practices Laws

A. EEOC Relationship with State FEP Agencies 7/2

    1. State agencies designated by the EEOC.. 7/2

    2. Dual-filing agreements 7/3

    3. No guarantees of effectiveness 7/4

B. Excluding Certain Employees 7/5

    1. Minimum number of employees 7/5

    2. Exclusion by type of employment... 7/5

C. Choosing a Remedy: The Importance of Damages... 7/7

    1. If no money damages are allowed... 7/7

    2. If money damages are allowed 7/8

D. Monetary Damages: State Differences... 7/8

    1. Administrative hearings... 7/9

    2. Punitive damages... 7/9

    3. Filing an administrative claim first... 7/9

E. Money Damages: State Summaries... 7/11

F. FEP Laws and Procedures: State Summaries.. 7/14

State fair employment practices (FEP) statutes provide a harassed employee with a legal remedy that is often similar to the U.S. Civil Rights Act. The effectiveness of these statutes varies considerably from state to state. Many states have a weak FEP statute that provides little help, but in other states, the FEP statute can be the single most effective legal weapon against sexual harassment.

SIMILARITIES TO EEOC PROCEDURES

Be sure to read Chapter 6. Although that chapter deals with the Civil Rights Act and the Equal Employment Opportunities Commission (EEOC), much of the discussion also applies to state FEP agencies—and is not repeated in this chapter.

Techniques for presenting your claim and for determining your eligibility are basically the same in dealing with a state FEP agency and with the EEOC. State FEP agencies use many of the same administrative processes as the EEOC, including the use of subpoenas to gather evidence, and negotiation and conciliation to settle cases. Unfortunately, EEOC problems of excessive caseload and delay are also present in most state FEP agencies as well.

A. EEOC Relationship with State FEP Agencies

The EEOC and most state FEP agencies work together to avoid unnecessary duplication of work, and to simplify their investigative procedures.

1. State agencies designated by the EEOC

The EEOC places most state FEP agencies in a category referred to as "designated." If an FEP agency is designated, it means that it meets certain standards set by the EEOC regarding staffing, funding and enforcement.

The EEOC and designated FEP agencies often defer to each other—that is, they accept each other's investigation of a case or refer cases back and forth in what is called a "work-sharing" agreement. Because the investigative work done by the designated state FEP agency must meet EEOC standards for this system to work, procedures will not vary that much from agency to agency or from state to state.

All of the agencies described in this chapter have been designated by the EEOC unless otherwise noted.

THE COURT IS SIMPLY NOT PREPARED TO SAY THAT A FEMALE WHO GOES TO WORK IN WHAT IS APPARENTLY A PREDOMINANTLY MALE WORKPLACE SHOULD REASONABLY EXPECT SEXUAL HARASSMENT AS PART OF HER JOB.—FROM *PRYOR V. UNITED STATES GYPSUM CO.*, 585 F. SUPP. 311 (W.D. MO. 1984)

2. Dual-filing agreements

The EEOC maintains dual-filing agreements with most—but not all—designated FEP agencies. This means that when you file a claim with one agency, it is automatically filed with the other agency as well. You then get the benefits of whatever rights are available under both the state and federal law.

Although dual-filing agreements are in force between the EEOC and most FEP agencies, they are subject to change without notice. If you file a claim with one agency, ask whether it will be dual-filed. (See Chapter 6, Section F.2.)

LOCAL AGENCIES MAY HAVE DIFFERENT LAWS

Many counties and cities also have their own laws prohibiting sexual harassment. Many of them have administrative agencies—similar to the EEOC or state FEP agencies—and some of these local agencies have also been designated by the EEOC.

If you are trying to decide where to file a harassment claim, find out whether there are any local agencies in your city or county that handle sexual harassment. Ask representatives at your local EEOC or state FEP office if they know of any—or look in the City and County Government listings in the telephone book under Employment Discrimination or Sexual Harassment.

Taking the time to do this bit of research could make a big difference in the outcome of your claim. Because local laws may be different from the laws of the state you live in, you may find that a city or county ordinance:

- Covers more categories of employees. For example, some states require a minimum number of employees, and a local law may not have this restriction.

- Covers more kinds of discrimination. A local law may define sexual harassment differently than the state law, or may prohibit other discrimination, such as discrimination based on sexual orientation.

- Gives better remedies. Even in a state which allows no compensatory or punitive damages, a local law may authorize such an award.

---

3. No guarantees of effectiveness

Each designated FEP agency has the power to stop ongoing acts of harassment and provide some help to the employee in recovering lost wages and other job-connected losses, but many FEP laws stop at that point. In about half of the states, the FEP agencies have only those minimum powers. In other states, the legislatures have gone further with their FEP laws and have established remedies in monetary damages for sexually harassed employees.

The mere fact that the EEOC has designated a state agency does not mean that agency administers an FEP law that offers an effective remedy.

B. Excluding Certain Employees

Most state FEP laws exclude various categories of employees from protection under the law. These exclusions vary greatly from state to state, but they fall into two general categories:

- Exclusions based on the number of employees, and

- Exclusions based upon the type of employment.

1. Minimum number of employees

Many states exclude employees from protection of the law unless the company has a certain minimum number of employees, but no state imposes a minimum that is higher than the 15-employee minimum under the U.S. Civil Rights Act. A few states set their own minimum number at 15, but most states that have a minimum set it at a lower number. For example, the Connecticut FEP statute covers companies with three employees or more, while Iowa covers companies with four or more.

If you fear you may be excluded from the protection of the state FEP law because your employer falls short of the minimum number of employees, ask the FEP agency for a copy of the statute or regulation and find out exactly what is required. In many instances, you can use some of the arguments suggested in Chapter 6, Section D, for making sure that the maximum number of employees are counted.

2. Exclusion by type of employment

Many state FEP laws exclude certain categories of employees. These categories also vary greatly from state to state, but there are certain similarities. Many states, for example, exclude women in domestic employment. Others exclude employees of religious groups or other non-profit groups. People employed by a parent, spouse or child is another common exclusion.

Be wary of any question on an FEP claim form that asks if you work in domestic employment or some similar type of work. If you answer yes, the FEP agency may decide that you are not protected by the law. If you have any doubt as to how to answer the question, ask to see the exact language of the statute or regulation. Sometimes the precise wording will clearly indicate that the exclusion does not apply to the particular type of work you do. Other times, you may be able to characterize the work you do in a way that the exclusion will not pertain to you.

> **Example:** Ken Arnold hires Jackie Baker. From the job interview, Jackie expected to do secretarial and editorial work for Ken's writing projects in his home office. But in reality, Jackie ends up spending most of her hours cleaning Ken's house, taking care of his kids and running errands for him. She does some secretarial work, but on those days, Ken sexually harasses her.
>
> When Jackie files her claim with the state FEP office, she describes her work as secretarial rather than domestic service for two reasons: That is the type of work she thought she was getting and, she considers that the most important part of her job.

Because sexual harassment is abusive and often violent, you may be able to convince a judge or the FEP agency not to apply these exclusions too strictly. These exclusions were written into the FEP laws mainly so that the anti-discrimination provisions of these laws would not apply in certain types of hiring situations. The state legislatures wanted to give employers the right to hire a close relative, despite equal opportunity restrictions—and to allow employers to hire whomever they wish for extremely personal work, such as domestic service or work that requires the employee to live in the employer's home, such as personal care.

But there is a big difference between allowing a man to hire whomever he wants as an assistant or a housekeeper and allowing him to sexually harass the woman that he does decide to hire. In other words, sexual discrimination and sexual harassment cases are different. You may be given the benefit of the doubt in some cases because of the possibility of serious injury and abuse in sexual harassment situations.

C. Choosing a Remedy: The Importance of Damages

The most significant difference among the various state FEP laws is between those that allow money damages to be awarded for personal injuries, and those that do not. About one-half of the states award these damages. This is a key issue, because the availability of money damages will often be the determining factor in deciding whether to pursue a claim under the state FEP law or deciding to pursue another remedy, instead.

1. If no money damages are allowed

If you feel you have a claim for personal injuries, there is no good reason for you to use a state FEP law that makes no provision for money damages. You should probably pursue your claim under the U.S. Civil Rights Act, instead, since that Act allows at least a limited award of money damages—between $50,000 and $300,000 based on the number of employees in the company. (See Chapter 6, Section B.)

The EEOC and the state FEP agencies are roughly equal in their investigative powers and their ability to provide other types of help to harassed employees, so the existence of a potential remedy in money damages under the federal law will often be the decisive consideration. Of course, not every sexual harassment case involves personal injuries. But if you have suffered personal injuries, you will want to be compensated adequately.

You may not be eligible under the Civil Rights Act because you work for a company with fewer than 15 people. (See Chapter 6, Section C.) This rules out the Civil Rights Act as a remedy in your case, but it doesn't make a poor FEP statute any more attractive. If you are in this situation, you will probably have to look for a common law tort lawsuit as your best option to recover damages for your personal injuries. (See Chapter 8.)

2. If money damages are allowed

If you work in a state with an FEP law that allows money damages for personal injuries, that statute may provide your best remedy for sexual harassment.

The FEP laws in these states often allow a remedy that is more generous than the remedy under the U.S. Civil Rights Act. State FEP laws that provide for money damages almost always allow them to be awarded in their actual amount, without any of the limitations contained in the Civil Rights Act.

For example, an employee in New York or California who can prove damages of $700,000 for pain and suffering is entitled to recover the full amount under the FEP law of either of those two states. By contrast, she would be limited to between $50,000 and $300,000 under the U.S. Civil Rights Act, depending upon the number of employees in the business. (See Chapter 6, Section B.)

Even if your state FEP law provides for damages for personal injuries, the U.S. Civil Rights Act may still be the best choice. Some state FEP laws, for example, permit damages to compensate the worker for her injuries, including pain and suffering, but do not allow punitive damages to punish the harasser when his actions were particularly outrageous. And sometimes, state court decisions put crippling restrictions on a state FEP law that looks good on its face. The best legal remedy in these situations may be a combination of claims under the U.S. Civil Rights Act, the state FEP law and various common law torts. (See Chapter 5, Section F for an example of this.)

D. Monetary Damages: State Differences

The FEP laws in roughly half of the states allow some form of monetary damages for personal injuries in sexual harassment cases. However, there are significant differences in these laws and how they are administered.

1. Administrative hearings

Several state FEP laws offer an alternative to going to court that allows a sexually harassed woman to be awarded money damages in an administrative hearing. This is usually an alternative procedure; you retain the right to go to court if you choose not to use this hearing process.

If you work in a state that allows money damages to be awarded through an administrative hearing, give serious thought to using it. This is simpler, and usually faster, than filing a lawsuit. It can be much cheaper as well, because some state agencies will either provide you with an attorney or act as your advocate at the hearing. You have the option, however, of filing a lawsuit instead of using the administrative hearing process if you or your attorney feel that you are likely to get a larger damage award from a judge or jury in court.

2. Punitive damages

In some states, the money damage award can include an amount for punitive damages—that is, damages that are awarded to punish the harasser for particularly outrageous acts. About half the states that allow money damages to be awarded also allow an award of punitive damages.

There are also differences in how punitive damages can be awarded. Some FEP laws allow punitive damages to be awarded along with compensatory damages through an administrative hearing. Other state FEP laws only allow punitive damages if you take your case to court.

These restrictions on punitive damages may be important if you are trying to decide whether to use the state FEP law or bring a common law tort suit.

3. Filing an administrative claim first

In some states, you must first file your claim with the FEP agency before you can file a private lawsuit. In California, for example, you must file your complaint with the Department of Fair Employment and Housing, the California FEP agency—and obtain a right-to-sue letter before filing the lawsuit.

However, in other states, such as Illinois, you don't have to file with the FEP agency before filing a lawsuit.

THE IMPORTANCE OF PHONING FIRST

Your state FEP agency can answer any questions you might have, tell you if the law has changed and send you documents, such as copies of the state laws and regulations, that may help you make your decision. A few things you should keep in mind when dealing with a state agency:

Call before you do anything else. Some state agencies require you to file your complaint over the phone, others require you to come in for an interview, and still others require you to file your complaint by mail. Before you make any decisions about whether to use your state FEP law, or waste any time doing the wrong thing, call and ask.

Be sure you are talking to the right person. The person who answers the phone will rarely know the answers to all of your questions. If you want to know when, where or how to file a complaint, ask to speak to an intake person or investigator. They can also answer questions about the investigation and conciliation process. If you have legal questions about the state FEP law, or want to know if the law has changed, ask to speak to someone on the legal staff, either a lawyer or someone who can give legal assistance.

Ask them to send you written materials. Most state agencies are willing to send you any pamphlets or other materials they have describing how their administrative procedures work, as well as copies of the state law and regulations. Also ask for a copy of the complaint form, or any other forms you will be asked to fill out.

Ask whether the law has changed. Many state legislatures are in the process of changing their FEP laws to conform to the changes in the U.S. Civil Rights Act. Always make sure the information you have is current.

Be persistent. State agencies tend to be understaffed and overworked. If you cannot get through to the person you need to reach, keep trying. Don't expect your call to be returned immediately. And if you find yourself on the line with someone who cannot or will not answer all of your questions, call back later and speak to someone else.

E. Money Damages: State Summaries

The chart below summarizes the state FEP laws on monetary damages. Where N/A is indicated in the chart, this means the information does not apply to the question posed.

AVAILABILITY OF MONETARY DAMAGES UNDER STATE FEP LAWS

	Agency hearing: can compensatory damages be awarded by FEP agency?	Agency hearing: can punitive damages be awarded by FEP agency?	Private lawsuit: can compensatory damages be awarded in a lawsuit?	Private lawsuit: can punitive damages be awarded in a lawsuit?	Private lawsuit: must employee file claim with agency first?
Alabama	no	no	no	no	N/A
Alaska	no	no	yes	no	no
Arizona	no	no	no	no	yes
Arkansas	no	no	no	no	N/A
California	no	no	yes	yes	yes
Colorado	no	no	no	no	yes
Connecticut	yes	no	yes	no	yes
Delaware	no	no	no	no	yes
Dist. of Columbia	yes	yes	yes	yes	no
Florida	no	no	no	no	yes
Georgia	no	no	no	no	yes
Hawaii	yes	yes	unclear	unclear	unclear
Idaho	no	no	no	no[1]	N/A
Illinois	yes	no	yes	no	no
Indiana	no	no	no	no	yes
Iowa	yes	no	yes	no	yes

---

[1] Idaho: Punitive damages of $1,000 are available. Given the costs of litigation, this is of no practical benefit.

	Agency hearing: can compensatory damages be awarded by FEP agency?	Agency hearing: can punitive damages be awarded by FEP agency?	Private lawsuit: can compensatory damages be awarded in a lawsuit?	Private lawsuit: can punitive damages be awarded in a lawsuit?	Private lawsuit: must employee file claim with agency first?
Kansas	no[2]	no	no	no	yes
Kentucky	yes	no	yes	no	no
Louisiana	unclear	unclear	yes	unclear	N/A
Maine	yes	yes[3]	yes	yes	yes[4]
Maryland	no	no	no	no	yes
Massachusetts	yes	no	yes	yes	yes
Michigan	yes	no	yes	no	no
Minnesota	yes	yes[5]	yes	yes[6]	no
Mississippi	N/A	N/A	no	no	N/A
Missouri[7]	yes	no	yes	yes	yes
Montana	yes	no	yes	no	yes
Nebraska	no	no	no	no	unclear
Nevada	no	no	no	no	N/A

[2] Kansas: The Kansas Commission on Human Rights can award compensatory damages up to $2,000 in an administrative hearing, but it is unclear whether the same low dollar restrictions apply to a damage award in a private lawsuit.

[3] Maine: The amount of punitive damages is limited to $10,000 for the first violation, $25,000 for the second violation, and $50,000 for the third violation.

[4] Maine: An employee can sue for compensatory damages without first filing her claim with the Maine Human Rights Commission. But if she wants to claim punitive damages (see footnote 3), she has to file her claim initially with that state FEP agency.

[5] Minnesota: The employee can recover up to $8,500 in punitive damages. But she can also have the amount of her compensatory damages "trebled"—that is, entered for three times their actual amount; this additional amount of money is also a form of punitive damages for all practical purposes.

[6] Minnesota: The employee can recover up to $8,500 in punitive damages. But she can also have the amount of her compensatory damages "trebled" —that is, entered for three times their actual amount; this additional amount of money is also a form of punitive damages for all practical purposes.

[7] Missouri: Workers' compensation may bar your claim. (See Chapter 8, Section D.)

	Agency hearing: can compensatory damages be awarded by FEP agency?	Agency hearing: can punitive damages be awarded by FEP agency?	Private lawsuit: can compensatory damages be awarded in a lawsuit?	Private lawsuit: can punitive damages be awarded in a lawsuit?	Private lawsuit: must employee file claim with agency first?
New Hampshire	no	no	no	no	N/A
New Jersey	yes	yes	yes	yes	no
New Mexico	no	no	unclear	unclear	yes
New York	yes	no	yes	yes	no
North Carolina	no	no	no	no	N/A
North Dakota	no	no	no	no	N/A
Ohio	no	no	yes	yes	no
Oklahoma	no	no	no	no	N/A
Oregon	yes	no	unclear	no	no
Pennsylvania	no	no	yes	no	no
Rhode Island	yes	no	yes	yes	yes
South Carolina	no	no	no	no	N/A
South Dakota	no	no	yes	yes	yes
Tennessee	yes	yes	yes	yes	no
Texas	no	no	no	no	N/A
Utah	no	no	no	no	N/A
Vermont	no	no	yes	yes	no
Virginia	no	no	no	no	N/A
Washington	no[8]	no	yes	yes	no
West Virginia	no[9]	no	yes	no	no
Wisconsin	no	no	no	no	N/A
Wyoming	no	no	yes	no	yes

[8] Washington: Compensatory damages are theoretically available through an administrative hearing, but they are limited to $1,000.

[9] West Virginia: Compensatory damages are theoretically available through an administrative hearing, but they are limited to $2,500.

MEN HARDLY EVER ASK SEXUAL FAVORS OF WOMEN FROM WHOM THE CERTAIN ANSWER IS NO.—ANTI-FEMINIST PHYLLIS SCHLAFLY, TESTIFYING AT 1981 LABOR COMMISSION HEARINGS ON THE EEOC SEXUAL HARASSMENT GUIDELINES

F. FEP Laws and Procedures: State Summaries

This section gives some basic information about each state's FEP law and administrative procedures. We have compiled the most up-to-date facts available, but be careful. The law of sexual harassment is changing rapidly—and many states are amending their laws. Before you take action based on the information given here, call your state agency and make sure it remains accurate.

How To Use These Listings

The information here is divided into a number of categories.

Statute. The legal citation to your state FEP law, if there is one. (See Chapter 10, Section B4. on how to read statute citations.)

State agency. The name, address and phone number of the state organization responsible for administering and enforcing the FEP law. Only the main office is listed here. There may also be local offices that are more convenient. Call the state agency for information on how and where to file a claim.

Exclusions. Groups who are not entitled to the protections of the state FEP law. If you think you may fall under one of these categories, see Section B and Chapter 6, Section B.

Time limits. The time within which you must file a claim. Unless otherwise indicated, the time limit starts with the incident of harassment. So, for example, in Alaska, an employee would have 300 days from the date she was harassed to bring a claim with the Commission. If she tried to bring a claim after 300 days, she would not be allowed to do so. It is very important to keep on top of these limits. Call your state agency if you have questions about when to file. When in doubt, file early.

Exhaustion. Whether you must file a claim with your state agency before bringing a private lawsuit based on the state FEP law. The term is shorthand for "exhaustion of administrative remedies." Some states require you to follow all available administrative procedures before you can resort to a lawsuit. If there is a "yes" listed for your state, you must file a claim with the state agency as a prerequisite to a lawsuit. If there is a "no" listed, you are not required to file a claim before bringing a lawsuit. Some states follow a procedure like the EEOC. They require you to file a claim with the state agency, but they will give you permission to bring a private lawsuit—either through a right-to-sue letter or by some other method—after a certain number of days.

Monetary damages. The kinds of damages that can be awarded under the state FEP law. We specify here whether these damages are available from an administrative hearing, a private lawsuit, or both. Unless otherwise indicated, all states will award job-connected losses, such as back pay and lost benefits. In addition, some states award:

- compensatory damages, or money to compensate for personal injuries, pain and suffering, mental distress and humiliation, and

- punitive damages, or money to punish the harasser for particularly heinous behavior.

Administrative procedure. Some details about how your state agency works. Unless otherwise indicated, every agency will investigate your claim and make an attempt to reach a settlement between you and your employer. Some agencies will also hold an administrative hearing, like a court case. Many agencies provide an attorney to argue for your complaint at this hearing; others require that you hire your own attorney. Some states will also award attorney's fees.

Private lawsuit. The requirements for bringing a private lawsuit based on state law. Some states don't allow you to bring a lawsuit at all. Others require you to obtain a right-to-sue letter before bringing a lawsuit or impose other limitations.

Note: An asterisk (*) indicates that the state agency has not been designated by the EEOC. This means that there is no guarantee of the quality of the agency's work, and your claim will probably not be dual-filed automatically. (See Section A.2.)

ALABAMA

No state FEP law.

ALASKA

Statute: Alaska Stats. §§18.80.010-300
State agency: Alaska State Commission for Human Rights
    800 A Street, Suite 202
    Anchorage, AK 99501
    (907) 276-7474
Exclusions: Domestic employment, social clubs and nonprofit religious, fraternal,
    charitable or educational organizations
Time limits: 300 days
Exhaustion: No
Monetary damages: Compensatory damages can be awarded in a private lawsuit,
    but not by the administrative agency.
Administrative procedure: If you choose to bring your complaint to the Commission,
    an administrative hearing is available. The complaint will be represented by the
    Commission, but you can also hire your own attorney. Attorney's fees are
    available.
Private lawsuit: You can bring a lawsuit directly in state court. You must file this
    suit within two years.

ARIZONA

Statute: Arizona Rev. Stats. §41-1461 to 1465, 1481 to 1484
State agency: Arizona Civil Rights Division
    1275 West Washington Street
    Phoenix, AZ 85007
    (602) 542-5263
Exclusions: Employers of fewer than 15 employees, the United States, Native
    American tribes, bona-fide tax exempt private membership clubs, appointed staff
    of elected officials
Time limits: 180 days

Exhaustion: Yes. After 90 days, if the Division has not completed its administrative process, you can request a right-to-sue letter.

Monetary damages: No compensatory or punitive damages are available under state law.

Administrative procedure: The Division does not hold an administrative hearing. If, after investigation, the Division decides that there is reasonable cause to believe that harassment took place, the Division can bring an action on your behalf in state court against your employer, but it is not required to do so.

Private lawsuit: You can bring a private action only with a right-to-sue letter. If the Division decides not to bring a lawsuit itself, you can bring your own lawsuit starting 90 days after the complaint was originally filed. You can apply for a court-appointed attorney to represent you in this suit, or can petition the court for permission to begin the action without paying fees or court costs. Attorney's fees are available.

ARKANSAS

No state FEP law.

CALIFORNIA

Statute: Cal. Govt. Code §§12900 to 12996
State agency: California Dept. of Fair Employment and Housing
  2014 T Street, Suite 210
  Sacramento, CA 95814
  (916) 739-4621
Exclusions: Nonprofit religious groups
Time limits: One year
Exhaustion: Yes. If the Department has not completed its administrative process after 150 days, you can request a right-to-sue letter.
Monetary damages: Compensatory and punitive damages can be awarded in a private lawsuit, but the Department cannot award compensatory or punitive damages.
Administrative procedure: The Department will hold an administrative hearing. At this hearing, an attorney for the Department will represent the complaint.
Private lawsuit: You can bring a lawsuit for up to one year after receiving a right-to-sue letter.

COLORADO

Statute: Colorado Rev. Stats. §§24-34-301 to 406
State agency: Colorado Civil Right Commission
  1560 Broadway, Suite 1050
  Denver, CO 80202
  (303) 894-2997
Exclusions: Domestic employment, religious organizations not supported by public taxes
Time limits: 180 days
Exhaustion: Yes. If the complaint is dismissed after a finding of no probable cause, you can bring a private lawsuit within 90 days. You can also bring a private lawsuit if there has been no administrative hearing 180 days after you filed your

complaint, or 120 days after your employer was notified that it would have to respond to your complaint in a hearing.

Monetary damages: No compensatory or punitive damages can be awarded under state law.

Administrative procedure: The Commission will hold an administrative hearing. The complaint will be represented by an attorney for the Commission.

Private lawsuit: You can bring a private lawsuit only under the circumstances listed above, under Exhaustion.

CONNECTICUT

Statute: Conn. Gen. Stats. §46a-51 to 99

State agency: Connecticut Commission on Human Rights and Opportunities
  90 Washington Street
  Hartford, CT 06106
  (203) 566-4895

Exclusions: Employers with fewer than three employees, domestic employment, those employed by their parent, spouse or child

Time limits: 180 days

Exhaustion: Yes. After 210 days, you can request a right-to-sue letter if the Commission has not completed its administrative process.

Monetary damages: Compensatory damages can be awarded both by the Commission and in a private lawsuit. Punitive damages cannot be awarded under state law.

Administrative procedures: The Commission will hold an administrative hearing. The complaint will be represented by the Commission. You can hire your own attorney if you wish. Attorney's fees are not available from the Commission.

Private lawsuit: You can bring a lawsuit only with a right-to-sue letter.

DELAWARE

Statute: 19 Del. Code Ann. §§710 to 718

State agency: Delaware Department of Labor, Anti-Discrimination Section
  820 North French Street, 6th Floor
  State Office Building
  Wilmington, DE 19801
  (302) 571-3929

Exclusions: Employers with fewer than four employees, agricultural workers, domestic employees, those employed by their parent, spouse or child, those who live with their employers as part of their job

Time limits: 90 days

Exhaustion: Yes

Monetary damages: No compensatory or punitive damages can be awarded under state law.

Administrative procedure: If the Department finds that there is cause to believe harassment took place, there will be a hearing before the Equal Opportunity Review Board. Once this Board issues a ruling, the employer has 30 days to comply or appeal to the state court. If the employer does not comply, the Department will file an action in state court to enforce the ruling. You may request an attorney from the Commission or hire your own attorney, but no attorney's fees are available from the Board.

Private lawsuit: You cannot bring a private lawsuit.

DISTRICT OF COLUMBIA

Statute: D.C. Code §1-2501 to 2557

State agency: D.C. Office of Human Rights
2000 14th Street, NW, 3d Floor
Washington, DC 20009
(202) 939-8740

Exclusions: Domestic employment in the employer's home, those employed by their parent, spouse or child

Time limits: One year

Exhaustion: No

Monetary damages: Compensatory and punitive damages can be awarded both by the Office and in a private lawsuit.

Administrative procedure: The Office will hold an administrative hearing, called a fact-finding conference. You can hire an attorney for this conference, but you are not required to have one. If you do get an attorney, attorney's fees are available.

Private lawsuit: You can bring a lawsuit directly in district court.

FLORIDA

Statute: Fla. Stats. Ann. §760.01 to .10

State agency: Florida Commission on Human Relations
325 John Knox Road
Building F, Suite 240
Tallahassee, FL 32399
(904) 488-7082

Exclusions: Employers with fewer than 15 employees

Time limits: 180 days

Exhaustion: Yes. After 180 days, you may withdraw your complaint and bring a private lawsuit.

Monetary damages: No compensatory or punitive damages can be awarded under state law.

The Commission will hold an informal hearing, at which attorneys are ordinarily not present. You may request a more formal hearing before the Department of Administrative Hearings; the Commission suggests that you hire an attorney for this hearing. Attorney's fees are available.

Private lawsuit: You can bring a lawsuit only after withdrawing your complaint from the Commission.

GEORGIA

Note: Only applies to employees of the state of Georgia

Statute: Code of Georgia Ann. §45-19-20 to 45.

State agency: Georgia Office of Fair Employment Practices
156 Trinity Avenue, SW; Suite 208
Atlanta, GA 30303
(404) 656-1736

Exclusions: Employees of private employers, appointed staff of elected officials

Time limits: 180 days

Exhaustion: Yes

Monetary damages: No compensatory or punitive damages can be awarded under state law.

Administrative procedure: Only state employees are protected, and they are limited to this state remedy. All actions are confidential. The Office holds an administrative hearing, at which you will be represented by an appointed attorney.

Private lawsuit: You cannot bring a private lawsuit.

HAWAII

Statute: Hawaii Rev. Stats. §368-1 to 17, §378-1 to 9

State agency: Hawaii Civil Rights Commission
888 Mililani Street, 2d Floor
Honolulu, HI 96813
(808) 586-8655

Exclusions: The United States, domestic employment

Time limits: 180 days

Exhaustion: Unclear. You probably should file a complaint with the Commission first, to be safe.

Monetary damages: Both compensatory and punitive damages can be awarded by the Commission. The damages that can be awarded in a private lawsuit are unclear, as workers' compensation may severely limit any recovery in state court. You should talk to an attorney if you are planning to bring a lawsuit.

Administrative procedure: The Commission will hold an administrative hearing. If you choose to hire an attorney for this hearing, attorney's fees are available.

Private lawsuit: State law is unclear as to whether you can bring a private lawsuit directly.

IDAHO

Statute: Idaho Code Ann. §67-5901 to 5912

State agency: Idaho Human Rights Commission
450 West State Street
Boise, ID 83720
(208) 334-2873

Exclusions: Employers with fewer than five employees, private clubs not open to the public, domestic employment

Time limits: One year

Exhaustion: No

Monetary damages: No compensatory damages can be awarded under state law. Punitive damages of up to $1,000 can be awarded if you or the Commission bring a lawsuit on your behalf in state court.

Administrative procedure: The Commission has no administrative hearing. If there is cause to believe that sexual harassment has occurred, the Commission will bring a lawsuit on your behalf in state court. You may hire your own attorney, if you are bringing claims that do not fall within the state statute, such as a common law tort action. Attorney's fees are available.

Private lawsuit: You can bring a lawsuit directly in state court. You must file the suit within two years.

ILLINOIS

Statute: Ill. Ann. Stats., chapter 68, §§1-101 to 2-105, §7A-101 to 104, §8-101 to 105, §8A-101 to 104

State agency: Illinois Department of Human Rights
100 West Randolph Street, 10th Floor
Chicago, IL 60601
(312) 814-6245

Exclusions: Domestic employment, appointed staff of elected officials, nonprofit religious groups, administrative officers of state and municipal governments, evaluees or trainees in vocational rehabilitation facilities

Time limits: 180 days

Exhaustion: No

Monetary damages: Compensatory damages can be awarded both by the Commission and in a private lawsuit, but no punitive damages can be awarded under state law.

Administrative procedure: The Commission will hold an administrative hearing. You can hire an attorney for this hearing, and attorney's fees are available.

Private lawsuit: You can bring a lawsuit directly in state court.

INDIANA

Statute: Indiana Stats. Ann. §22-9-1-1 to 13, §22-9-4-1 to 6

State agency: Indiana Civil Rights Commission
32 East Washington Street, Suite 900
Indianapolis, IN 46204
(317) 232-2612

Exclusions: Employers with fewer than six employees, domestic employment, those employed by their parent, spouse or child, nonprofit fraternal or religious groups, clubs that are exclusively social

Time limits: 90 days, or 90 days from the end of a valid company or union grievance procedure

Exhaustion: Yes

Monetary damages: No compensatory or punitive damages can be awarded under state law.

Administrative procedure: The Commission will hold an administrative hearing. An attorney will be provided for you. No attorney's fees are available.

Private lawsuit: You cannot bring a private lawsuit.

IOWA

Statute: Iowa Code Ann. §601A.1 to .19
State agency: Iowa Civil Rights Commission
   Grimes State Office Building
   211 East Maple Street, 2d Floor
   Des Moines, IA 50319
   (515) 281-4121
Exclusions: Employers with fewer than four employees, domestic employment, employment for personal services
Time limits: 180 days
Exhaustion: Yes. After 60 days, you can request a right-to-sue letter. However, you can't get a right-to-sue letter if there has already been a finding of no probable cause, if a conciliation agreement has already been reached or if notice of the administrative hearing has already issued.
Monetary damages: Compensatory damages can be awarded, both by the Commission and in a private lawsuit, but not punitive damages.
Administrative procedure: The Commission will hold an administrative hearing. The complaint will be presented by a Commission attorney. You can also hire your own attorney. Attorney's fees are available.
Private lawsuit: You can bring a lawsuit only with a right-to-sue letter.

KANSAS

Statute: Kan. Stats. Ann. §44-1001 to 1311
State agency: Kansas Commission on Human Rights
   Landon State Office Building, Suite 851-S
   900 S.W. Jackson Street
   Topeka, KS 66612
   (913) 296-3206
Exclusions: Employers with fewer than four employees, domestic employment, those employed by their parent, spouse or child, non-profit fraternal or social associations
Time limits: Six months
Exhaustion: Yes. After 30 days, you can request a right-to-sue letter.
Monetary damages: The Commission can award compensatory damages, but only up to $2,000. It is unclear whether compensatory or punitive damages can be awarded in a private lawsuit.
Administrative procedure: The Commission holds a public hearing if there is probable cause to believe discrimination has taken place. You will be provided with an attorney at this hearing.
Private lawsuit: You can bring a private suit only after receiving a right-to-sue letter.

KENTUCKY

Statute: Ky. Rev. Stats. §344.010 to .450
State agency: Kentucky Commission on Human Rights*
   701 West Muhammed Ali Boulevard
   P.O. Box 69
   Louisville, KY 40201
   (502) 588-4024

Exclusions: Employers with fewer than eight employees, domestic employment, those employed by their parent, spouse or child

Time limits: 180 days

Exhaustion: No

Monetary damages: Compensatory damages can be awarded both by the Commission and in a private lawsuit, but punitive damages cannot be awarded under state law.

Administrative procedure: If there is probable cause to believe that discrimination has occurred, there will be an administrative hearing. You can hire an attorney for this hearing, but the Commission will provide an attorney for you, if you wish. Attorney's fees are available, in the Commission's discretion.

Private lawsuit: You can file your own lawsuit directly.

LOUISIANA

Statute: La. Rev. Stat. Ann. §23-1006

State agency: None

Exclusions: Employers of fewer than 15 employees, religious organizations, non-profit corporations

Time limits: None indicated. If you are planning to bring a lawsuit, consult with an attorney about the appropriate statute of limitations.

Exhaustion: No, because there is no administrative procedure.

Monetary damages: Compensatory damages can be awarded in a private lawsuit.

Administrative procedure: None

Private lawsuit: You must bring a private lawsuit.

MAINE

Statute: Maine Rev. Stats. Ann., title V, §4551-4632

State agency: Maine Human Rights Commission
Statehouse Station 51
Augusta, ME 04333
(207) 289-2326

Exclusions: Those employed by their parent, spouse or child

Time limits: Six months

Exhaustion: No. However, civil penal damages and attorney's fees are only available if you filed a complaint with the Commission that: was dismissed after a finding that there were no reasonable grounds to believe that discrimination took place, or that could not be conciliated within 90 days of a reasonable grounds finding.

Monetary damages: Compensatory damages are available in state court. Punitive damages of $10,000 for the first violation, $25,000 for the second violation and $50,000 for the third violation, can be awarded in a private lawsuit if you initially filed your complaint with the Commission, or if the Commission brings a lawsuit on your behalf.

Administrative procedure: There is no administrative hearing. After investigating and attempting to conciliate, the Commission will refer the case to its attorneys, who will bring a lawsuit on your behalf in state court. If the Commission cannot bring a lawsuit within a reasonable time, you will be given the right to sue. Attorney's fees are available.

Private lawsuit: The same remedies are available as through the administrative process if you initially filed a complaint with the Commission (see Exhaustion). If you did not bring a complaint, no attorney's fees or punitive damages are available.

MARYLAND

Statute: Ann. Code of Md. Article 49B, §1 to 39
State agency: Maryland Commission on Human Relations
20 East Franklin Street
Baltimore, MD 21202
(301) 333-1715
Exclusions: Employers with fewer than 15 employees, bona-fide private membership clubs, appointed staff (not civil service) of elected officials
Time limits: Six months
Exhaustion: Yes
Monetary damages: No compensatory or punitive damages can be awarded under state law.
Administrative procedure: The Commission will hold an administrative hearing. You can hire an attorney if you wish, but no attorney's fees are available.
Private lawsuit: You cannot bring a private lawsuit.

MASSACHUSETTS

Statute: Ann. Laws of Mass. chapter 151B, §§1 to 10
State agency: Massachusetts Commission Against Discrimination
One Ashburton Place, Room 601
Boston, MA 02108
(617) 727-3990
Exclusions: Employers of fewer than six employees, domestic employment, those employed by their parent, spouse or child, nonprofit clubs, associations or fraternal organizations
Time limits: Six months
Exhaustion: Yes. However, if you want to bring a private lawsuit, you may request a right-to-sue letter at any time. After 90 days, you can bring a private lawsuit even without a right-to-sue letter
Monetary damages: Compensatory damages can be awarded by the Commission, and both compensatory and punitive damages can be awarded in a private lawsuit.
Administrative procedure: You can file your complaint anonymously if you wish. The Commission will hold an administrative hearing. An attorney will be provided by the Commission.
Private lawsuit: You can bring a lawsuit only after initially filing with the Commission.

MICHIGAN

Statute: Mich. Compiled Laws Ann. §37.2101 to .2804
State agency: Michigan Department of Civil Rights
  Executive Plaza Building
  1200 6th Street
  Detroit, MI 48226
  (313) 256-2615
Exclusions: Those employed by their parent spouse or child
Time limits: 180 days
Exhaustion: No
Monetary damages: Compensatory damages can be awarded, both by the
  Department and in a private lawsuit. No punitive damages can be awarded
  under state law.
Administrative procedure: The Commission will hold a hearing. An attorney from
  the Commission will represent you, but you can also hire your own attorney if
  you wish. Attorney's fees are available.
Private lawsuit: You can bring a lawsuit directly in state court.

MINNESOTA

Statute: Minn. Stats. Ann. §363.01 to .15
State agency: Minnesota Department of Human Rights
  Bremer Tower
  Seventh Place and Minnesota Street
  St. Paul, MN 55101
  (612) 296-5665
Exclusions: Domestic employment, those employed by their parent, spouse or child
Time limits: One year
Exhaustion: No. However, if you do file with the Commission, you must wait 45
  days before bringing a private lawsuit.
Monetary damages: Unlimited damages can be recovered for mental suffering. In
  addition, you can recover up to three times the amount of your actual damages,
  and up to $8,500 in punitive damages. These damages can be awarded both by
  the Commission and in a private lawsuit.
Administrative procedure: The Commission will investigate and attempt to conciliate
  and will often hold a fact-finding conference. After 180 days have passed since
  the complaint was filed, you can request that the case be heard by the
  Department of Administrative Hearings. The Commission will pay your costs,
  but you must get your own attorney.
Private lawsuit: You can bring a lawsuit directly in state court.

MISSISSIPPI

Statute: Miss. Code Ann. § 25-9-149
  Although there is a state law prohibiting discrimination against state employees,
  no damages, exclusions or other specifics are mentioned in the statute.

MISSOURI

Statute: Vernon's Ann. Missouri Stats. §213.010 to .130
State agency: Missouri Commission on Human Rights
3315 West Truman Boulevard
P.O. Box 1129
Jefferson City, MO 65102
(314) 751-3325
Exclusions: Employers with fewer than six employees, religious groups
Time limits: 180 days
Exhaustion: Yes. You can request a right-to-sue letter 180 days after the harassment occurred if the Commission has not completed its administrative process.
Monetary damages: Compensatory damages can be awarded, both by the Commission and in a private lawsuit. Punitive damages are available in a private lawsuit only.
Administrative procedure: The Commission will conduct an administrative hearing. At this hearing, the complaint will be presented by the attorney general. You can join in the hearing and have your own attorney, if you wish. No attorney's fees are available.
Private lawsuit: You can bring a lawsuit only with a right-to-sue letter.

MONTANA

Statute: Montana Code Ann. §§49-1-101 to 49-2-601
State agency: Montana Human Rights Division
Department of Labor and Industry
Post Office Box 1728
1236 6th Avenue
Helena, MT 59624
(406) 444-2884
Exclusions: Nonprofit fraternal, charitable or religious groups
Time limits: 180 days. However, if you are using a valid company or union grievance procedure, this time can be extended by the amount of time spent using the grievance procedure, up to an additional 120 days.
Exhaustion: Yes. You can get a right-to-sue letter if the Commission makes a finding that there is no reasonable cause to believe that discrimination has occurred.
Monetary damages: Compensatory damages can be awarded both by the Commission and in a private lawsuit. No punitive damages can be awarded under state law.
Administrative procedure: If there is a finding of reasonable cause, your claim will be certified for an administrative hearing. At this hearing, you can have an attorney. No attorney's fees are available from the Commission, but you can petition the state court for a rehearing solely on the issue of attorney's fees. Attorney's fees are routinely granted in this manner.
Private lawsuit: You can bring a lawsuit only after the Commission has made a finding of no reasonable cause.

NEBRASKA

Statute: Nebraska Rev. Stats. §48-1101 to 1126
State agency: Nebraska Equal Employment Opportunity Commission
   301 Centennial Mall South, 5th Floor
   P.O. Box 94934
   Lincoln, NE 68509
   (402) 471-2024
Exclusions: Employers with fewer than 15 employees, the United States, Indian tribes, religious organizations and private membership clubs, domestic employment, those employed by their parent, spouse or child
Time limits: 180 days
Exhaustion: Unclear. You should probably file your complaint with the Commission first, to be safe.
Monetary damages: No compensatory or punitive damages can be awarded under state law.
Administrative procedure: The Commission has no enforcement power. Thus, even if the Commission finds that you have been harassed, it cannot enforce an order unless your employer agrees. If your employer does not cooperate, you must sue your employer in state court.
Private lawsuit: See Exhaustion.

NEVADA

Statute: Nev. Rev. Stats. Ann. §613.310 to .430
State agency: Nevada Equal Rights Commission
   1515 East Tropicana, Suite 590
   Las Vegas, NV 89158
   (702) 486-7161
Exclusions: Employers with fewer than 15 employees, private membership clubs, the United States, Indian tribes
Time limits: 180 days
Exhaustion: Yes. If the Commission finds that there is probable cause to believe that you have been harassed, you can bring a private lawsuit.
Monetary damages: No compensatory or punitive damages are available under state law.
Administrative procedure: There is no administrative hearing, and the Commission has no enforcement power. After investigation and conciliation efforts, if the Commission finds that there is probable cause to believe that discrimination has occurred, it will advise you to go to the EEOC or to state court.
Private lawsuit: You may bring a lawsuit only after the Commission makes a finding of probable cause.

NEW HAMPSHIRE

Statute: N.H. Rev. Stats. Ann. §354-A:1 to A:14
State agency: New Hampshire Human Rights Commission
   163 Loudon Road
   Concord, NH 03301
   (603) 271-2767

Exclusions: Employers of fewer than six employees, fraternal, charitable or religious organizations, domestic employment, those employed by their parent, spouse or child

Time limits: 180 days

Exhaustion: No

Monetary damages: No compensatory or punitive damages can be awarded under state law.

Administrative procedure: The Commission will hold a hearing. The complaint will be presented by an attorney for the Commission, but you can have your own attorney if you wish. Attorney's fees are available.

Private lawsuit: You may bring a lawsuit directly in state court.

NEW JERSEY

Statute: N.J. Stats. Ann. §10:5-1 to 38.

State agency: New Jersey Division on Civil Rights
31 Clinton Street
Newark, NJ 07102
(201) 648-2700

Exclusions: Domestic employment, those employed by their parent, spouse or child

Time limits: None indicated. Call the state agency for more information.

Exhaustion: No

Monetary damages: Compensatory and punitive damages can be awarded, both by the Division and in a private lawsuit, according to a recently enacted law. Check with the Division about how this law is being interpreted.

Administrative procedure: The Division will hold an administrative hearing. The complaint will be presented by an appointed attorney.

Private lawsuit: You may bring a lawsuit directly in state court. Attorney's fees are available.

NEW MEXICO

Statute: N.M. Stats. Ann. §28-1-1 to 15

State agency: New Mexico Human Rights Commission
Aspen Plaza
1596 Pacheco Street
Santa Fe, NM 87502
(505) 827-6838

Exclusions: Employers with fewer than four employees

Time limits: 180 days

Exhaustion: Yes. If the Commission has not settled the complaint or held a hearing within 180 days, you can request a letter of no determination, which will allow you to bring a private lawsuit.

Monetary damages: The Commission cannot award compensatory or punitive damages. State law is unclear as to whether compensatory damages can be awarded in a private lawsuit.

Administrative procedure: The Commission will hold an administrative hearing. You must get your own attorney for this hearing. Attorney's fees are available.

Private lawsuit: You can bring a lawsuit directly in state court only after the Commission has issued a letter of non-determination or held its hearing.

NEW YORK

Statute: N.Y. Executive Law §§290 to 301
State agency: New York State Division of Human Rights
    55 West 125 Street, 13th Floor
    New York, NY 10027
    (212) 870-8566
Exclusions: Employers with fewer than four employees, domestic employment
Time limits: None is indicated in the state law. Call the agency to find out when you
    should file.
Exhaustion: No
Monetary damages: Compensatory damages can be awarded both by the Division
    and in a private lawsuit, but punitive damages can be awarded only in a private
    lawsuit.
Administrative procedure: There is an administrative hearing, and the state will
    provide you with an attorney.
Private lawsuit: You can bring a lawsuit directly in state court.

NORTH CAROLINA (has two state agencies)

Statute: Gen. Stats. of N.C. §143-422.1 to .3

For state and county employees and employees of the University of North Carolina:

State agency: North Carolina Office of Administrative Hearings
    Post Office Drawer 27447
    Raleigh, NC 27611
    (919) 733-0431
Exclusions: Private employers
Time limits: 180 days
Exhaustion: Yes
Monetary damages: No compensatory or punitive damages can be awarded under
    state law.
Administrative procedure: There will be an administrative hearing, at which you
    must provide your own attorney. Attorney's fees are available.
Private lawsuit: You cannot bring a private lawsuit.

For private employees:

State agency: North Carolina Human Relations Commission*
    21 West Jones Street
    Raleigh, NC 27603
    (919) 733-7996
Exclusions: Employers with fewer than 15 employees
Time limits: 180 days
Exhaustion: Yes
Monetary damages: No compensatory or punitive damages can be awarded under
    state law.
Administrative procedure: The Commission has no enforcement power. If your
    employer will not cooperate, the Commission will defer the claim to the EEOC.
Private lawsuit: You cannot bring a private lawsuit.

NORTH DAKOTA

Statute: N.D. Century Code Ann. §14-02,4-01 to 21
State agency: North Dakota Department of Labor
    State Capitol Building
    600 East Boulevard
    Bismarck, ND 58505
    (701) 224-2660
Exclusions: Appointed staff of elected officials, domestic employment, those
    employed by their parent, spouse or child
Time limits: 300 days
Exhaustion: No
Monetary damages: No compensatory or punitive damages can be awarded under
    state law.
Administrative procedure: There is no administrative hearing. After investigation and
    conciliation, if the Department finds that there is cause to believe harassment
    has occurred, you will be given the right to sue in state court.
Private lawsuit: You can bring a lawsuit directly in state court.

OHIO

Statute: Page's Ohio Rev. Code Ann. §4112.01 to 99
State agency: Ohio Civil Rights Commission
    220 Parsons Avenue
    Columbus, OH 43215
    (614) 466-5928
Exclusions: Employers with fewer than four employees, domestic employment
Time limits: Six months
Exhaustion: No
Monetary damages: Compensatory and punitive damages can be awarded in a
    private lawsuit. No compensatory or punitive damages can be awarded by the
    Commission.
Administrative procedure: The Commission will hold a hearing, at which the
    Attorney General will present the complaint. You may also have your own
    attorney, if you wish.
Private lawsuit: You may bring a lawsuit directly in state court.

OKLAHOMA

Statute: 25 Oklahoma Stats. §§1101 to 1802
State agency: Oklahoma Human Rights Commission
    2101 North Lincoln Boulevard, Room 480
    Oklahoma City, OK 73105
    (405) 521-2360
Exclusions: Employers with fewer than 15 employees, domestic employment, those
    employed by their parent, spouse or child, bona-fide nonprofit private
    membership clubs, Indian tribes
Time limits: 180 days
Exhaustion: Yes. If the Commission has not completed its administrative process in
    180 days, you can request a right-to-sue letter.

Monetary damages: No compensatory or punitive damages can be awarded under state law.

Administrative procedure: The Commission will hold a hearing, at which the complaint will be presented by Commission staff. You may also have your own attorney, if you wish. Attorney's fees are available. The Commission's order has no legal effect without a corresponding order from the state court. The Commission must bring an action for review by the state court to get such an order.

Private lawsuit: You can bring a private lawsuit only with a right-to-sue letter.

OREGON

Statute: Or. Rev. Stats. §659.010 to .990
State agency: Oregon Bureau of Labor and Industry
Civil Rights Division
P.O. Box 800
Portland, OR 97207
(503) 229-6601
Exclusions: Domestic employment, those employed by their parent, spouse or child
Time limits: One year
Exhaustion: No
Monetary damages: Compensatory damages can be awarded by the Division. State law is unclear as to whether compensatory damages can be awarded in a private lawsuit. No punitive damages are available under state law.

Administrative procedure: The Division will hold a hearing, and a Division attorney will present the complaint. You may also have your own attorney, if you wish. Attorney's fees are available.

Private lawsuit: You may file a lawsuit directly in state court. You must bring this suit within one year of the harassment, if you don't file a complaint with the Division.

PENNSYLVANIA

Statute: 43 Penn. Stats. Ann. §§951 to 962.2
State agency: Pennsylvania Human Rights Commission
2971 East North 7th Street
Harrisburg, PA 17110
(717) 787-4412
Exclusions: Employers with fewer than four employees, agricultural workers, domestic employment, those employed by their parent, spouse or child
Time limits: 180 days
Exhaustion: No
Monetary damages: Compensatory damages can be awarded in a private lawsuit, but not by the Commission. No punitive damages can be awarded under state law.

Administrative procedure: The Commission will hold a hearing, at which you can have an attorney. However, only limited attorney's fees are available from the Commission.

Private lawsuit: You can bring a lawsuit directly in state court.

RHODE ISLAND

Statute: Gen. Laws of R.I. §28-5-1 to 40
State agency: Rhode Island Commission for Human Rights
    10 Abbott Park Place
    Providence, RI 02903
    (401) 277-2661
Exclusions: Employers with fewer than four employees, domestic employment, those employed by their parent, spouse or child
Time limits: One year
Exhaustion: Yes. After 120 days, you can request a right-to-sue letter.
Monetary damages: Compensatory damages can be awarded both by the Commission and in a private lawsuit. Punitive damages can be awarded only in a private lawsuit.
Administrative procedure: The Commission will hold a hearing, at which you must be represented by your own attorney. Attorney's fees are available.
Private lawsuit: You can bring a private lawsuit only with a right-to-sue letter.

SOUTH CAROLINA

Statute: Code of S.C. title 1, §1-13-10 to 110
State agency: South Carolina Human Affairs Commission
    P.O. Box 4490
    Columbia, SC 29240
    (803) 253-6336
Exclusions: Employers with fewer than 15 employees, bona-fide private membership clubs, Indian tribes, appointed staff of elected officials
Time limits: 180 days
Exhaustion: Yes. If the Commission doesn't bring a civil lawsuit within 180 days, you can get a right-to-sue letter.
Monetary damages: No compensatory or punitive damages can be awarded under state law.
Administrative procedure: There is no administrative hearing. If the Commission makes a finding of probable cause, it can bring a lawsuit against your employer. If the Commission doesn't bring suit within 180 days, you can bring a private lawsuit.
Private lawsuit: You may bring a private lawsuit only with a right-to-sue letter.

SOUTH DAKOTA

Statute: S.D. Codified Laws, Chapter 20-13
State agency: South Dakota Division of Human Rights
    500 East Capitol Street
    Pierre, SD 57501
    (605) 773-4493
Exclusions: None
Time limits: 180 days
Exhaustion: Yes. A right-to-sue letter is available after 60 days.
Monetary damages: Compensatory and punitive damages can be awarded in a private lawsuit, but not by the Division.

Administrative procedure: If the division finds probable cause to believe that discrimination has occurred, there will be an administrative hearing. You must get an attorney for this hearing, but no attorney's fees are available.

Private lawsuit: You may bring a private lawsuit only with a right-to-sue letter. Attorney's fees are available.

TENNESSEE

Statute: Tenn. Code Ann. §4-21-101 to 408

State agency: Tennessee Human Rights Commission
226 Capitol Boulevard, Suite 602
Nashville, TN 37219
(615) 741-5825

Exclusions: Employers with fewer than eight employees

Time limits: 180 days

Exhaustion: No

Monetary damages: Compensatory and punitive damages can be awarded, both by the Commission and in a private lawsuit.

Administrative procedure: You are entitled to an attorney at the administrative hearing. You can choose your own attorney, or have one appointed for you. Attorney's fees are available.

Private lawsuit: You can file a lawsuit directly in state court within one year. If you file a complaint with the Commission, you can withdraw it at any time to file your own lawsuit.

TEXAS

Statute: Tex. Stats. Ann., Article 5221(k) §§1.01 to 10.05

State agency: Texas Commission on Human Rights
8100 Cameron Road, #525
P.O. Box 13493
Austin, TX 78753
(512) 837-8534

Exclusions: Employers with fewer than 15 employees, appointed staff of elected officials.

Time limits: 180 days

Exhaustion: Yes. After 180 days, you can bring a private lawsuit.

Monetary damages: No compensatory or punitive damages are available under state law.

Administrative procedure: If the evidence supports the complaint, the Commission will recommend a finding of harassment to an administrative panel. If two of the three members of this panel agree that harassment has taken place, conciliation will be attempted. If conciliation efforts fail, the Commission can decide to file suit in the state court to enforce its finding. You can join this lawsuit, with or without an attorney. The case for the complaint will be presented by Commission staff. Attorney's fees are available.

Private lawsuit: You must first file a complaint with the Commission. Once 180 days have passed, you then have a right to sue in state court. You can also sue in state court if the Commission determines that the complaint has no merit—that there is no reason to believe that harassment has occurred. Finally, if the

Commission decides that harassment has taken place, but doesn't bring a suit in state court to enforce this finding, you may bring your own lawsuit to do so.

UTAH

Statute: Utah Code Ann. §34-35-1 to 7.1
State agency: Utah Industrial Commission, Anti-Discrimination Division
160 East 300 South
Salt Lake City, UT 84111
(801) 530-6801
Exclusions: Employers with fewer than 15 employees, religious organizations
Time limits: Must file within 180 days
Exhaustion: Yes
Monetary damages: No compensatory or punitive damages are available under state law.
Administrative procedure: You may have an attorney at the administrative hearing. Attorney's fees are available.
Private lawsuit: You cannot bring a private action.

VERMONT

Statute: 21 Vermont Stats. Ann. §495
State agency: Vermont Attorney General's Office
Civil Rights Division
109 State Street
Montpelier, VT 05609
(802) 828-3171
Exclusions: None
Time limits: Unclear. A federal district court recently held that there is a three-year statute of limitations. However, you may have as long as six years to file.
Exhaustion: No
Monetary damages: Compensatory and punitive damages can be awarded in a private lawsuit only.
Administrative procedure: There is no administrative hearing. If, after investigation and conciliation efforts, no solution has been reached, you must litigate in state court.
Private lawsuit: You may bring a lawsuit directly in state court.

VIRGINIA

Although there is a state law prohibiting harassment of state employees only, there is no state agency.

WASHINGTON

Statute: Rev. Code of Wash. Ann. §49.60.010 to .330
State agency: Washington State Human Rights Commission
Evergreen Plaza Building, Suite 402
711 South Capitol Way
Olympia, WA 98504
(206) 753-6770

Exclusions: Employers with fewer than eight employees, nonprofit religious organizations, domestic employment, those employed by their parent, spouse or child
Time limits: Six months
Exhaustion: No
Monetary damages: The Commission can award up to $1,000 in compensatory damages, but no punitive damages. Unlimited compensatory and punitive damages can be awarded in a private lawsuit.
Administrative procedure: There will be an administrative hearing, at which the Commission will represent the complaint. If you wish to have your own attorney, you may do so. Attorney's fees are available.
Private lawsuit: You may bring a lawsuit directly in state court.

WEST VIRGINIA

Statute: W. Va. Code §5-11-1 to 19
State agency: West Virginia Human Rights Commission
   1321 Plaza East, Room 106
   Charleston, WV 25301
   (304) 348-2616
Exclusions: Employers with fewer than 12 employees, domestic employment, those employed by their parent, spouse or child
Time limits: 180 days
Exhaustion: No
Monetary damages: Compensatory damages are limited to $2,500 from the Commission, but are unlimited in state court. No punitive damages can be awarded under state law.
Administrative procedure: At the administrative hearing, the attorney general will present the complaint. You can have your own attorney, if you wish. If you do retain an attorney, attorney's fees are available from the Commission.
Private lawsuit: You can bring a lawsuit directly in state court.

WISCONSIN

Statute: Wis. Stats. Ann. §11.31 to 39
State agency: Wisconsin Equal Rights Division
   Department of Industry, Labor and Human Relations
   P.O. Box 8928
   201 East Washington Avenue
   Madison, WI 53708
   (608) 267-9678
Exclusions: Those employed by their parent, spouse or child
Time limits: 300 days
Exhaustion: Yes
Monetary damages: No compensatory or punitive damages can be awarded under state law.
Administrative procedure: You may have an attorney at the administrative hearing. Attorney's fees are available.
Private lawsuit: You cannot bring a private lawsuit.

WYOMING

Statute: Wyoming Stats. Ann. §27-9-101 to 108

State agency: Wyoming Fair Employment Commission
Herschler Building
2nd East
Cheyenne, WY 82002
(307) 777-7261

Exclusions: Employers with fewer than two employees, religious organizations

Time limits: 90 days

Exhaustion: Yes. You can get a right-to-sue letter if the Commission decides that its investigation will take more than 200 days.

Monetary damages: Compensatory damages can be awarded in a private lawsuit, but not by the Commission. Punitive damages cannot be awarded under state law.

Administrative procedure: You may have an attorney at the administrative hearing if you wish; however, no attorney's fees are available.

Private lawsuit: You can bring a private lawsuit only with a right-to-sue letter.

Common Law Tort Actions

A. When To File a Tort Action 8/2

    1. If you work for a small employer 8/3

    2. If your injuries are severe 8/3

    3. If your claim is unclear 8/4

    4. If your claim is filed late 8/4

B. Common Tort Actions Against Sexual Harassment 8/4

    1. Assault and battery 8/4

    2. Intentional infliction of emotional distress 8/8

    3. Defamation 8/14

    4. Interfering with an employment contract 8/16

    5. Intrusion 8/20

    6. Wrongful discharge 8/22

    7. Rape 8/24

C. Disadvantages of Tort Actions 8/26

    1. Federal and state laws may be stronger 8/26

    2. Unpredictability 8/26

    3. Proving intent 8/27

    4. Proving personal harm 8/27

    5. Getting a lawyer 8/28

D. Workers' Compensation: Employers' Defense 8/28

T itle VII of the U.S. Civil Rights Act and state fair employment practices (FEP) laws that prohibit discrimination and other unfair employment practices (discussed in Chapters 6 and 7) provide some measure of relief for those who are subjected to sexual harassment on the job. This chapter discusses several additional legal actions, referred to broadly as common law torts, often filed in sexual harassment cases.

Common law torts, or civil wrongs, include assault and battery, intentional infliction of emotional distress, interference with contract and defamation. They are filed in state courts like any other lawsuit based on a personal injury. And they may provide a wider range of remedies than those available under the Civil Rights Act and most states FEP laws, including both compensatory damages for the emotional and physical distress suffered because of the workplace harassment and the possibility of large punitive damages aimed at punishing the wrongdoer.

CLAIMS WILL USUALLY OVERLAP

Although several of the principal common law tort actions are discussed here separately, in practice, a number of them are often filed in the same sexual harassment lawsuit, along with claims for violations of federal and state laws banning harassment.

Lawyers often recommend that you file as many claims as possible, even though they may be repetitious. The reasoning is that you'll have a number of different legal alternatives to fall back on if some prove unsuccessful.

A. When To File a Tort Action

However welcome and needed the state and federal anti-discrimination laws are, they offer limited relief. In many states, fair employment practices laws compensate only for easily-documented losses, such as back pay for time lost from work. Even the U.S. Civil Rights Act—which does allow damages to compensate women for physical and mental injuries—limits covered employers to those with 15 or more employees and caps the damages at $300,000 even for the largest employers.

There are a number of situations in which filing a common law tort may be the best action you can take against sexual harassment.

1. If you work for a small employer

While a tort action may be the best option for some harassed workers, it's the only possible remedy for others. As mentioned, if your employer has 14 or fewer employees, you are not covered by the U.S. Civil Rights Act and cannot file an EEOC complaint or a federal lawsuit for damages.

And unfortunately, while the local laws in some bigger cities may provide relief for employees of any size company, many state laws either do not cover employees who work for small companies at all, or limit damages to compensation for lost pay—and sometimes medical expenses—due to physical injuries. Not many state laws allow compensation for stress-related claims or punitive damages—that is, damages charged to the wrongdoer to specifically punish him for his actions.

2. If your injuries are severe

Common law tort actions allow, at least in theory, unlimited dollar verdicts for some of the most severe injuries wrought by the harassment: emotional and physical harm. These tort actions are particularly appropriate where a woman has suffered extreme trauma from the psychological remnants of harassment—embarrassment, fright, humiliation—which can cause a permanent loss of self-esteem. Also, the daily prospect of facing a workplace fraught with unpleasantness commonly takes a heavy toll on a worker's emotional and physical health. Tort actions can often compensate for these harms.

3. If your claim is unclear

Claims brought under state FEP laws or the Civil Rights Act look much the same legally. Employees must prove to administrative authorities or a court that, according to previous interpretations and the guidelines set out, they were sexually harassed at work.

But if a situation does not quite fit within the bounds of a sexual discrimination claim under federal or state law—for example, you are an independent contractor and not an employee—picking and choosing among the suitable tort actions may allow you to tailor your case more specifically to the actual workplace wrong. A woman who has been sexually harassed at work in various ways will often combine several tort actions when seeking legal relief for the wrong.

4. If your claim is filed late

Both state and federal laws prohibiting sexual harassment have strict time limits, called statutes of limitation, within which claims must be filed—either 180 or 300 days from the harassment incident. There are statutes of limitations on tort actions, too, but they are less stringent. Depending on which tort you are suing for and in which state you live, you usually have one year to three years to file.

B. Common Tort Actions Against Sexual Harassment

While creative legal minds have been able to shoehorn harassment actions into a number of different legal theories, the actions discussed here have been the most successful.

1. Assault and battery

Assault and battery are actually two separate legal wrongs. But because they frequently occur together, they are very often paired in legal complaints.

These offenses may also be crimes and, if they are particularly serious, should be reported to local law enforcement authorities. The two actions forbid physical contact in the workplace, or the threat of contact, that you consider to be harmful or offensive.

STRIKING BACK AT HARASSMENT: THE OLD-FASHIONED WAY

Filing assault and battery charges was one of the first ways to legally combat workplace harassment. As early as 1875, a Wisconsin woman was awarded $1,000 in damages in an assault and battery action for both mental suffering and "being wronged" when a male train conductor put his soiled hand in the muff she was wearing to keep her hands warm—and then kissed her five or six times.[1]

Still, even the most sympathetic early courts that considered workplace harassment were skeptical—and hesitant. When evaluating evidence of outrageous and sometimes brutal attacks by a male co-worker, court opinions would quaintly ponder for pages whether a man had "put his hands upon a woman with a view to violate her person."

---

a. Assault

To prove an assault, you must show that:

- the person who assaulted you intended to cause physical contact, and
- you feared or apprehended the contact.

Generally, more than verbal abuse is required for a legal claim of assault, although repeated verbal threats accompanied by menacing gestures may qualify.

---

[1] *Croaker v. Chicago and Northwestern Ry. Co.*, 36 Wis. 657 (1875).

b. Battery

Battery is actual contact that is harmful, offensive or insulting. You must show that the person who battered you:

- intended to touch you—although he need not have intended to harm you, and

- contacted you physically.

Clearly, when a battery—which may include touching, kissing, embracing or rubbing up against your body—occurs in the workplace, you may often anticipate or fear the action, so it also qualifies as an assault. That may not always be the case, however, if the abuse took you by surprise. Nevertheless, if your harasser has physically contacted you, or if you have had reason to expect that he will, it is usually best to file both assault and battery charges unless an attorney advises you to limit your pleadings to one action or another.

If, during an assault, your harasser had or attempted to have intercourse with you, it is advisable to file rape charges against him, also. (See Section B.7.)

If your harasser's offensive conduct has been limited to verbal attacks—slurs, insults or threats to fire you—you will not likely succeed with an assault or battery claim. Most courts will require that there be some actual harmful or offensive touching or threat of touching. Some courts will even require that the touching cause an observable physical injury.

Example: While they were attending an out-of-town convention, a male supervisor asked his female employee to come to his hotel room to discuss an upcoming business meeting. When she did, she walked in on a decidedly unbusinesslike setting: brimming glasses of wine and the television tuned to pornographic films on a pay channel. When the woman protested and attempted to leave the room, her boss grabbed her by both shoulders and blocked her way. The court held that while the touching was intentional and "it may have been mildly offensive to her," there was no assault and battery since the woman was not physically or mentally harmed.[2]

---

[2] *Boyd v. James S. Hayes Living Health Care Agency,* 671 F. Supp. 1155 (W.D. Tenn. 1987).

Fortunately, a growing number of courts that require that an injury as a result of an assault and battery produce are enlightened enough to realize that mental suffering is also a serious injury. Even one offensive instance may be enough for a battery charge. But again, the reality is that if you are able to prove the abuse took place more than once, you will have a better chance of winning your lawsuit.

Example: A female executive secretary filed a lawsuit for assault and battery against the plant manager after he repeatedly touched her breasts and buttocks, ignoring her pleas to stop. The court held that while the offensive touching caused no cuts or bruises, the emotional and psychological harm she suffered from the frequent abuse was sufficient to support a common law legal action for assault and battery.[3]

If you have been subjected to assault and battery in the workplace, it is especially important to notify your employer of the abuse. If your supervisor has assaulted you, the company may automatically be liable; but if it was a co-worker who did wrong, the company may not be liable unless it knew or had reason to know of the offense.

THE WAY PROFESSOR HILL WAS TREATED WAS SHAMEFUL. . . . THE MESSAGE TO WOMEN THROUGHOUT AMERICA WILL BE A CHILLING ONE: SUFFER IN SILENCE OR PAY A TERRIBLE PRICE.—SENATOR EDWARD KENNEDY [D-MASS.] WHO VOTED AGAINST THE NOMINATION OF CLARENCE THOMAS TO THE SUPREME COURT IN OCTOBER 1991

---

[a] *Newsome v. Cooper-Wiss, Inc.*, 347 S.E.2d 619 (1986).

ADDED PROTECTION: RESTRAINING ORDERS

If you have been assaulted or battered at work, causing you to fear for your own safety, consider filing a formal complaint with local law enforcement authorities. You should also consider getting a civil or criminal restraining order against your harasser.

A restraining order is a judgment issued by a court that is tailored to stop the harassment. Restraining orders may state, for example, that your harasser must stay a certain distance away from you, must stop contacting you at home or work, or must not contact you by mail. Those who violate a restraining order can, at a minimum, be held in contempt of court and in more severe cases, may be fined or even jailed.

One advantage of a restraining order is that police are more likely to respond to future pleas for help if you can produce a judge's order requiring that the harassment stop. In most communities, specialists at women's rights groups or victim witness counselors working within local police departments to counsel those subjected to violent wrongs can advise you on how to get a restraining order—and may refer you to other local resources to help you with the necessary paperwork.

---

2. Intentional infliction of emotional distress

Intentional infliction of emotional distress, sometimes simply called outrage, is one of the broadest common law tort actions—and one of the most difficult to define precisely. Aimed at preserving a person's peace of mind, it is the most common of the tort actions filed in sexual harassment situations—and historically, the one most likely to secure money for harassed workers who have suffered mental anguish.

You can file an action for intentional infliction of emotional distress against a co-worker, supervisor or your employer. To win such a case, you must prove that:

- your harasser acted outrageously

- your harasser either intentionally caused you emotional distress, or at least should have known that his actions would distress you

- you suffered severe emotional distress, and

- your distress was caused by the harasser's conduct.

The biggest problem with the legal action of intentional infliction of emotional distress is defining it. To win this type of lawsuit, the harasser's conduct must be pretty outrageous, but it is unclear just how appalling the conduct must be before courts will allow you to base a legal action on it.

Courts grappling for a description of a case that might meet the legal requirements for outrageousness often fall back on a pseudo-definition set out long ago by legal scholar William Prosser:

> *Liability has been found only where the conduct has been so outrageous in character, and so extreme in degree, as to go beyond all possible bounds of decency, and to be regarded as atrocious, and utterly intolerable in a civilized community. Generally, the case is one in which the recitation of facts to an average member of the community would arouse his resentment against the actor, and lead him to exclaim, "Outrageous!"*

Obviously, those looking for real guidance from this definition find scant help. Probably the best that can be said is that the conduct required to prove intentional infliction of emotional distress must evoke a strong gut reaction approaching revulsion, an I-know-it-when-I-see-it response.

This points up another problem with the tort of intentional infliction of emotional distress: It is extremely subjective. In this tort, more than most other legal actions, cases with nearly the same facts, brought in different states, or in different years or before different judges, commonly produce different results. Even in the same state in the same year, each court will analyze the evidence according to its own standards.

Theoretically, all sexual harassment in the workplace should qualify as outrageous. Just as racial slurs against workers of color should not be tolerated, lewd comments about a female worker's body and other harassing conduct are abhorrent and inappropriate.

But the reality is that the type of harassment that will be considered an intentional infliction of emotional distress must meet a tougher standard. A few lewd remarks—even a few very obnoxious ones—probably will not qualify. Physical injury is not required to prove the intentional infliction of emotional distress, but it is much easier to prove a case if there have been some physical repercussion—illness, shock, nausea, insomnia. Generally speaking, the more outrageous a harasser's conduct, the less severe the harassed woman's injuries need to be to prove her case.

> **Example:** A union officer, representing employees in California restaurants and bars, sexually harassed several women who came to him to discuss grievances. He solicited them to have sex with him and with others—and forewarned that his position with the unions and connections to underworld figures made it risky for them not to comply.
>
> The harassed women claimed they were fearful and intimidated by the harassment and they were able to show by evidence from their physician or psychiatrist that this affected them physically. Based on this evidence, the court upheld their claims for intentional infliction of emotional distress.[4]

Several courts have attempted to eliminate some of the nebulousness in intentional infliction of emotional distress cases by listing requirements for bringing a case. For example, in 1984, a Pennsylvania court ruled that a claim for intentional infliction of emotional distress based on workplace harassment must include evidence of:

- direct sexual advances
- threats of retribution
- unconsented physical contact, or
- sexual references about the employee to other workers.

Courts in other states have adopted similar standards, but most are less concrete. In general, courts seem to prefer the guesswork of deciding whether particular behavior is sufficiently outrageous or shocking on a case-by-case basis. Sadly, from the view of the harassed woman, the guesses of the predominantly male judges evaluating the cases too often seem to miss the mark.

---

[4] *Seritis v. Lane,* 30 Fair Empl. Prac. Cas. (BNA) 423 (Cal. Super. Ct. 1980).

Example: A female professor whose contract was not renewed sued the university, charging the male dean's persistent unwanted sexual advances not only were the reason she lost her job, but were also the reason she developed hypertension and required counseling. While the first court to review the claim found the dean's behavior to be degrading and humiliating, it held he was guilty of "social impropriety" rather than any legal offense. On appeal, however, the court held that the complaint sufficiently stated an action for intentional infliction of emotional distress.[5]

Example: A woman claimed her co-workers taunted her about being a new mother and overloaded her schedule at an optical lab, forcing her to work so hard and fast that she made numerous mistakes. When she collapsed on the job, presumably from overwork, no one helped her. After she was fired, she brought an action for intentional infliction of emotional distress against her co-workers and supervisor. The court dismissed the claim, holding that the conduct the woman complained of was not so outrageous that it "went beyond all bounds of decency."[6]

Example: Three women who worked as waitresses at a country club alleged that they had been harassed by the manager and a co-worker, causing them mental and emotional distress. The first woman claimed the club manager assigned her work that she was physically unable to do because she was pregnant. The second woman claimed the manager screamed and shouted at her, called her names, interfered with her supervision of the other waitresses and once threw a menu at her in anger.

The third woman complained about the chef at the club, alleging that he shouted profanities at her, threatened her and made sexually derogatory remarks and sexual advances toward her, causing her to fear he would harm her. She also claimed she was fired in retaliation for reporting the harassment to the club manager. The court held that only the third woman had a valid claim for emotional distress. It noted that while the manager's conduct toward the first two women was "intemperate," it did not "exceed all bounds usually tolerated by a decent society" and so was not sufficiently outrageous to support a legal claim.[7]

---

[5] *Howard Univ. v. Best*, 484 A.2d 958 (DC 1984).

[6] *Hooten v. Pennsylvania College of Optometry*, 601 F. Supp. 1151 (E.D. Pa. 1984).

[7] *Hogan v. Forsyth Country Club Co.*, 340 S.E.2d 116 (1986).

Retaliation may boost your intentional infliction of emotional distress claim. It seems evident that retaliation accelerates the level of a harassed woman's workplace angst. So courts generally consider evidence that you were shunned, ostracized or threatened after complaining about harassment to weigh heavily in your favor.

Example: An Illinois woman complained that her supervisor caused her to suffer severe emotional distress. For two months, he told her sex-related jokes daily, bragged of his sexual exploits with multiple partners, invited her and other co-workers out for weekend sex orgies, interrogated them about their preferences for anal and oral sex and described his penis to them in grand terms.

When the woman complained about his behavior to the vice president of the company, her supervisor retaliated—threatening that he would get even, undermining her authority and making it more difficult for her to do her job well. The court ruled that, taken on its own, the harassing sexual comments did not amount to intentional infliction of emotional distress, but the retaliation did.[8]

One additional point: Evidence of retaliation may also help establish an employer's liability if company management participates in the retaliation or pays no heed to it.

INTERCOURSE AND WOMEN'S INEQUALITY ARE LIKE SIAMESE TWINS, ALWAYS IN THE SAME PLACE AT THE SAME TIME, PISSING IN THE SAME POT.—FROM *INTERCOURSE*, BY ANDREA DWORKIN (MACMILLAN, 1987)

---

[8] *Class v. New Jersey Life Ins. Co.*, 746 F. Supp. 776 (N.D. Ill. 1990).

A CHECKLIST TO HELP YOU EVALUATE YOUR CASE

Here are some factors to look at when evaluating workplace behavior to see whether it is likely to be considered sufficiently outrageous to support a claim of intentional infliction of emotional distress.

Coercion. Where the harasser has some power over you in the workplace, such as supervising your work or controlling your raises or promotions, your chances of success increase. Some courts have actually required that some work benefit—a raise, promotion, new job—be denied or threatened before they will find any intentional infliction of emotional distress.

Frequency. A claim is more likely to succeed where the harassing behavior happens regularly, or recurs several times, as opposed to an isolated instance.

Duration. Again, a single instance of harassment may be enough, but if the bad behavior has continued over a long span of time, it may be more likely to be considered outrageous.

Physical contact. While there is no legal requirement that your harasser actually touch you, some courts seem more inclined to find intentional infliction of emotional distress if there has been unwanted touching as opposed to solely verbal heckling or threats.

Physical symptoms. If the sexual harassment you endured also caused physical suffering, a court is more likely to find that the harassment was outrageous—and illegal. Symptoms range from nervousness, depression and sleeping disorders to headaches, rashes and severe stress-related circulatory problems. Proof that you have been treated by a physician, psychiatrist or psychologist is not essential for a legal claim, but is very persuasive evidence with a court.

Retaliation. Evidence of retaliation bolsters your claim. Evidence of co-workers shunning you, or your harasser interfering with your ability to get your work done, can often mean the difference between success and failure for a claim of intentional infliction of emotional distress.

Union members beware: Your claim of infliction of emotional distress may be barred by a court if you are a union employee and your collective bargaining agreement states that the Railway Labor Act or the National Labor Relations Act controls workplace disputes. Other union employees, however, are not banned from filing this legal action.

3. Defamation

Defamation is a legal action with the chivalrous-sounding intent of protecting a person's reputation and good standing in the community.

To sue for defamation, you must show that the person who defamed you:

- made a false or damaging statement about you

- told or wrote that statement to at least one other person

- was negligent or intentional in communicating the statement, and

- the communication harmed you in some way, such as by causing others to shun you, or resulted in you losing a job or a promotion.

Defamation cases are often difficult to prove. To win a case of defamation, you must prove that the hurtful words were more than malicious watercooler gossip: "She wore that same suit to work yesterday. Kind of makes you wonder where she spent the night," probably would not qualify.

The words must also be more than a personal opinion. It is ordinarily legal for anyone to voice an opinion, no matter how unflattering: "She looks awful in that puce dress."

Statements that have been ruled to sufficiently harm a worker and qualify as defamation are false claims that she:

- committed a crime

- performed job duties incompetently

- improperly used drugs or alcohol, or

- acted in some other way that clearly implies she was unfit for a particular job.

Because a few unflattering comments or even a small dose of mean-spiritedness don't usually qualify as defamation, it is extremely important to scrupulously document cases where false or damaging statements are made. You can do this by recording not only the exact offensive words that were said and who said them, but when and where they were said and whether there were any witnesses. (See Chapter 3, Section F, for details on documentation.) Again, courts will generally be most persuaded by words that clearly damaged your work reputation. For example, your defamation case may be stronger if you can show that a formerly friendly co-worker began to shun you after hearing the false, damaging statements about you.

In workplace harassment situations, the strongest cases are where the defamatory statements have a lasting sting—resulting in additional job-related harm, such as where a woman is passed over for a job or promotion because of the damaging words. In fact, most successful defamation cases have been against employers who have made false statements about an employee to co-workers or to other prospective employers.

> **Example:** After firing a female employee, the media conglomerate ABC packed and removed all documents and other work paraphenalia from her former office. When curious co-workers asked what was going on, members of management told them "they didn't want to know" and should "mind their own business." They also made derisive comments about the woman's mental and emotional health to co-workers. Although the trial court threw out her case, an appellate court ruled that the woman may have a valid claim for defamation and that she should be given the chance to prove that the statements were made with malice.[9]

Some cases against co-workers have succeeded where it is shown that the defamatory words or actions were likely to harm a woman's reputation among co-workers. To be defamatory, the statements must usually call into question her ability to do her job well or her suitability to hold the position.

> **Example:** An appellate court held that a female police officer may have been defamed when several male officers photographed a nude, lifesize inflatable doll and posted the pictures in the squadroom under a teletyped message that the doll was "Wanted" for impersonating her. It sent the case back to the original court that heard it to determine whether the officer was defamed by the squadroom antics.[10]

---

[9] *Coleman v. American Broadcasting Corp,* 38 Fair Empl. Prac. Cas. (BNA) 65 (D.D.C. 1985).

[10] *Carpenter v. County of Chenango,* 522 N.Y.S.2d 339 (1987).

DAMNED IF THEY ARE, DAMNED IF THEY AREN'T

As a practical matter for litigation, it might be noted, "attractiveness" will likely arise as an implicit credibility issue that cuts two ways—both of them against the women. A conventionally attractive woman will be more likely to be believed when she charges sexual harassment. But it will also be believed that she asked for it, since attractiveness in women so largely consists in the projection of sexual availability, although in veiled and denied ways. Conventionally unattractive women, who would be more credible in asserting that they did not ask for it, by the same token, would be less credible in asserting, over a man's derogatory denial, that it happened at all.

—From *Sexual Harassment of Working Women*, by Catherine MacKinnon (1979)

---

4. Interfering with an employment contract

Another tort action sometimes filed in workplace sexual harassment cases is quaintly called tortious interference with contractual relations or, in some states, intentional interference with an economic relationship. More simply put, this mouthful means that it is illegal for a person to make it impossible for you to get or keep employment. This legal action may be appropriate whenever there are negative employment consequences from a woman's refusal to meet sexual demands placed on her.

Under this legal theory, you may recover damages directly from the person who harassed you if you can prove that:

- you were validly working when the harassment took place

- the person who harassed you knew of the employment relationship

- your harasser intentionally and improperly interfered with your employment relationship, and

- you suffered damages such as loss of your job, a demotion or a failure to get a promotion because of the interference.

In addition, if you are able to prove that a harassing co-worker or supervisor acted maliciously in interfering with your employment relationship, you may be able to get punitive damages—an award of money aimed at punishing the wrongdoer.

This legal action is most appropriate and most common where the harasser is a supervisor or a co-worker who persuades your employer to retaliate against a woman worker by firing or demoting her.

Unfortunately, there are potentially severe limits to this legal action. The most significant is that some courts allow it only for employees who work under a written employment contract that spells out the length of employment.

While workers in upper-echelon executive positions sometimes have written employment contracts, the vast majority of workers do not have such arrangements and are considered to be employees-at-will. This means they can be fired or quit their jobs for any legal reason. Thus, if a court requires a written employment contract as a prerequisite to a lawsuit for interference with a contractual relationship, very few women employees who are sexually harassed can use this legal remedy. (However, see the discussion of wrongful discharge in Section B.6.)

Fortunately, a growing number of courts recognize that even at-will employees should be able to bring actions for interference with employment in some situations. A few courts reason that where a company has an employee manual setting out specific workplace rights such as paid time off, health plan policies and pension rights, that manual may legally be considered an employment contract for purposes of this legal action. Other courts have gone much further, and allowed the action based on the simple and persuasive reasoning that at-will employees have as much interest in the integrity and security of their employment relationship as those working under a written contract.

Example: An Oregon woman took a position as a beauty supply warehouser and was soon promoted to head the company's telemarketing operations. When she spurned the sexual advances of a co-worker who was the business owner's son, he became belligerent, swearing and throwing things at her. He told co-workers that she would not be working at the company much longer and then refused to provide her with the information she needed to do her job. After management ignored her complaints, she resigned. The court found that the woman suffered harassment that was intentionally aimed at forcing her to leave her job.[11]

Example: One of the few female industrial engineers in the computer department of a large plant claimed that her supervisors and co-workers forced her to quit by making her work environment intolerable. She testified that her co-workers ridiculed and harassed her, calling her irrational and advising her that she "should become a school teacher, the best profession a woman can have."

She also presented copious statistical evidence showing that her employer tacitly approved of discrimination against its women workers, by clustering them in the lowest grades of jobs and systematically banning them from training programs that could lead to advancement. The court ruled that several supervisors and co-workers had "acted to intentionally deprive her of an economic benefit" and so had maliciously interfered with her employment contract.[12]

There are limitations on the types of damages that can be recovered in these actions. Employees are usually limited to damages for job-connected losses, such as loss of pay and other employment benefits. Normally, they cannot recover for mental distress or other mental injuries they may have experienced when their harasser interfered with their employment contract. For most employees, this also bars compensation for medical problems that result from being harassed.

Also, such a claim may only be brought against a third person who interfered with employment, not against your employer. The essence of this legal action is that the person who has harassed you has somehow come between you and your employer and harmed that employment relationship. For that reason, the actions are not attributed to the employer in a legal sense.

---

[11] *Lewis v. Oregon Beauty Supply Co.,* 733 P.2d 430 (1987).

[12] *Kyriazi v. Western Elec. Co.,* 461 F. Supp. 894 (1978).

If you sue your harasser under this legal theory, you will not be able to reach the likely larger financial resources of his employer. This may make no difference if the person causing the problem is financially solvent, but suing the harasser and getting a money judgment only against him will do you little good if he is a co-worker who owes more than he earns.

BIG CASES, BIG MONEY

While suffering through sexual harassment to file a tort action is not a preferred method for getting rich quick, there have been a number of cases recently in which large amounts of money were awarded.

Because most cases that are filed are settled, and the terms of settlements of sexual harassment cases are often kept secret, there is no way of keeping tabs on all of their final tallies. But some jury verdicts have reached as high as several million dollars for emotional distress, lost wages and wrongful discharge. While such high stakes are a rarity, a few settlements in recent sexual harassment cases speak loudly.

O'Connell v. Local Union 25
October 1989 settlement: $1.1 million
A 30-year-old apprentice asbestos worker received more than $1 million after claiming she suffered sexual harassment, sex discrimination and wrongful discharge at a Wayne, Illinois plant. Her employer claimed she was fired for excessive absenteeism.

Bihun v. AT&T Information Systems
May 1990 settlement: $2 million
A 37-year-old personnel manager in Los Angeles was awarded $2 million after suffering mental distress she said was caused by unwelcomed advances from her supervisor. She took time off from work to recover, and when she returned, her job had been eliminated.

Gaffke v. U-Haul of Oregon
February 1988 settlement: $1,448,969
An executive at an Oregon shipping and vehicle rental company recovered nearly a million-and-a-half in lost wages and other damages after her employer discriminated against her by paying her less than co-workers, subjecting her to sexual harassment and then wrongfully terminating her.

DO NOT SUFFER YOUR HAND TO BE HELD OR SQUEEZED WITHOUT SHOWING THAT IT DISPLEASES YOU BY INSTANTLY WITHDRAWING IT.—*GUIDE TO GOOD MANNERS FOR YOUNG WOMEN*, PUBLISHED IN 1853

5. Intrusion

A number of tort offenses are grouped under the general heading of invasion of privacy. Of them, intrusion is the one most likely to arise in a sexual harassment situation. Unlike the broader claim of intentional infliction of emotional distress that protects your mental well-being, the tort of intrusion is meant to protect your solitude. Simply put, it prohibits offensive nosiness.

To prove a case of intrusion, you must show:

- that your harasser intentionally intruded upon your private matters or concerns

- the intrusion would be highly offensive to a reasonable woman, and

- you were damaged by the intrusion.

While it is not a legal requirement, some courts will strictly require that there be some actual physical violation for this action.

Example: A woman employed at a paper processing plant was found to have a legal case of intrusion against several male co-workers who heckled her and put an air hose between her legs, simulating a penis.[13]

---

[13] *Waltman v. International Paper Co.*, 47 Fair Empl. Prac. Cas. (BNA) 671 (W.D. La. 1988).

To prove intrusion, most courts do not require a physical touching, but some require that the harasser physically enter a place where he is clearly unwanted and that the harassed woman would reasonably think was private, such as a restroom or locked office. Fortunately, the strong trend is also to find intrusion where a workplace harasser follows, telephones or questions a co-worker about her sex life. Here, intruding into a person's privacy is often key. In addition, the more that the workplace harasser's comments seem to venture from the strictly work-related and the more they fixate on a woman's personal and sexual life, the more likely an illegal intrusion will be found.

> **Example:** An assistant manager at a hotel and restaurant claimed that her supervisor not only frequently pestered her at work with telephone calls in which he regularly steered the conversation to her personal and sex life, but telephoned her at home asking the same prying types of questions. The court, strongly swayed by the fact that the phone calls were made to the woman's home, found there was an intrusion—that the supervisor had clearly transgressed "the sphere from which the woman could reasonably expect her supervisor should be excluded."[14]

An increasing number of courts are becoming more lenient, and find that intrusion claims may be pressed against those who violate not only physical space, but psychological bounds of privacy. This is particularly true if the harasser's offensive conduct seems especially outrageous, persistent and inappropriate.

> **Example:** A woman whose employer constantly pestered her with questions about her sex life and frequently demanded that she have sex with him was held to have a valid complaint for intrusion. The court seemed particularly taken by the fact that the harasser was relentless and pestering in his demands for sex, causing the woman to suffer extreme and obvious health problems requiring medication and counseling. It noted that a person's "emotional sanctum is certainly due the same expectations of privacy as one's physical environment."[15]

---

[14] *Rogers v. Loews L'Enfant Plaza Hotel,* 526 F. Supp. 523 (D.D.C. 1981).

[15] *Phillips v. Smalley Maintenance Servs. Corp.,* 435 So. 2d 705 (Ala. 1983).

CAN YOU COLLECT IF YOU WIN?

Even a multi-million dollar court award will be worth only the paper it's written on unless the person or company found liable is able to pay. In most sexual harassment cases, collecting what's due and owing to you is not a problem because your employer as well as the harasser is liable—and either or both are likely to be solvent. Some larger employers also purchase a form of specialized insurance that covers attorneys' costs in defending against a harassment lawsuit.

As a general rule, employers are responsible for sexual harassment by supervisors and managers who work there. And they may even be held financially responsible for harassment you suffer at the hands of a co-worker if a supervisor either knew or should have known about the wrongful behavior.

Where a co-worker commits one act of harassment with no prior history or workplace pattern of such treatment, the employer may not be liable. When the employee alone is liable, it will probably be difficult to collect. And if the employer is small and has limited cash supply and no insurance to cover attorney's fees for defending a sexual harassment lawsuit, it may be impossible to collect a large judgment.

---

6. Wrongful discharge

Workers who have been fired illegally may be able to sue their former employers for wrongful discharge—and if they succeed, may be able to claim compensation for all injuries suffered in the process, including lost wages and mental distress.

Historically, there was a nearly insurmountable impediment to bringing this legal action: the doctrine of employment-at-will. (See Section B.4.) Most workers are legally deemed to be employees-at-will, meaning that they can be fired for any legal reason, without violating the law. While the legal doctrine of employment-at-will is still technically the law in many states, there is also a well-recognized exception that provides many sexually harassed employees a way around it. Courts in nearly every state have held that an employee cannot legally be fired for refusing to tolerate conduct that violates a public policy—such as sexual harassment on the job.

One of the strongest arguments that a woman who has been fired after being subjected to harassment can make is this: Sexual harassment violates public policy—and that she has the right to a workplace free from it. This argument sets the stage for a lawsuit for wrongful discharge.

Example: A plumber's all-male co-workers and supervisor subjected her to gender-related jokes, teasing and condescending behavior that demeaned her skills while she worked at a jobsite. After a week's work, the woman was laid off, ostensibly because there was not sufficient work, although all her male co-workers were retained. In ruling that she had a valid claim for wrongful discharge, the court held that because she had presented sufficient evidence to establish a civil rights violation under the U.S. Civil Rights Act, her lay-off was contrary to an express public policy.[16]

Many courts also reason that sexual harassment on the job is a form of illegal discrimination, and they conclude that workers also have an important public interest in not being fired for resisting such harassment.

Example: Several women who worked at a catering company were subjected to the harassing behavior of their general manager. To their great consternation, he commented daily on their breasts, buttocks and physical appearance, intimated that they had better "show him a good time" and established a dress code for women employees, admitting that he required them to wear skirts, nylons and heels so he could admire their legs. Men had no dress restrictions.

When one woman complained to company supervisors about his behavior, he abruptly changed his tack toward her—constantly criticizing her work and cajoling her about her appearance. Shortly after she complained, he fired her. The court held that her wrongful discharge action was properly based on the evidence that she acted in an important public interest—eliminating sexual harassment in her workplace.[17]

---

[16] *Hallquist v. Max Fish Plumbing & Heating,* 46 FEP 1854 (1987).

[17] *Dias v. Sky Chefs, Inc.,* 919 F. 2d 1370 (9th Cir. 1990).

THE BEST OF TORTS, THE WORST OF TORTS

Chapters 5, 6 and 7 discuss how the U.S. Civil Rights Act and state fair employment practices (FEP) laws ban most serious forms of sexual harassment.

And those laws as statements of public policy can also form the basis for a common law tort claim of wrongful discharge when an employee is fired for refusing to tolerate or attempting to put an end to sexual harassment. An employee who is fired as a result of sexual harassment will often have at least three claims that she can join together in one legal action: a claim for violating the Civil Rights Act, a claim for violating the FEP and a claim for wrongful discharge.

But beware: Courts in Hawaii, Illinois, Pennsylvania and Wisconsin have ruled that their FEP laws are the only remedy for wrongful discharge claims based on violations of public policy. It may be too strong to conclude that wrongful discharge lawsuits based on charges of sexual harassment in the workplace under federal law will be absolutely banned in these states. However, it seems likely that you will have a tougher task pleading and proving this legal action.

Also, your claim of wrongful discharge may be barred if you are a union employee and your collective bargaining agreement states that the Railway Labor Act or the National Labor Relations Act controls disputes. Other union employees, however, are not banned from filing this legal action.

---

7. Rape

The most outrageous and egregious form of workplace harassment is rape. Generally, rape requires that a man have sexual intercourse with a woman without her consent. But the specifics of the offense differ from state to state.

Until the mid 1970s, rape laws in most states covered only situations where a man forced a woman to have intercourse under the threat of bodily injury. Practically speaking, these cases were rarely proven unless the woman resisted strenuously—and there was outside corroboration for the attack. So most rapes went unprosecuted. For example, in the state of New York, which had this type of restrictive law in the early '70s, there was a paltry total of less than 20 rape convictions annually, although several thousand charges were filed. Of course, the poor likelihood of getting a conviction meant most women didn't bother filing charges.

Most laws still require proof that some force was used during a rape, but, fortunately, force is typically interpreted to include verbal threats in addition to physically overpowering a woman.

Today, most state laws include several degrees of rape charges under various names, such as sexual assault, which cover a broader range of situations. For example, the most serious charge under Florida's rape law prohibits sexual battery—which requires proof of penetration, nonconsent, use or display of a deadly weapon or use or threat of physical force likely to cause serious injury. A lesser charge, sexual assault, requires proof of physical force or violence not likely to cause physical injury.

And in some states, no force is required. For example, Wisconsin's law defines third degree sexual assault to include sexual intercourse with a women who has not agreed to it, even if she remained silent and he used no force.

Newer, tougher laws have meant that more cases of rape are filed and prosecuted. In 1990, according to a Senate Judiciary Committee report, the number of rapes reported in the United States rose to 100,433. Experts estimate that in as many as 85% of all reported rape cases, the woman knew the offender. Since work is obviously a place where a lot of social contact takes place, rape in the workplace—which usually fits under the informal designation of acquaintance rape—is being prosecuted more often.

There are special circumstances to consider in workplace rape. Often, the rapist is a woman's supervisor who also uses threats of firing or demoting her if she resists. Many courts will view such threats as sufficient force or coercion to satisfy that demand in the law.

In addition, there has been a slow-to-emerge recognition that most women will not cry rape frivolously. Women's testimony about rape and assault is generally being given more credence—and an increasing number of women believe that the rape charges they file will be given proper consideration by the courts.

One issue that is still unsettled is whether an employer can be held liable when a co-worker or supervisor rapes an employee. The handful of courts that have considered this issue have differed.

C. Disadvantages of Tort Actions

Despite these encouraging words about tort actions you can file to fight back against sexual harassment, there are also a number of legal and practical reasons that may weigh against doing so.

1. Federal and state laws may be stronger

The 1990s are certain to be fraught with rapid changes in sexual harassment laws and how they're interpreted. In the late 1960s through the '70s, most harassment claims were filed with the EEOC under Title VII, as women hoped that the Civil Rights Act of 1964 would give them significant protection. The sands shifted drastically in the '80s. More women found Title VII and state discrimination laws came up short in curing the ills of sexual harassment on the job. As a result, state tort claims, especially those seeking lucrative damages for emotional distress, increasingly became the legal action of choice.

Today, we are at a new crossroad. Amendments to the Civil Rights Act passed in 1991 now make it possible for women filing Title VII actions to collect up to $300,000 in compensatory and punitive damages. (See Chapter 6, Section B.) Surely this will mean that these lawsuits will become more common. Also, the rights and remedies available to a harassed woman under many state FEP laws have been improved. It is unclear what effect that legal change will have on the number of common law tort actions filed against harassment.

2. Unpredictability

Another possible disadvantage of common law torts is that the rules and interpretations are much less well-defined and more open to subjective interpretation than actions for harassment filed under the Civil Rights Act or through state FEP agencies. For example, whether an employee has suffered mental distress or has been defamed requires a subjective evaluation of her mindset and reactions. Once you file one of these actions, you are at the mercy of the particular sensibilities and sensitivities of the judge or jury that will be evaluating your situation—mulling over whether the harassment you have suffered was sufficiently outrageous or sufficiently damaging to form the basis of a significant dollar judgment.

By contrast, when you file a sexual harassment claim with a state FEP agency or the EEOC, your proof problems are somewhat easier. The statutes not only define sexual harassment in fairly broad terms, they offer specific—albeit limited—types of relief. In addition, these investigations and subsequent hearings are less public and somewhat less prying than a lawsuit is likely to be.

3. Proving intent

For many women, there are additional practical drawbacks to bringing a lawsuit based on a common law tort charge as opposed to a claim under a state FEP law or the Civil Rights Act. To succeed in a tort case, you must typically prove the wrongdoer's bad intent. Proving intent can be difficult. It requires that you get inside the wrongdoer's mind.

An alarming number of male judges, for example, have reached the ludicrous conclusion that a man who repeatedly pinches, fondles or strokes a female co-worker did not intend to harass her.

4. Proving personal harm

Also, to win in most of the state court actions based on the torts discussed in this chapter, you must prove that you were harmed personally by the harassment. Typically, this means you must have suffered a fairly serious physical injury or illness that required extensive medical treatment. It is not enough that your job status suffered—that you were denied a promotion or fired.

This also means that you will likely need to speak up about painful personal history and intensely private facts of your life—your mental state, your physical health, your lifestyle, your feelings. And you may face hostile cross-examination on all of these issues.

For some women, that price is too high.

5. Getting a lawyer

Finally, to bring most state court common law cases, you will need to hire a lawyer to help—and that can be expensive, difficult and frustrating. The average legal costs of pursuing a sexual harassment case that goes to trial has been estimated at $80,000—with an additional $4,000 to $25,000 in fees for deposition transcripts and expert witnesses.

Few women can afford this, so almost all will have to find a lawyer to handle their case on a contingency fee basis—that is, taking a fee as a percentage of the final judgment (usually 33% to 40%), but not requiring the client to pay any money upfront. Since many more women hope to hire lawyers experienced in sexual harassment cases than there are lawyers, you will likely only find one to handle your case for a contingency fee if he or she is convinced that your case is sufficiently shocking to pay off big. (See Chapter 9, Section A.4.)

But by learning about your possible legal alternatives, you will be able to save great amounts in time and stress—not to mention legal fees. You may also be able to get a free or low-cost evaluation of whether your situation is likely to merit one of the legal actions described here by contacting a local law clinic or an attorney affiliated with women's special interest groups. (See the Appendix for contact information on many such groups.)

D. Workers' Compensation: Employers' Defense

Workers' compensation is a system most states have established to deal with workers who are injured on the job. It works much like an insurance policy: Employers pay a certain amount per month into a general fund. Then, employees who are injured at work can file a claim and get some payment from the fund. Created partially in response to employers' fears of high-damage lawsuits by employees injured in industrial accidents, workers' compensation represents a compromise. Employees are paid quickly, but only a limited amount—and employers pay premiums to avoid other lawsuits.

Workers' compensation is a poor remedy in most sexual harassment cases, because it pays so little. You can recover only for physical injuries—not emotional injuries, and frequently not for stress-related injuries. And you can collect only your medical bills and some fraction of the wages you lost if your injury forced you to take time off work. That's all.

As a result, very few employees use workers' compensation in sexual harassment situations. But increasingly, employers seeking to avoid expensive tort judgments are arguing that sexual harassment claims should be handled exclusively under the workers' compensation system.

Unfortunately for some women, state tort actions may not be available to fill in the gap because courts in some states have absolutely ruled that their state's workers' compensation law is the sole remedy for sexual harassment—barring a harassed worker from bringing any other state tort legal action for the injury caused. This presents some harassed workers with a Catch-22: The only relief available to them is under the state's workers' compensation laws, which is inadequate for their injuries.

A few courts—in Florida, Missouri and Wisconsin—have even gone so far as to ignore their own state's fair employment laws in broadly ruling that workers' compensation is the only system for compensating injured workers. In fashioning such findings, these courts have had to resort to novel stretches of definitions and have sometimes seemed to completely overlook common sense.

Florida. A grocery store cashier sued her supervisor for battery and intentional infliction of emotional distress, claiming that while discussing store business during work hours, he reached over and grabbed her breast. The court dismissed the claims, holding that because the injuries were physical, "not due to fright or excitement only," and occurred during the natural course of employment, the exclusive remedy for them was under the workers' compensation laws.[18]

In another recent sexual harassment case in Florida, two women alleged that their supervisor had committed vintage physical harassment—repeatedly pinching, patting and grabbing their buttocks, shoulders and breasts. He also kissed them and tore at their clothing several times. The court, however, characterized the

---

[18] *Brown v. Winn-Dixie Montgomery, Inc.*, 469 So.2d 155 (Fla. Dist. Ct. App. 1985).

pinching and kissing as accidental, and limited legal recovery to the workers' compensation laws.[19]

Missouri. An employee who worked at a women's college sued her supervisor for intentional infliction of emotional distress, claiming that he harassed her in various ways. The court ruled that her injuries were accidental and so she was restricted to bringing an action under the workers' compensation law. It also held that because the harasser acted "outside the scope of his employment," the college could not be found liable in any civil action based on the harassment.[20]

Wisconsin. A woman sued her employer, three supervisors, her union and four co-workers for intentional infliction of emotional harm, claiming she was subjected to invidious sexual harassment at work. The court flatly rejected her arguments that the injuries she suffered were neither accidental nor unexpected because the harassment occurred daily. It held that the state workers' compensation statute provided the exclusive remedy for the harassment.[21]

But most courts do not buy into this argument of workers' compensation as the exclusive remedy. In fact, courts in several states have taken the step of holding that injuries brought on by workplace sexual harassment are outside the scope of workers' compensation laws. These decisions advance the enlightened view that harassment is not a natural part of the workday and encourage employers not to tolerate it.

---

[19] *Schwartz v. Zippy Mart, Inc.*, 470 So. 2d 720 (Fla. Dist. Ct. App. 1985).

[20] *Miller v. Lindenwood Female College*, 616 F. Supp. 860 (E.D. Mo. 1985).

[21] *Zabkowicz v. West Bend Co.*, 789 F.2d 540 (7th Cir. 1986).

Example: While they were out of town on a business trip, a woman recently hired as an educational programs assistant charged that her supervisor continually pressured her to have sex with him, insulted her for refusing his advances and fraudulently got access to her hotel room as she slept. She sued for assault, battery and intentional infliction of emotional distress.

The employer advanced the argument that all her claims were barred by the workers' compensation statute. But the Massachusetts Supreme Court on appeal held that not only is sexual harassment intolerable in the workplace, it is also unconstitutional and must be corrected through any legal claim available.[22]

THE PARAMOUNT DESTINY AND MISSION OF WOMAN ARE TO FULFILL THE NOBLE AND BENIGN OFFICES OF WIFE AND MOTHER. THIS IS THE LAW OF THE CREATOR.—FROM *BRADWELL V. ILLINOIS*, 83 U.S. 130 (1873)

---

[22] *O'Connell v. Chasdi*, 511 N.E.2d 349 (1987).

CHAPTER

9

Lawyers and Legal Research

A. Hiring A Lawyer.. 9/2
    1. Where to look for a lawyer... 9/2
    2. Deciding on a particular lawyer 9/4
    3. The initial interview 9/5
    4. Paying your lawyer.. 9/6
    5. Managing your lawyer... 9/7
    6. Firing a lawyer 9/9

B. Legal Research 9/9
    1. Libraries... 9/11
    2. An overview of research tools.. 9/11
    3. EEOC publications.. 9/12
    4. Statutes 9/15
    5. Regulations.. 9/16
    6. Cases... 9/17
    7. Treatises 9/22
    8. Law review articles 9/23

I f you have read this far, you now have a solid understanding of what sexual harassment is—and what your options are for dealing with it. However, there may be situations when you will need to move beyond the information provided in this book. In this chapter, we give you some guidelines on how to select and work with a lawyer and how to do additional legal research on your own.

A. Hiring A Lawyer

Many readers who are subjected to sexual harassment on the job will need to hire a lawyer to get more information about laws and legal strategies. For example, you will likely need a lawyer's help if:

- You have used the formal procedures for filing a complaint against harassment in your workplace, but the company representatives do not seem willing to negotiate with you fairly or openly.

- You have filed a complaint with your state fair employment practices (FEP) agency or with the Equal Employment Opportunities Commission (EEOC), but you would like to find out more about your specific options. Lawyers on staff at the EEOC handle a few cases in court for harassed women, but very few—only 50 or so in 1990. If you wish to pursue a claim for sexual harassment, you will most likely need to hire a lawyer to represent you.

- You have suffered serious injuries from the harassment, which make it appropriate for you to file a lawsuit.

1. Where to look for a lawyer

If you decide to hire a lawyer, the first task is to find one who best suits your needs. The legal field of sexual harassment is new and evolving very quickly, and you need a lawyer who has experience in handling the nuances and complications of a sexual harassment lawsuit. Out of the nearly 800,000 lawyers in the United States, only a few thousand have such training or experience.

Depending on your circumstances and location, there are a number of places to turn for a referral to a lawyer in this group. They include:

Your state fair employment practices agency or the federal EEOC office. Some, but not all, of these offices maintain lists of lawyers who are experienced in handling sexual harassment lawsuits. Frankly, the help you get from these agencies depends greatly on the knowledge and helpfulness of the person who answers the telephone. It will be worth your while to persist until you find the person in the agency with the willingness and moxy to really tell you which local lawyers know what they are doing.

Legal aid clinics. Many local legal aid clinics or legal services offices have sexual harassment lawyers on staff—a phenomenon that developed in the last few years. Most of these offices have income or geographical restrictions on the clients they can accept, but even if you don't qualify, someone there may be able to refer you to a competent attorney. Locate your community's legal aid clinics by looking in the telephone directory under Legal Aid Society or Legal Services—or check with the nearest law school.

Local women's organizations. Most larger cities have helplines established by women's groups—often affiliated with a local law school—that answer legal questions about sexual harassment. Many other women's groups maintain lists of attorneys with experience in handling sexual harassment and discrimination problems. Check the Yellow Pages of the telephone book under Women's Organizations & Services or Crisis Services.

National women's organizations. Several groups that concentrate on women's legal rights, such as NOW, the ACLU and National Women's Political Caucus, also maintain lists of experienced lawyers from which they'll make referrals. (See the Appendix for contact details.)

Employee groups. Specialized employees may have access to legal help offered by special interest groups. Union workers, for example, can contact the Coalition for Labor Union Women for legal guidance and referrals to experienced attorneys. (See the Appendix for additional specialized listings.)

BEWARE OF LAWYER REFERRAL SERVICES

Bar associations and other lawyer groups often maintain and advertise lawyer referral services. Usually, there is little or no screening before a lawyer can get listed in these services. While it is always possible you will find a good lawyer through one of these services, your chances are hit and miss.

---

2. Deciding on a particular lawyer

Once you have a referral to a lawyer—or even better, several referrals—you'll want to contact each and see whether he or she meets your needs. Come forearmed with some inside knowledge:

- Most lawyers are guided by the principle that Time Is Money. And time and money should also be your guiding concerns in deciding whether to hire a lawyer to help with your sexual harassment claim.

- Even the simplest problems can take a long time to be resolved through the legal system. And problems involving sexual harassment do not often present themselves in straightforward issues. Unless a case is settled—most cases are—a court proceeding can take from five to eight years before a final judgment is reached.

- A lawyer's help rarely comes cheap. Legal organizations estimate that harassment cases eat up an average of between $8,000 to $30,000 in lawyers' time and other legal costs such as court filings and witness interviews.

- Lawyers usually take on sexual harassment cases for little or no money upfront. They depend on court-ordered fees and often a percentage of your recovery, or a contingency fee. (See Section A.4.) This means that a lawyer will be assessing whether your case is likely to pay off so that he or she will be compensated.

Given these dire circumstances, you will want to be as certain as possible that any lawyer you hire will be doing the utmost to represent you fairly and efficiently—and that you are comfortable with his or her representation. Also, depending on your own interest and energy level, you may be able to help out on your case—by gathering documents and organizing information—which can go a long way toward saving time and money.

WHAT A LAWYER WANTS TO HEAR

From a lawyer's point of view, a good case has these attributes:

• Fairly serious harassment—usually either a few incidents of clearly bad conduct or a longstanding pattern of harassment that continues even after requests have been made that it stop.

• Personal injuries—the more serious, the better. If there are medical bills and loss of work time you can trace to sexual harassment, that will help get the lawyer's attention.

• A solvent defendant—large employers that are sensitive to maintaining a good public image may be the most willing to agree to a quick and sizeable settlement.

If your situation includes some or all of these items, make sure the lawyer knows it.

---

3. The initial interview

Start by asking for an appointment. Some lawyers will try to screen you over the phone by asking you to discuss the basics of your case. A little of this can be appropriate—most experienced sexual harassment lawyers are inundated with potential clients these days, so he or she will want to be sure you need expert legal advice.

Many lawyers will agree not to charge you for an initial consultation to decide whether your situation requires legal action. But be prepared to pay a reasonable fee for legal advice. A charge of between $75 and $150 for a one-hour consultation is typical. If you organize the facts in your case well before going to your consultation, an hour should be more than enough to explain your case and obtain at least a basic opinion on how it might be approached and what it is likely to cost. If you find the right lawyer and can afford the charge, it can be money well spent. A good way to bring order to your case facts is to fill out a copy of the sexual harassment complaint form (Chapter 4, Section D.1) and bring it with you to the interview.

4. Paying your lawyer

FEE ARRANGEMENTS—GET IT IN WRITING

Most disagreements between lawyers and clients involve fees, so be sure to get all the details involving money in writing—including the per hour billing rate or the contingency fee arrangement, the frequency of billing and how the attorney will handle any funds you're required to deposit in advance to cover expenses.

Most sexual harassment cases are handled on some form of contingent fee arrangement. Under a contingent fee, a lawyer agrees to handle your case for a fixed percentage of the amount you finally recover in a lawsuit. If you win the case, the lawyer's fee comes out of the money awarded to you. If you lose, neither you nor the lawyer will get any money.

A lawyer's willingness to take your case on a contingent fee is a hopeful sign of faith in the strength of your claim. A lawyer who is not firmly convinced that your case is a winner is unlikely to take you on as a contingency fee client. Be very wary of a lawyer who wants to take your case on an hourly payment basis. That usually signals that he or she does not think your case is very strong in terms of the money you might be able to recover. It could also mean financial disaster for you, as your legal bills are likely to mount up with no useful results. At the very least, insist that the lawyer writes down some specific objectives to be accomplished in your case—and puts a limit on how high the fees can accumulate.

Although there is no set percentage for contingency fees in most types of cases, the standard amount demanded by lawyers in most areas is about 35% if the case is settled before a lawsuit is filed with the courts, and 40% if a case has to be tried. Keep in mind that the terms of a contingency fee agreement may be negotiable. You can try to get your lawyer to agree to a lower percentage—especially if the case is settled quickly—or to absorb some of the court costs.

Sometimes, a lawyer working for you under a contingency agreement will require that you pay all out-of-pocket expenses, such as filing fees charged by the courts and the cost of transcribing witness depositions. If this is so, the lawyer will want you to deposit a substantial amount of money—a thousand dollars or more—with the law firm to cover these expenses. From your standpoint, it is a much better arrangement for the lawyer to advance such costs and get repaid out of your recovery. A common sense arrangement might involve you advancing a little amount of money for some costs, with the attorney advancing the rest.

In Civil Rights Act and FEP cases, there is also the possibility of the court awarding you attorney's fees as part of final judgment. However, this award may not be large enough to cover the entire amount owed to your attorney under the legal fee contract. Therefore, the contingency fee contract should spell out what happens to a court award of attorney's fees. One approach is to have the fees paid to the attorney in their entirety—and subtract that amount from the contingency fee to which you have agreed.

5. Managing your lawyer

A great many complaints against lawyers have to do with their failure to communicate with their clients. Your lawyer may be the one with the legal expertise, but the rights that are being pursued are yours—and you are the most important person involved in your case. You have the right to demand that your lawyer be reasonably available to answer your questions and to keep you posted on your case.

You may need to put some energy into subtly managing your lawyer.

Carefully check every statement. Each statement or bill should list costs that the lawyer has paid or that you are expected to pay. If any one lacks sufficient detail for you to verify that it complies with your written fee agreement, call your lawyer and politely demand that a new, more detailed version be sent before you pay it. Don't feel as though you're being too pushy by demanding more detail: The laws in many states actually require thorough detail in lawyers' statements.

Learn as much as you can about the laws and decisions involved in your case. By doing so, you'll be able to monitor your lawyer's work and may even be able to make a suggestion or provide information that will move your case along faster. Certainly if the other side offers a settlement, you will be in a better position to evaluate whether or not it makes sense to accept it.

Keep your own calendar of dates and deadlines. Note when papers and appearances are due in court. If you rely on your lawyer to keep your case on schedule, you may be unpleasantly surprised to find that an important deadline has been missed. Many a good case has been thrown out simply because of a lawyer's forgetfulness. Call or write to your lawyer at least a week before any important deadline in your case to inquire about plans to meet it.

Maintain your own file on your case. By having a well-organized file of your own, you'll be able to discuss your case with your lawyer intelligently and efficiently—even over the telephone. Being well-informed will help keep your lawyer's effectiveness up and your costs down. Be aware that if your lawyer is working on a hourly basis, you'll probably be charged for telephone consultations. But they're likely to be less expensive than office visits.

DISAGREEING ON A SETTLEMENT OFFER

In many case, your employer may offer a cash amount to settle the case. The problem is that you and your lawyer may have different interests at heart. If your lawyer is rushed or needs money, he or she may be ready to settle your case quickly for an inadequate amount. You, on the other hand, may want to hold out for what you consider to be more adequate. At this critical juncture, you may wish to get a second legal opinion as to whether the amount offered is realistic given the facts of your situation.

---

6. Firing a lawyer

Change lawyers if you feel that's necessary. If the relationship between you and the lawyer you chose doesn't seem to be working out, or if you feel that your case isn't progressing as it should, think about asking another lawyer to take over. Be clear with the first lawyer that you are taking your business elsewhere, and immediately put your decision in writing.

You could end up receiving bills from both lawyers—both of whom will claim they handled the lion's share of your case. Before you pay anything, be sure that the total amount of the bills does not amount to more than you agreed to pay. If you have a contingency fee arrangement, it is up to your new lawyer and former lawyer to work out how to split the fee.

Take prompt action against any behavior by a lawyer that appears to be deceptive, unethical or otherwise illegal. A call to the local bar association, listed in the telephone directory under Attorneys, should provide you with guidance on what types of lawyer behavior are prohibited and how to file a complaint. In most states, attorney regulatory bodies are biased toward lawyers. Unless the lawyer's conduct is plainly dishonest or he or she has abandoned your case, you will probably not get much satisfaction. However, sometimes the threat of filing a complaint can move your lawyer into action. And if worst comes to worst, filing a formal complaint will create a document that you'll need should you end up later filing a lawsuit against a lawyer for malpractice.

B. Legal Research

Legal research is by no means necessary for everyone. This book gives more than enough details on sexual harassment law for most people. However, there are times when specific legal knowledge can give you additional control over your situation—and save you time and money. Think of legal knowledge as a form of power—the more you know, the more you can make informed choices, demand the treatment you're entitled to and plan an effective strategy for settlement and litigation. Some examples of when you might want to consider doing some legal research:

Presenting the facts of your case to a government agency. The first statement you make to an investigator for the EEOC or your state FEP agency is very important: It will form the basis for your claim and for any lawsuit you may want to bring later. Therefore, if your case involves particularly complex or unsettled legal issues—for example, whether local courts have been allowing more or fewer tort actions for sexual harassment since the U.S. Civil Rights Act was amended—it would probably be wise to do some hands-on research.

Getting more details on the law of your state. Sexual harassment law varies somewhat in all 50 states. Chapter 7 gives you some details of each state's law. But to learn how state FEP policies have been applied by state courts, and to see how traditional common law torts have been used in sexual harassment cases in each state, you'll need to do some additional research.

Choosing and working with a lawyer. If you decide to hire a lawyer, you will need to find one with some expertise in sexual harassment. Your own legal knowledge will help you determine whether your lawyer is well-qualified and will allow you to participate fully in your case.

DON'T START FROM SCRATCH

For more general information about sexual harassment, check the Appendix. You will find that many legal and special interest groups publish helpful bibliographies and pamphlets on the legal aspects of sexual harassment. Before you do extensive research on your own, first check on what others have done.

If you are new to legal research, you may find that you need more guidance than we provide here. Excellent resources on legal research for the novice include *Legal Research Made Easy*—a 2-½ hour video that explains how to do technical legal research and how to set priorities to get results in a reasonable time. Also, *Legal Research: How to Find and Understand the Law*, by Steve Elias, contains clear explanations and examples of all legal research techniques. Both are published by Nolo Press.

1. Libraries

The reference sections in most larger public libraries contain a set of local and state laws, as well as a set of the federal statutes. The librarians there should be able to help you look up any laws—including your state fair employment practices law—that might affect your situation. However, if you want to look up a court case or a ruling by agencies such as the Equal Employment Opportunity Commission or your state's fair employment practices agency, you'll probably have to visit a law library.

In many states, county law libraries are free and open to the public. You can also try the library of the nearest law school, particularly if it's affiliated with a public university funded by tax dollars. Law school libraries offer one big advantage: They are usually open from early in the morning until late at night—even on weekends and some holidays. Whatever library you choose, you'll find that most librarians are not only well-versed in legal research techniques, but also are friendly and open to helping you through the mazes of legal citations.

2. An overview of research tools

There are several types of research materials concentrating on sexual harassment that you'll find useful: secondary sources such as books and law review articles, and also primary sources such as statutes and cases. These resources serve different purposes.

Secondary sources—books such as this one and articles—are primarily used to get an overview of a particular topic. If you find a good article or chapter on a topic you're interested in, it will give both an explanation of the law and citations to other materials—especially cases—that may prove helpful.

Primary sources—statutes (state and federal laws) and cases (published decisions of state and federal courts)—tell you the current status of the law. Very often, your goals in doing legal research are first to find the statutes that apply to you, and then to find the court cases that interpret the statutes in sexual harassment situations similar to yours. There may be cases with similar facts—for example, a supervisor who persistently asked a female employee to go out with him after she repeatedly said no. Or there may be a court case that raises a similar issue or legal question—for example, whether an employer is legally responsible for harassment by a co-worker or whether a state fair employment law covers a particular kind of employee. These court decisions may give you some indication of how a government agency or court is likely to decide your case.

With all this in mind, where should you begin your research? It depends on your situation. If you want some additional general information about sexual harassment, or an update on the law since this book was published, you will probably find a recent book or article more than adequate. However, if you want very specific legal information—for example, whether the common law tort of wrongful discharge is a valid legal theory in your state— you will probably need to look at both your state fair employment practice law and any judicial decisions dealing with the issue. The sections that follow describe several types of resources, how to find them and how to use them to learn about the law that applies to your situation.

YOU DO NOT CONDUCT PERSONAL LIFE AT THE OFFICE.—JUDITH MARTIN, AKA MISS MANNERS

3. EEOC publications

The EEOC periodically publishes guidelines on the changing shape of how sexual harassment is defined by courts around the nation. The most recent, "EEOC: Policy Guidance on Sexual Harassment," was issued in March 1990. Because EEOC office personnel are instructed to apply these guidelines in evaluating sexual harassment cases, they are a good barometer for how your own problem is likely to be analyzed.

And for those on the research trail, the guidelines are also a storehouse of information about recent cases. Pay particular attention to the footnotes, which generally list recent court decisions and explain legal embellishments on particular issues. Many law libraries will have copies of the EEOC policy guidelines—or you can get a copy from your state or the federal EEOC office.

The EEOC also publishes regulations detailing how the U.S. Civil Rights Act is to be interpreted and enforced. If you cannot find them in your library, you can get a copy of them from your local EEOC office as well.

THE TWO RESEARCH TRACKS: FEDERAL AND STATE

By now you know that there are two separate sets of laws on sexual harassment—federal law and state law. Each has separate statutes, regulations and court cases, so you must decide which law you are relying on before you start to research.

The U.S. Civil Rights Act is a federal law, and the court decisions which interpret it—including those involving the EEOC—are federal cases. However, not all federal decisions carry equal weight. The cases which will be most persuasive in federal court are those from the highest court in that jurisdiction: the United States Supreme Court. On the second level in the hierarchy are the federal courts of appeal. You should look first for cases in the same judicial circuit or geographical region as yours, since these will be more authoritative. And finally, on the lowest level are the federal district courts—again, look first for cases in your geographical area.

If you are researching your state's FEP law or common law tort theories, you will be looking at state court cases. Most state court systems are similar to the federal system, in that there are three hierarchical levels of courts. The most authoritative cases will be those from your state's highest court (usually called the supreme court), followed by decisions issued by your state appellate court, followed by decisions issued by your state trial court.

SEXUAL HARASSMENT LAW IS CHANGING FAST—WATCH FOR KEY DATES

A few important cases and legislative developments have substantially changed the legal complexion of sexual harassment—often wiping out all the decisions and developments that came before. When doing research on sexual harassment, some of the older resources may give you interesting historical perspectives, but check the following dates to be sure that the information they give on specific points has not become obsolete.

July 1964   Congress passes the Civil Rights Act outlawing sex discrimination in employment and creating the Equal Employment Opportunity Commission.

April 1976   A Washington, D.C., judge becomes the first to recognize sexual harassment as a form of sex discrimination—and allows a lawsuit by a Department of Justice employee who claims her supervisor harassed and fired her after she refused to have sex with him. *Williams v. Saxbe,* 413 F. Supp. 654 (1976).

September 1982   A federal judge in Wisconsin upholds a verdict in favor of a male social services worker who claims he was sexually harassed by his female supervisor. *Huebschen v. Dep't of Health and Social Services,* 547 F. Supp. 1168 (1982).

June 1986   The U.S. Supreme Court decides its first sexual harassment case, ruling that harassment is sex discrimination—and illegal under Title VII of the Civil Rights Act. *Meritor Sav. Bank v. Vinson,* 477 U.S. 57 (1986).

March 1990   The EEOC issues guidelines on how to define and prevent sexual harassment, updating the guidelines it issued in 1980.

January 1991   An appellate court in Florida rules that nude pin-ups in the workplace can be illegal sexual harassment. *Robinson v. Jacksonville Shipyards,* 760 F. Supp. 1486 (1991). About a week later, an appellate court in California recognizes that, in considering what qualifies as sexual harassment, the behavior should be evaluated by the reasonable woman standard, as opposed to the reasonable man standard that was formerly applied. *Ellison v. Brady,* 924 F.2d 872 (1991).

October 1991   The Civil Rights Act is amended to allow compensatory and punitive damages in sexual harassment cases.

4. Statutes

When people refer to "the law," they are usually talking about statutes. Statutes are the written laws created by state and federal legislatures. The federal statute prohibiting sexual harassment is the Civil Rights Act of 1964. It can be found in title 42 of the U.S. Code, Section 2000.

Most states—although not all—also have their own laws prohibiting sexual harassment. To find your state's discrimination statute, locate the citation listed after your state in Chapter 7. Then ask the librarian where you can locate the state laws—often called codes—find the appropriate volume and read on. For example, if you live in California, look at the Fair Employment and Housing Act, found in the California Government Code beginning at Section 12900. If there is no citation listed for your state, that means there is no state statute prohibiting sexual harassment and you should probably concentrate your research on federal law.

OUR SUPERVISOR TELLS US WHAT KIND OF MAKE-UP TO WEAR, WHAT KIND OF LIPSTICK TO WEAR, IF OUR HAIR IS NOT THE RIGHT STYLE FOR US, IF WE'RE NOT SMILING ENOUGH. THEY EVEN TELL US HOW TO ACT WHEN YOU'RE ON A PASS.—TERRY MASON, 26, A FLIGHT ATTENDANT, IN *WORKING* BY STUDS TERKEL (AVON, 1972)

HOW TO READ STATUTE CITATIONS

Federal statutes are contained in the United States Code. For example, if you are looking for the Civil Rights Act, 42 U.S.C. 2000, locate title 42 of the United States Code and turn to Section 2000.

Finding state statutes is a bit trickier, because states use slightly different systems to number and organize their statutes. Most states use one of the following methods:

By topic. California uses this type of organization. To find Cal. Gvt. Code §12900, locate the volumes that contain the state's government code and turn to Section 12900.

By number. Florida, for example, lists statutes numerically, without flagging the topics the laws cover. To find Fla. Stat. §760.01, turn to Section 760.01.

By title. Vermont, for example, divides its statutes into titles, similar to the federal citation system. To find 21 Vt. Stat. §495, locate Title 21 of the Vermont Statutes—and turn to Section 495.

Inside the back cover of the volume, you will find an unbound supplement called a "pocket part." This material will update the information in the main volume, telling you about any amendments or changes to the law that have happened since the main volume was published. It is organized just like the main volume, using the same numerical system. Be sure to consult this every time you use a statute: If you don't, you may be relying on law that is no longer valid.

5. Regulations

In some situations, you may also want to consult the regulations that pertain to a statute. Regulations are the rules created by administrative agencies for carrying out legislation. If, for example, a statute requires an agency to investigate sexual harassment complaints, there will probably be regulations that give more detail about what form the investigation will take, who will conduct it and how it will be done.

Federal regulations can be found in the Code of Federal Regulations—usually abbreviated as CFR. The EEOC regulations on sex discrimination can be found in volume 29 of the CFR, beginning at Section 1604.1. This set of books will be available in most law libraries, or you can request a copy of the regulations from the EEOC.

Most state fair employment agencies also publish regulations. Finding these regulations can be difficult. Often, all of the regulations for a given state will be gathered into an Administrative Code. Look in the index of the Code to determine if your state's fair employment agency regulations are published there. Other state agencies publish their regulations separately, in manuals. These may be available at the law library—ask the librarian for more information. Or contact your state FEP agency and ask it to send you a copy of the regulations, or at least to tell you where they can be found.

DON'T FORGET LOCAL LAWS

Many major cities and some counties—especially those with larger populations—also have their own laws prohibiting sexual harassment, and regulations detailing how these laws should be carried out. Don't neglect these in your research. Sometimes a local law will contain the best protections against sexual harassment or provide the best remedies. Ask your law librarian how to find and use your city or county code.

---

6. Cases

Sometimes, you will find all the information you need in the statutes and regulations. However, laws can be deceptively straightforward, impossibly complex—or somewhere in between. To be sure you get the point, it's wise to also look at court cases that involve the statute and see how the courts apply and interpret it. Courts have been known to take a law with an apparently obvious meaning and turn it on its head.

And sometimes, there will be no statute that applies to your situation. For example, when you are researching whether common law tort theories such as assault and battery or the intentional infliction of emotional distress apply to your situation, you will absolutely need to look at some court decisions, since these issues are decided on a case-by-case basis.

START WITH THE CASE CITATIONS IN THIS BOOK

Many court cases are cited throughout this book. Be sure to look at them as possible leads. If the discussion here makes a case seem similar in some way to your situation, you might want to look it up and read the court's ruling. For information on how to interpret case citations, see subsection c, below.

---

a. Finding a case interpreting a statute

If you want to track down how a certain statute has been referred to by the courts in a case, your research task will be fairly simple: All you have to do is consult an annotated code. An annotated code is a version of the state or federal statutes that contains summaries of cases that have interpreted various provisions of a statute. There are two sets of federal annotated codes: the United States Code Service and the United States Code Annotated. Most states also have annotated codes. Ask the law librarian where you can find them.

To use an annotated code, first look up the U.S. Civil Rights Act or the FEP statute for your state. Then look for the numbered section of the statute that is relevant to your situation. If there have been any court cases interpreting that statute, they will be listed after the specific section of the statute, along with a sentence or two describing the case. If the summary of the case leaves you wanting to know more about it, you can track down the case and read it by following the citation given there.

b. Finding a case using secondary sources

In some situations, you will want to find court decisions on a particular topic without referring to a statute. For example, if you want to find out whether some uncomfortable situation at work might form the basis of a common law tort action in your state (discussed in Chapter 8), you should probably not begin your research with a statute. Common law tort actions were developed almost exclusively by case decisions. Sometimes these torts are also written into code, such as a state criminal statute defining and setting out the punishment for assault—but more likely, you will have to hunt down a few cases.

One good way to find relevant cases is through secondary sources (discussed in Section B.2). Quite often, a law review article or book—including this one—will discuss key cases and give citations for them. If you find a source that analyzes an issue that is important in your case, you will likely get some good leads there.

c. Digests

Another good resource for finding cases is the West Digest System. These digests, published by the West Publishing Company, provide brief summaries of cases organized by topic. There are many sets of digests, divided by geographic region. If you are looking for cases interpreting the U.S. Civil Rights Act and regulations on sexual harassment, consult the federal practice digest—which contains all federal cases. If you are looking for cases about common law torts or cases involving your state's FEP agency, look at the state digests, which are published in nearly every state.

To use the digest system to find cases, first choose the relevant volumes—regional, state or federal. Next, look in the descriptive word index; most listings on sexual harassment can be found under the headings of Civil Rights or Discrimination. You will find a number of categories listed under each heading—such as Sex Discrimination, Remedies and Men/Women. Look in the digest under topics that are relevant to your search. Under each topic, there will be short summaries of cases, arranged chronologically. If a case interests you, you can find the complete decision in the state or regional reporter by using the case citation.

The digests have a handy feature: the key number system. All of the digests use the same headings to categorize cases. Topics are divided into subtopics; each subtopic is given a number. If you find a topic in the state digest that seems relevant, and want to find federal cases on the same point, look in the federal practice digest under the same key number.

HOW TO READ A CASE CITATION

There are several places where a case may be reported. If it is a case decided by the U.S. Supreme Court, you can find it in either the United States Reports (U.S.) or the Supreme Court Reporter (S.Ct.). If it is a federal case decided by a court other than the U.S. Supreme Court, it will be in either the Federal Reporter, Second Series (F.2d) or the Federal Supplement (F. Supp.).

Most states publish their own official state reports. All published state courts decisions are also included in the West Reporter System. West has divided the country into seven regions—and publishes all the decisions of the supreme and appellate state courts in the region together. These reporters are:

A. and A.2d. Atlantic Reporter (First and Second Series), which includes decisions from Connecticut, Delaware, the District of Columbia, Maine, Maryland, New Hampshire, New Jersey, Pennsylvania, Rhode Island and Vermont.

N.E. and N.E.2d. Northeastern Reporter (First and Second Series), which includes decisions from New York,* Illinois, Indiana, Massachusetts and Ohio.

N.W. and N.W.2d. Northwestern Reporter (First and Second Series), which includes decisions from Iowa, Michigan, Minnesota, Nebraska, North Dakota, South Dakota and Wisconsin.

P. and P.2d. Pacific Reporter (First and Second Series), which includes decisions from Alaska, Arizona, California,* Colorado, Hawaii, Idaho, Kansas, Montana, Nevada, New Mexico, Oklahoma, Oregon, Utah, Washington and Wyoming.

S.E. and S.E.2d. Southeastern Reporter (First and Second Series), which includes decisions from Georgia, North Carolina, South Carolina, Virginia and West Virginia.

So. and So.2d. Southern Reporter (First and Second Series), which includes decisions from Alabama, Florida, Louisiana and Mississippi.

S.W. and S.W.2d. Southwestern Reporter (First and Second Series), which includes decisions from Arkansas, Kentucky, Missouri, Tennessee and Texas.

---

* All California appellate decisions are published in a separate volume, the California Reporter (Cal. Rptr.) and all decisions from New York appellate courts are published in a separate volume, New York Supplement (N.Y.S.).

A case citation will give you the names of the people or companies on each side of a case, the volume of the reporter in which the case can be found, the page number on which it begins and the year in which the case was decided. For example:

Thoreson v. Penthouse Int'l, 563 N.Y.S.2d 968 (1990)

Thoreson and Penthouse are the names of the parties having the legal dispute. The case is reported in volume 563 of the New York Supplement, Second Series, beginning on page 968; the court issued the decision in 1990.

d. Employment law reporters

Perhaps the best way to find cases is through one of two specialized legal publications that gather both state and federal cases on employment law issues:

- Fair Employment Practices Cases (Fair Empl. Prac. Cas.) published by the Bureau of National Affairs, and

- Employment Practices Decisions (Empl. Prac. Dec.) published by Commerce Clearing House.

To use these publications, look in the index volumes under Sexual Harassment—and glance through for specific topics that interest you. You might try: Investigation, Retaliation, Employer Liability, State Law Claims. Then use the case citations listed to look for relevant court decisions in the reporter volumes.

e. Finding similar cases

Once you find a case that seems relevant to your situation, you can determine if there are more by using a publication called *Shepard's Citations. Shepard's* collects and lists every reference to a particular case. In other words, you can look up any case—state or federal—in the *Shepard's* volumes, and get a list of every case decided after it that has mentioned your case. This is very valuable for finding cases on the same subject, as well as for determining whether the original case you found has been influential or discredited.

7. Treatises

There are several books—sometimes called treatises—that cover sexual harassment. The drawbacks of most treatises is that nearly all of them are written by and for lawyers—with little effort made to translate legalese into English. Also, these books oftentimes devote many pages to lawyerly concerns, such as how to plead and prove picayune points of law. Still, these volumes will often provide you with helpful background information on sexual harassment—and will also often lead you to cases that pertain to your situation. When using a legal treatise, be sure to check the back inside cover; most publishers update the books periodically by issuing pocket parts, bound pamphlets noting changes and additions to the text.

One of the most current treatises on sexual harassment is:

Sexual Harassment in the Workplace: Law and Practice, by Conte, published by John Wiley & Sons, Inc.

There are also a number of books that cover employment discrimination in general, some of which contain good discussions of sexual harassment issues. They include:

- *Employment Discrimination,* by Larson, published by Matthew Bender (a five-volume set)

- *Employment Discrimination Law,* by Schlei and Grossman, published by BNA (The book comes in two volumes. One is the main text, written in 1983; the second is a supplement to this text, written in 1988)

- *Employee Rights Litigation,* by the National Employment Lawyers' Association, published by Matthew Bender (a three-volume set)

- *Sex-Based Employment Discrimination,* by Omiliam and Kamp, published by Callahan & Co.

You should be able to find these books at most large law libraries.

8. Law review articles

There are also many law review articles on sexual harassment. Law reviews
are periodicals containing articles written by lawyers, law professors and law
students—usually covering a unique or evolving legal topic. Since sexual
harassment is of great current interest, you'll find lots of articles about it. The
inside joke about law review articles is that they're made up mostly of
footnotes. While annoying to many readers, these footnotes—which contain
references (citations) to other relevant cases, statutes and articles—can be
goldmines for researchers. Look especially for articles that are published in law
reviews from schools in your state, since these will be most likely to discuss
your state's FEP law and court decisions.

There are two tools in every law library that can help you find law review
articles on topics that interest you: the Current Law Index and the Index to
Legal Periodicals. These volumes are published annually, except for the most
recent listings, which are published every month. Both list articles by subject,
by author and by the cases and statutes referred to in the article. If you don't
have a case name or a specific statute in mind to guide you, turn to Sexual
Harassment or Sex Discrimination in the index and peruse the listings of
articles there.

HOW TO READ LAW REVIEW CITATIONS

Both the Current Law Index and the Index to Legal Periodicals will give you the
author, title and citations of law review articles. The citations will give the title of
the publication and the volume and page numbers of the articles you want to
look at. For example, if you look under Sexual Harassment—Analysis, you will
see a listing for Susan Estrich's article "Sex at Work." The citation reads:

   43 Stan. L. Rev. 813 (1991)

This article can be found in volume 43 of the Stanford Law Review, beginning
on page 813; 1991 is the year of publication. If you have trouble deciphering the
law review names, check the listing of abbreviations in the index—or ask a law
librarian for help.

Appendix

Sexual Harassment Resources

How to Use These Listings

These organizations can give you additional information or assistance on sexual harassment. Some groups offer a wide variety of services, and others are more limited. To help you use these listings most effectively, we have organized them in two ways. First, there is a chart that shows which groups provide particular services. These services are divided into five categories:

1. Publications and written materials. Call first for price and order information, as these materials are rarely free.

2. Sexual harassment telephone counseling and hotlines for advice on your particular situation.

3. Support groups or in-person counseling for women who have been sexually harassed.

4. Attorney referrals—if you want to consult a lawyer, these groups will give you names of attorneys in your area. Note that a referral is not necessarily a recommendation. Some referral services are really just like advertising—if the attorney pays, he or she will be listed. Be sure to ask how attorneys are chosen for referrals, and whether they have experience in sexual harassment cases.

5. Workplace training resources including on-site training programs and written and video training materials. These can be very expensive. Ask first for a catalog and price list.

We have also included an alphabetical listing of organizations on the chart, including their addresses and telephone numbers, and a brief description of their work. A few groups listed here are not included in our chart because their services are not easily reduced to a chart format.

Some organizations restrict their services to their members or to a limited geographic area, and we have indicated these limitations in our listings. However, some groups may have additional restrictions that don't appear here, so be sure to ask whether you're eligible to use their services.

Unions

Many unions and groups for union members are especially active in the fight against sexual harassment. We have listed several larger unions and union organizations here, but this list is by no means exhaustive. Contact your local to find out if they offer any special services or guidance. Also, the Coalition for Labor Union Women, listed below, is an excellent resource.

Other Sources of Help

Don't forget the Equal Employment Opportunity Commission (EEOC) and your state or local Fair Employment Practices (FEP) agency. Many will send you written materials on sexual harassment, and can provide information on local training programs, support groups and attorneys. For the address and telephone number of the EEOC office nearest you, see Chapter 6. For the address and telephone number of your state FEP office, see Chapter 7.

Some states and larger cities also have a Commission on the Status of Women, or a state or local agency dealing specifically with women's issues. The services these groups provide range from referrals to local women's rights groups, to advice and counseling, to legal referrals. Check your phone book to see if there is such a group in your area.

Finally, some law schools have clinics that deal with women's rights or employment law. These clinics are usually staffed by students, who are assisted by experienced attorneys. Many provide in-person or telephone counseling and legal advice, and some will even represent you in court. Their services are low-cost, often free. A few of these clinics are listed here. Call law schools in your area and ask if they have such a clinic.

SPECIAL MENTION: 9TO5

One group is doing so much to end sexual harassment that it deserves special mention. Be sure to see the writeup for 9to5, National Association for Working Women, which has been fighting to end sexual harassment since the early 1970s.

Resources at a Glance

	publications	telephone counseling	support groups	attorney referrals	training
AFL-CIO: Union Privilege				•	
Alexander Hamilton Institute	•				•
American Bar Association (ABA)	•			•	
American Civil Liberties Union (ACLU)		•		•	
American Federation of State, County and Municipal Employees (AFSCME)	•				•
American Federation of Teachers (AFT)	•				
American Psychological Association	•				
American Society for Training and Development					•
Asian-American Legal Defense and Education Fund		•		•	
Association for Union Democracy		•	•	•	
Bureau of National Affairs (BNA) Communications	•				•
Bureau of Law & Businesses, Inc.	•				•
Business and Professional Women/USA	•				
Center for Women in Government	•				•
Center for Women Policy Studies	•				
Center for Working Life			•		•
Coalition of Labor Union Women (CLUW)	•			•	
College and University Personnel Association	•				•
Commerce Clearing House	•				•
Communications Workers of America	•				•
Coronet MTI Film and Video					•
Equal Rights Advocates		•		•	

	publications	telephone counseling	support groups	attorney referrals	training
Federally Employed Women (FEW)	●				
Federation of Organizations for Professional Women	●	●	●		
Fund for the Feminist Majority	●	●			
Haimes Associates	●				●
Institute for Women and Work	●				●
9to5, National Association of Working Women	●	●	●	●	●
National Association for Women in Education	●				
National Council for Research on Women	●				
National Education Association (NEA)	●				●
National Employment Lawyers Association				●	
National Lawyers Guild				●	
NOW Legal Defense and Education Fund	●			●	
National Resource Center for Consumers of Legal Services	●			●	
Pacific Resource Development Group	●				●
Society for Human Resource Management	●				●
Tele-Lawyer		●			
United Auto Workers Union (UAW)	●				●
U.S. Department of Labor, Women's Bureau	●				
Wider Opportunities for Women (WOW)	●				●
Women's Alliance for Job Equity (WAJE)			●	●	●
Women Employed Institute	●	●		●	●
Women's Law Project				●	
Women's Legal Defense Fund	●				
Women's Rights Litigation Clinic	●	●			
Workers' Rights Clinic		●			

List of Organizations

AFL-CIO: Union Privilege

1444 I Street, NW, 8th Floor
Washington, DC 20005
(202) 842-3500
Nationwide legal services plan free to most members of AFL-CIO. Initial consultation and follow-up are free, and other attorney's fees are discounted 30%. Many locals also have their own legal services plan.

Alexander Hamilton Institute

197 West Spring Valley Avenue
Maywood, NJ 07607
(800) 879-2441
Institute specializing in human resource management issues, publishes booklet for managers on how to prevent sexual harassment, and materials on personnel training issues.

American Arbitration Association

140 West 51st Street
New York, NY 10020
(212) 484-4000
National nonprofit organization offering mediation and arbitration services through local offices across the country. Also provides fact-finding teams for neutral investigations of workplace disputes, including sexual harassment.

American Association of University Women Legal Advocacy Fund

1111 16th Street, NW
Washington, DC 20036
(202) 785-7744
Fund sexual harassment cases brought by university women students, faculty and staff against institutions of higher education.

American Bar Association (ABA)

750 North Lakeshore Drive
Chicago, IL 60611
(312) 988-5555
Booklet listing local lawyer referral services by state and county. Many state bar associations will also give legal referrals.

American Civil Liberties Union (ACLU)

Legal advice and counseling, as well as attorney referrals provided by local offices throughout the country. Contact your state ACLU office.

American Federation of State, County and Municipal Employees (AFSCME)

1625 L Street, NW
Washington, DC 20036
(202) 429-5090
Booklet available to state and local union members of AFSCME on how to stop sexual harassment. Training workshops for AFSCME members.

American Federation of Teachers (AFT)

Human Rights Department
555 New Jersey Avenue, NW
Washington, DC 20001
(202) 879-4400
Booklet on sexual harassment, available to AFT union members.

American Psychological Association

750 1st Street, NE
Washington, DC 20002
(202) 336-5500
Referrals to state and local associations that provide names of specialists who deal with the psychological problems associated with sexual harassment. Also pamphlets on how to choose a therapist.

American Society for Training and Development

1640 King Street
Alexandria, VA 22313
(703) 683-8100
National organization of professional workplace trainers, provides information and referral services on sexual harassment training.

Asian-American Legal Defense and Education Fund

99 Hudson Street, 12th Floor
New York, NY 10013
(212) 966-5932
Legal advice and attorney referrals for Asians and Asian-Americans.

Association for Union Democracy

Women's Project
500 State Street
Brooklyn, NY 11217
(718) 855-6650
Nationwide attorney referrals, legal advice, counseling and organizational assistance for women in unions. Also training, workshops and educational programs on sexual harassment.

Bureau of National Affairs (BNA) Communications

9439 Key West Avenue
Rockville, MD 20850
(800) 233-6067
Books, special reports, audio-video materials and training programs on sexual harassment.

Bureau of Law & Businesses, Inc.

39 Academy Street
Madison, CT 06443
(203) 245-7448
Handbooks, video and other training materials on sexual harassment.

Business and Professional Women/USA

2012 Massachusetts Avenue, NW
Washington, DC 20036
(202) 293-1100
National membership organization of working women in over 3,000 local chapters, publishes position paper on sexual harassment.

Center for Women in Government

University of Albany, Draper Hall 310
135 Western Avenue
Albany, NY 12222
(518) 442-3900
Sexual harassment training for New York state employees. Also serves workers nationwide through training videos, digests of important sexual harassment cases and laws, and pamphlets on sexual harassment.

Center for Women Policy Studies

2000 P Street, NW, Suite 508
Washington, DC 20036
(202) 872-1770
Written materials on sexual harassment.

Center for Working Life

600 Grand Avenue, Suite 305
Oakland, CA 94610
(510) 893-7343
National nonprofit organization providing workshops and sexual harassment training in the workplace. Support groups for women who have been sexually harassed, including a group specifically for blue-collar women workers. Short-term counseling for women who have been sexually harassed.

Coalition of Labor Union Women (CLUW)

15 Union Square
New York, NY 10003
(212) 242-0700
National organization with 70 local chapters, provides education on sexual harassment, organizes conferences and workshops, testifies and lobbies for legislation, supports strikes and boycotts, and publishes a newsletter and other written materials for union women. Referrals to attorneys and legal rights groups for union workers. Sample contract language, resolutions and policies on sexual harassment.

College and University Personnel Association

1233 20th Street, NW
Washington, DC 20036
(202) 429-0311, extension 23
Book on sexual harassment in business, industry and education, and a video on sexual harassment in higher education.

Commerce Clearing House

4025 West Peterson Avenue
Chicago, IL 60646
(312) 583-8500
Training manual for managers and supervisors.

Communications Workers of America

501 3rd Street
Washington, DC 20001
(202) 434-1110
Internal training for union members and staff. Written materials on sexual harassment.

Coronet MTI Film and Video

108 Wilmot Road
Deerfield, IL 60015
(800) 621-2131
Training videotapes on sexual harassment for businesses and schools.

Equal Rights Advocates

1663 Mission Street, Suite 550
San Francisco, CA 94103
(415) 621-0672 (General information)
(415) 621-0505 (Advice and counseling
hotline)
Legal advice and counseling, in both
English and Spanish. Referrals to
women's groups nationwide.

Federally Employed Women (FEW)

1400 Eye Street, NW, Suite 425
Washington, DC 20005
(202) 898-0994
National nonprofit membership organization of federally employed women
with chapters throughout the United
States. Written materials on how federal
workers can stop sexual harassment,
find and select an EEO attorney and go
to court.

Federation of Organizations for Professional Women

2001 S Street, NW, Suite 500
Washington, DC 20009
(202) 328-1415
Telephone advice and counseling on
sexual harassment. Written sexual harassment materials. Support groups in
Washington, DC area. Limited legal assistance may be available through the
Professional Women's Legal Fund.

Fund for the Feminist Majority

1600 Wilson Boulevard
Arlington, VA 22209
(703) 522-2214 (General information)
(703) 522-2501 (Sexual harassment hotline)
Hotline gives feminist strategies for
dealing with sexual harassment and
advice on how to file a claim and deal
with the EEOC. Free special report on
sexual harassment also available.

Haimes Associates

708 South Washington Square
Philadelphia, PA 19106
(215) 922-1617
Handbooks for managers and supervisors on sexual harassment.

Institute for Women and Work

School of Industrial and Labor
Relations
Cornell University
15 East 26th Street, 4th Floor
New York, NY 10010
(212) 340-2812
Bibliography of sexual harassment resource materials. Occasional training
seminars on sexual harassment, primarily for union members.

9to5, National Association of Working Women

614 Superior Avenue, NW,
Cleveland, OH 44113
(216) 566-9308 (General information)
(800) 522-0925 (Hotline)
National nonprofit membership organization for American office workers with local chapters throughout the country. Toll-free confidential telephone hotline, staffed by trained job counselors, provides information and referrals on how to deal with sexual harassment and other problems on the job. Books and reports on sexual harassment, available at a discount to members. Members also get legal referrals to attorneys specializing in sexual harassment. Newsletter published five times a year. Some 9to5 local chapters offer sexual harassment support groups and referrals to training resources.

National Association for Women in Education

1325 18th Street, NW, Suite 210
Washington, DC 20036
(202) 659-9330
Written materials on sexual harassment on college campuses.

National Council for Research on Women

Sexual Harassment Information Project
47-49 East 65th Street
New York, NY 10021
(212) 570-5001
Coalition of 70 centers and organizations that support and conduct feminist research, policy analysis and educational programs. Guide to research and resources on sexual harassment, including lists of key researchers and expert witnesses on sexual harassment.

National Education Association (NEA)

Human and Civil Rights Department
1201 16th Street, NW
Washington, DC 20036
(202) 833-4000
Training, videos and brochures on sexual harassment, available to union members only. Contact local or state NEA office for more information.

National Employment Lawyers Association

535 Pacific Avenue
San Francisco, CA 94133
National directory of 1,100 employment law attorneys, including brief descriptions of their practices. Send self-addressed stamped envelope for more information.

National Lawyers Guild

Anti-Sexism Committee
131 George Street
San Jose, CA 95110
(408) 287-1916
Referrals to experienced attorneys who are members of the Guild, an association of progressive attorneys.

NOW Legal Defense and Education Fund

99 Hudson Street, 12th Floor
New York, NY 10013
(212) 925-6635
Legal resource kit on sexual harassment that is specifically geared towards attorneys, plus other publications on sexual harassment. Legal referrals are available through the mail.

National Resource Center for Consumers of Legal Services

P.O. Box 340
Gloucester, VA 23061
(804) 693-9330
Nationwide legal referrals to attorneys experienced in sexual harassment cases. Publishes materials on how to choose a lawyer.

National Women's Law Center

1616 P Street, NW, Suite 100
Washington, DC 20036
(202) 328-5160
National nonprofit organization focuses on policy areas important to women including sexual harassment. Research and testimony on sexual harassment.

National Women's Political Caucus

1275 K Street, NW, Suite 750
Washington, DC 20005
(202) 898-1100
Model sexual harassment policy for congressional members, and honor roll of members of Congress who have adopted sexual harassment policies.

Pacific Resource Development Group

145 NW 85th Street, Suite 104
Seattle, WA 98117
(800) 767-3062
Employee handbooks and videotape training package on sexual harassment, monthly newsletter and training manuals for managers. In-house training workshops and presentations.

Society for Human Resource Management

606 North Washington Street
Alexandria, VA 22314
(703) 548-3440
Membership organization for human resources managers. Written information for members, including advice on developing sexual harassment policy. Video training program.

Tele-Lawyer

19671 Beach Boulevard, Suite. 207
Huntington Beach, CA 92648
(800) 835-3529
Legal advice over the phone at a reasonable per-minute charge. Staff lawyers will also review documents, such as employment contracts, and do legal research.

United Auto Workers Union (UAW)

800 East Jefferson
Detroit, MI 48214
(313) 926-5212
Written and video training materials and workshops for UAW and other union members.

U.S. Department of Labor, Women's Bureau

200 Constitution Avenue, NW
Room S3311
Washington, DC 20210
(202) 523-6665
Detailed list of sexual harassment resources, including organizations, training materials, court cases and articles.

Wider Opportunities for Women (WOW)

1325 G Street, NW
Washington, DC 20005
(202) 638-3143
National nonprofit organization, primarily focusing on women in nontraditional employment. Reports and materials on sexual harassment. Consulting and training services for employers.

Women's Alliance for Job Equity (WAJE)

1422 Chestnut Street, Suite 1100
Philadelphia, PA 19102
(215) 561-1873
Information and public education seminars in Philadelphia area. Regular job problem meetings, peer support program and legal referrals for WAJE members, primarily women working in nonmanagement jobs. On-site training program for local employers.

Women Employed Institute

22 West Monroe, Suite 1400
Chicago, IL 60603
(312) 782-3902
Membership organization providing telephone counseling on sexual harassment in Chicago area. Local attorney referrals. Factsheet on sexual harassment. Sexual harassment prevention training for area employers.

Women's Law Project

125 South 9th Street, Suite 401
Philadelphia, PA 19107
(215) 928-9801
Information and legal referrals in the Philadelphia area.

Women's Legal Defense Fund

1875 Connecticut Ave., NW, Suite 710
Washington, DC 20009
(202) 986-2600
National nonprofit membership organization providing public education, written information, advocacy and targeted litigation on sexual harassment.

Women's Rights Litigation Clinic

Rutgers University Law School
15 Washington Street
Newark, NJ 07102
(201) 648-5637
Legal advice and counseling, written materials on sexual harassment, and technical legal support in some cases.

Workers' Rights Clinic

Rotates among several locations. Call for more information.
(415) 864-8208
Legal clinic for low income workers in the San Francisco Bay Area with employment problems, including sexual harassment. Telephone and in-person legal advice and counseling.

Index

Appearance of Employee
 Blaming the victim, 3/12
 Court's consideration of, 2/23-24, 3/13
Assault and Battery
 Defined, 8/5, 8/6
 Differences between, 8/4-5
 Proving assault, 8/5
 Reporting assault and battery, importance of, 8/7
Attorneys. *See* Lawyers
Attorney's Fees
 Common law tort cases, 8/28
 Written fee agreement, 9/6

Battery. *See* Assault and Battery

Causes of sexual harassment
 Discrimination as control, 1/9
 Economics, 1/8
 Violence and self-perceptions, 1/7
Civil Rights Act. *See* Equal Employment Opportunities Commission (EEOC)
Common Law Torts
 Assault and battery, 8/4-6
 Defamation, 8/14-15
 Intentional infliction of emotional distress, 8/8-13
 Interference with employment contract, 8/16-19
 Intrusion, 8/20-21
 Rape, 8/24-5
 Relief available
  Generally, 1/27, 5/4
  Personal injuries, monetary damages for, 5/11-12
  Recovering wages and other losses, 5/9
  Reforming the company, 5/14
 Selecting tort action over other remedies, 8/2-4
 Wrongful discharge, 8/22
Company Complaint Procedure. *See also* Workplace Policies
 Alternatives for dealing with harassment, 1/25
 Follow-up procedures, 4/24-25
 Investigation procedures, 4/11, 21-24
 Reporting guidelines, 4/10
 Sample complaint form, 4/17-20
Compensatory damages
 Defined, 5/9
Complaints
 Common law tort, filing lawsuit for, 1/27
 Company procedure. *See* Company Complaint Procedure
 Deciding best place to file, 5/7
 EEOC or FEP agency, filing complaint with, 1/26
 Right-to-sue letter, obtaining, 1/27, 5/13, 6/33-35
 Time for filing. *See* Time for Filing
Confidentiality
 Confidential claim filed by another, sample letter, 6/24-25
 Filing claim with EEOC under Civil Rights Act, 6/16-17
 Investigations, 4/11

Confrontation
    Alternative for dealing with harassment, 1/25
    Coping strategies instead of confrontation, 2/24
    Effectiveness of, 3/23
    Employers confronting harassment, 4/31
    Failure to confront harassment, later proof problems, 2/25
    How to say no, 3/30
    Letters to write, samples of, 3/25-29
    Procedures if harassment continues, 3/31-38
    Specific procedures, 3/24-25
Constructive discharge, 1/13
Costs
    Ignoring sexual harassment, cost to company of, 4/4
Co-Workers
    Assault and battery by co-worker, Breaking off relationship, 2/25-26
    Defamation, proving damage to reputation, 8/15
    Discussing harassment, 2/25, 3/34, 4/21
    Employer's liability for harassment, 4/5
    Hostile conduct based on gender, 2/12
    Lewd and vulgar behavior, 2/14-15
    Malicious interference with employment contract, 8/17
    Organizing co-workers, 3/35-36
    Pornographic materials, 2/14
    Rape by, 8/25
    Retaliation by, 4/12
    Severe or pervasive conduct, 2/18-21
    Unreasonable conduct, 2/15-18
Customers, harassment by, 2/9

Damages
    Collecting, 8/22
    Limitation on damages based on number of employees, 6/6-7
    Personal injuries, comparison of damages allowed, 1/27, 5/9-12, 7/7-13
    Punitive damages
        Availability under FEP, 7/9
        Malicious interference with employment contract, 8/16-17
    State summaries of money damages, 7/11-13
Defamation
    Defined, 8/14
    Proving damage to work reputation, 8/14-15
Discrimination
    FEP, exclusion of certain employees, 7/6
    Historical background, making sex discrimination illegal, 1/20
    Stereotyping as, 1/17
    Union's duty under National Labor Relations Act, 4/37
    Workplace control, discrimination as, 1/9
Dual-Filing, 6/14-15, 7/3

Effects of Sexual Harassment, 1/10-18
Emotional Distress. *See* Physical and Emotional Injuries
Employer liability for harassment, 4/5
Equal Employment Opportunities Commission (EEOC)
    District offices, list of, 6/37-40
    Enforcement power of, 1/23
    Filing claim under Civil Rights Act
        Conciliation after investigation, 6/32-33
        Confidentiality, filing by another to keep identity secret, sample letters, 6/16-17, 6/24-25
        Contents of claim, 6/21-22

　　　　Covered employees, 6/4
　　　　Dual-filing agreements with FEP agencies, 6/14-15
　　　　Filing in person or by mail, 6/16
　　　　Independent contractors, 6/12-13
　　　　Investigation procedures, 6/30-31
　　　　Lawsuit by EEOC, 6/34
　　　　Lawsuit by employee, 6/34-36
　　　　Letters to EEOC, samples of how to state information, 6/23-28
　　　　No-cause finding, effect of, 6/33
　　　　Number of employees, how to count, 6/5-12
　　　　Reasons to file claim with EEOC, 6/3-4
　　　　Remedies available, 6/4-6
　　　　Time limits and exceptions to, 6/18-21
　　　　Tips for writing effective claim, 6/29-30
　　　　When to file, 6/3-4
　　　　Where to file, 6/14
　　Filing deadlines, coordinating with company complaint procedure, 4/21
　　Historical background, 1/20-23
　　Legal definition of sexual harassment, 2/3
　　Regulations defining sexual harassment, 1/21
　　Relief available
　　　　Damages recovery under Civil Rights Act, 1/24, 5/10
　　　　Generally, 5/2-3
　　　　Recovering wages and other losses, 5/8
　　　　Reforming the company, 5/12-13
　　　　Stopping harassment, 5/5
　　Right-to-sue letter, 1/27, 5/13, 6/33-35
　　Severe or pervasive conduct, EEOC guidelines, 2/18-19
　　State FEP agencies, relationship with EEOC, 7/2-4
Evidence. *See* Proof
Expenses
　　Doctor's bills, coverage under Civil Rights Act, 6/7

Fair Employment Practices (State Laws)
　　Administrative claim, 7/9
　　Administrative hearing, award of damages at, 7/9
　　EEOC relationship with FEP
　　　　Designated agencies and work-sharing, 7/2-3
　　　　Dual-filing agreements, 7/3
　　Excluded employees, 7/5-6
　　Filing deadlines, coordinating with company complaint procedures, 4/21
　　Historical background of statutory law, 1/22
　　Minimum enforcement powers, 7/4
　　Relief available
　　　　Generally, 1/27, 5/3-4
　　　　Money damages for personal injuries, 5/11, 7/7-13
　　　　Punitive damages, 7/9
　　　　Recovering wages and other losses, 5/8
　　　　Reforming the company, 5/13
　　　　Stopping harassment, 5/6
　　Requiring employers to take action against harassment, 4/10
　　State laws and administrative procedures, 7/14-36
Federal Employees
　　Formal complaint procedures, 4/36-37
Filing Deadlines. *See* Time for Filing
Filing Lawsuit. *See* Complaints
Firing Lawyer
　　When to change lawyers, 9/9

Forms of Sexual Harassment
    Advances or demands by superiors, co-workers, customers and clients, 2/5-10
    Conduct of sexual nature, 2/4
    EEOC definition of sexual harassment, 2/3
    Hostility based on sex, 2/12
    Pornographic or vulgar behavior, 2/14
    Preferential treatment based on sexual conduct, 2/10-11
    Severe or pervasive conduct, EEOC guidelines, 2/18-21
    Unreasonable conduct, 2/15-18
    Unwelcome conduct
        Appearance of employee, effect of, 2/23-24
        Breaking off relationship, 2/25
        Coping strategies giving appearance of willingness, 2/24
        Limited consent of employee, 2/26
        Voluntary submission but unwelcome, 2/22

Gender differences in perception, 3/6-8

Historical Background, 1/19-22
Hostile Work Environment
    Defined, 2/5
    Hostile acts based on gender, 2/11-13
    Pornographic material and lewd conduct creating, 2/14
    Preferential treatment based on sexual conduct, 2/11
    Severe or pervasive harassment, 1/10, 2/18-19

Independent Contractors
    Determining status under Civil Rights Act, 6/12-13
Injunctions
    Relief available under Civil Rights Act, 6/5
Intentional Infliction of Emotional Distress
    Defined, 8/8-12
    Checklist for evaluation of case, 8/13
    Outrage, difficulty of defining, 8/8-11
    Proving, 8/8-9
    Retaliation as boost to tort claim, 8/12
Interference with Employment Contract
    Defined, 8/16
    Limitations, 8/18-19
    Malicious actions, punitive damages for, 8/16-17
    Proving elements, 8/16
    Requirement of written employment contract, effect of, 8/17
Intrusion
    Defined, 8/20
    Proving elements of, 8/20-21
Investigations. *See* Company Complaint Procedures and EEOC

Job, Effect of Harassment on
    Generally, 1/10
    Constructive discharge, 1/13
    Forced reassignment, 1/13
    Job option limitations, 1/16
    Loss of job, 1/11
    Loss of wages and benefits, 1/12
    Productivity decreased, 4/2, 4/4
    Retaliation for reporting harassment. *See* Retaliation

Stereotyped workers, 1/17-18
Jokes and Innuendos
 Gray areas, 3/15-18
 Sexually-poisoned workplace, 2/21

Labor Relations
 Unfair Labor Practices. *See* Unfair Labor Practices
 Unions. *See* Unions
Lawyers. *See also* Attorney's Fees
 Generally, 9/2-9
Legal Research
 Generally, 9/9-23
Lesbians
 Hostile acts against, 2/13
Local Law
 County and city laws prohibiting harassment, 7/4
 Legal research, city and county laws, 9/17

Misconceptions About Sexual Harassment, 1/4-6
Myths, 1/6

Office Romances
 Breaking off romance, 2/25-26
 Gray areas, 3/10-11

Personal Injuries. *See* Physical and Emotional Injuries
Physical and Emotional Injuries
 Availability of money damages, 7/7-13
 Common law torts, 1/22-23
 Examples of, 1/15
 Expenses for treatment. *See* Expenses
 Generally, 1/14-15
 Intentional infliction of emotional distress, 8/8-13
 Legal remedies available under different laws, 5/9-12
 Proving personal harm in common law torts, 8/27
 Stress
  Confiding in friends, 3/34
  Reducing stress, 3/37
  Statistics on, 1/14
Pornography Policies. *See* Workplace Policies
 Pin-ups in workplace, 3/13-15
 Sexually-poisoned workplace, 2/14, 2/21
Preferential Treatment
 Evaluating workplace for, 4/7
 Sexual conduct as basis for, 2/10-11
Productivity
 Effect of sexual harassment on, 4/2, 4/4
Proof
 Collecting evidence if harassment continues after confrontation, 3/31-36
 Common law torts, 1/27
 Co-workers
  Discussing harassment with as evidence, 2/25, 3/34, 4/21
  Harassment by, proving company's knowledge of harassing actions, 2/7
 Defamation, 8/14-15
 Going along with unpleasant situation, proof problems of, 2/25
 Intent, difficult proof problem of common law torts, 8/27

Intentional infliction of emotional distress, 1/27, 8/8-12
Intrusion tort, 8/20-21
Letters written to harasser, 3/29
Lewd and vulgar behavior, 2/15
Outrageous conduct, 1/27, 8/8-12
Personal harm, difficult proof problem, 8/27
Preferential treatment based on sexual conduct, 2/11
Rape, 8/25
Severe or pervasive conduct, 2/18-20
Sexually-poisoned workplace, 2/21
Unreasonable conduct, 2/18
Unwelcome conduct, 2/21-23
Voluntary submission to advance but unwelcome, 2/23
Witnesses, retaliation against, 3/34
Work records, obtaining copy of, 3/35

Quid pro quo, 2/5

Rape
        Defined, 8/24-25
Reasonable woman test, 2/16
Reinstatement of Job
        Legal remedies available under different laws, 5/8-9, 6/4
Reporting Harassment
        See also Confrontation and Confidentiality
        Assault and battery, importance of reporting, 8/7
        Company's guidelines making reporting easier, 4/8, 4/10
        Coping strategies of employee too fearful to report, 2/24
        Going along with unpleasant situation, later proof problems, 2/25
        Reasons why it's hard to speak up, 3/5
        Work records, obtaining copy, 3/35
Restraining Orders
        Stopping assault and battery, 8/8
Retaliation
        Defined, 1/13
        Co-workers
                Company's policy against retaliation by, 4/12
                Company's retaliation or threats against witnesses, 3/34
                Interfering with employment contract, 8/17
        Filing claim with EEOC, protecting identity to prevent retaliation, 6/17
        Intentional infliction of emotional distress, retaliation in tort claim, 8/12
        Preferential treatment based on sexual conduct, retaliation for complaints about, 2/11
        Reporting harassment, firing or demoting employee for, 1/13, 2/8
        Workplace policy against, 4/8, 4/11

Sex-for-Jobs, 2/6
Sexually-poisoned workplace, 2/14
State Laws. See Fair Employment Practices (State Laws)
Statute of Limitations. See Time for Filing
Stereotyping
        Generally, 1/10, 1/17
        Promotions affected by, 4/7
Stress. See Physical and Emotional Injuries
Subpoenas
        EEOC issuance of subpoena as part of investigation, 6/31-32

Threats
    Co-workers as witnesses, threat of firings to prevent cooperation, 3/34
    Element of rape case, 8/25
Time for Filing
    Coordinating EEOC and FEP complaint filing with company complaint filing, 4/21
    EEOC claim, 6/18-21
Tortious interference with contractual relations, 8/16
Torts. *See* Common Law Torts
Training Resources. *See* Workplace Policies

Unfair Labor Practices
    Filing lawsuit with NLRB, 4/39
Union Members
    Grievance or lawsuit against union, 4/37-39
    Wrongful discharge, remedy affected by collective bargaining agreement, 8/24
U.S. Government Employees. *See* Federal Employees
Unreasonable conduct, 2/15
Unwelcome conduct, 2/21-22

Violence
    Aspect of violence against women, 1/7
    Avoiding exclusion of certain employees under FEP due to violence and abuse, 7/6
    Procedures and alternatives for confronting violent harasser, 3/24

Wages
    Recovering lost wages, 5/8-9, 6/4
Work Records
    Obtaining copy, 3/35
Work-sharing, 7/3
Workers' Compensation, 8/28-31
Workplace Policies. *See also* Company Complaint Procedure
    Benefits of company policy to employers and employees, 4/3-4
    Effective policy, 4/9-12
    Evaluating workplace, 4/5-8
    Federal employees, 4/36-37
    Generally, 4/2
    Guidelines on reporting and investigating, 4/9-12
    Monitoring surveys, sample, 4/32-35
    Organizing other employees, 3/35-36
    Sample policy, 4/13-16
    Training resources, 4/25-30
    Union members, 4/37-39
Wrongful Discharge
    Defined, 8/22
    Historical background, 8/22
    Limited remedies in certain states and for certain union members, 8/24
    Recovering lost wages, 5/9

RECYCLE YOUR OUT-OF-DATE BOOKS
AND GET 25% OFF YOUR NEXT PURCHASE

OUT - O F - DATE = DANGEROUS

Using an old edition can be dangerous if information in it is wrong.
Unfortunately, laws and legal procedures change often. Generally speaking,
any book more than two years old is of questionable value. Books more than
four or five years old are a menace.

To help you keep up-to-date, we extend this offer:

If you cut out and deliver to us the title portion of the cover of any old Nolo
book, we'll give you a 25% discount off the retail price of any new Nolo book.
For example, if you have a copy of *Tenant's Rights,* 4th edition, and want to
trade it for the latest *California Marriage and Divorce Law,* send us the
Tenant' Rights cover and a check for the current price of *California Marriage
and Divorce,* less a 25% discount.

Information on current prices and editions is listed in the back of this book
and in the catalog in the *Nolo News* (see offer at the back of this book).

This offer is to individuals only.

CATALOG

SELF-HELP LAW BOOKS & SOFTWARE

ESTATE PLANNING & PROBATE

Plan Your Estate With a Living Trust

Attorney Denis Clifford
National 1st Edition
This book covers every significant aspect of estate planning and gives detailed specific, instructions for preparing a living trust, a document that lets your family avoid expensive and lengthy probate court proceedings after your death. *Plan Your Estate* includes all the tear-out forms and step-by-step instructions to let you prepare an estate plan designed for your special needs.
$19.95/NEST

Nolo's Simple Will Book

Attorney Denis Clifford
National 2nd Edition
It's easy to write a legally valid will using this book. The instructions and forms enable people to draft a will for all needs, including naming a personal guardian for minor children, leaving property to minor children or young adults and updating a will when necessary. Good in all states except Louisiana.
$17.95/SWIL

How to Probate an Estate

Julia Nissley
California 6th Edition
If you find yourself responsible for winding up the legal and financial affairs of a deceased family member or friend, you can often save costly attorneys' fees by handling the probate process yourself. This book also explains the simple procedures you can use to transfer assets that don't require probate, including property held in joint tenancy or living trusts or as community property.
$34.95/PAE

The Conservatorship Book

Lisa Goldoftas & Attorney Carolyn Farren
California 1st Edition
When someone becomes incapacitated due to illness or age, a conservator may need to take charge of their medical and financial affairs. *The Conservatorship Book* comes with complete instructions and all the forms necessary to file conservatorship documents, appear in court, be appointed conservator and end a conservatorship.
$24.95/CNSV

software

WillMaker

Nolo Press
Version 4.0
This easy-to-use software program lets you prepare and update a legal will—safely, privately and without the expense of a lawyer. Leading you step-by-step in a question-and-answer format, *WillMaker* builds a will around your answers, taking into account your state of residence. *WillMaker* comes with a 200-page legal manual which provides the legal background necessary to make sound choices. Good in all states except Louisiana.
IBM PC
(31/2 & 51/4 disks included)
$69.95/WI4
MACINTOSH $69.95/WM4

Nolo's Personal RecordKeeper

(formerly For the Record)
Carol Pladsen & Attorney Ralph Warner
Version 3.0
Nolo's Personal RecordKeeper lets you record the location of personal, financial and legal information in over 200 categories and subcategories. It also allows you to create lists of insured property, compute net worth, consolidate emergency information into one place and export to *Quicken*® home inventory and net worth reports. Includes a 320-page manual filled with practical and legal advice.
IBM PC
(3-1/2 & 5-1/4 disks included)
$49.95/FRI3
MACINTOSH $49.95/FRM3

Nolo's Living Trust
Attorney Mary Randolph
Version 1.0

A will is an indispensable part of any estate plan, but many people need a living trust as well. By putting certain assets into a trust, you save your heirs the headache, time and expense of probate. *Nolo's Living Trust* lets you set up an individual or shared marital trust, make your trust document legal, transfer your property to the trust, and change or revoke the trust at any time. The 380-page manual guides you through the process step-by-step, and over 100 legal help screens and an on-line glossary explain key legal terms and concepts. Good in all states except Louisiana.
MACINTOSH $79.95/LTM1

GOING TO COURT

Everybody's Guide to Municipal Court
Judge Roderic Duncan
California 1st Edition
Everybody's Guide to Municipal Court explains how to prepare and defend the most common types of contract and personal injury law suits in California Municipal Court. Written by a California judge, the book provides step-by-step instructions for preparing and filing all necessary forms, gathering evidence and appearing in court.
$29.95/MUNI

Fight Your Ticket
Attorney David Brown
California 5th Edition
This book shows you how to fight an unfair traffic ticket—when you're stopped, at arraignment, at trial and on appeal.
$17.95/FYT

Collect Your Court Judgment
Gini Graham Scott, Attorney Stephen Elias & Lisa Goldoftas
California 2nd Edition
This book contains step-by-step instructions and all the forms you need to collect a court judgment from the debtor's bank accounts, wages, business receipts, real estate or other assets.
$19.95/JUDG

How to Change Your Name
Attorneys David Loeb & David Brown
California 5th Edition
This book explains how to change your name legally and provides all the necessary court forms with detailed instructions on how to fill them out.
$19.95/NAME

Everybody's Guide to Small Claims Court
Attorney Ralph Warner
National 5th Edition
California 10th Edition
These books will help you decide if you should sue in Small Claims Court, show you how to file and serve papers, tell you what to bring to court and how to collect a judgment.
National $15.95/NSCC
California $15.95/ CSCC

The Criminal Records Book
Attorney Warren Siegel
California 3rd Edition
This book shows you step-by-step how to seal criminal records, dismiss convictions, destroy marijuana records and reduce felony convictions.
$19.95/CRIM

LEGAL REFORM

Legal Breakdown: 40 Ways to Fix Our Legal System
Nolo Press Editors and Staff
National 1st Edition
Legal Breakdown presents 40 common-sense proposals to make our legal system fairer, faster, cheaper and more accessible. It advocates abolishing probate, taking divorce out of court, treating jurors better and a host of other fundamental changes.
$8.95/LEG

BUSINESS/WORKPLACE

Sexual Harassment on the Job
Attorneys William Petrocelli & Barbara Kate Repa
National 1st Edition
This is the first comprehensive book dealing with sexual harassment in the workplace. It describes what harassment is, what the laws are that make it illegal and how to put a stop to it. This guide is invaluable both for employees experiencing harassment and for employers interested in creating a policy against sexual harassment and a procedure for handling complaints.
$14.95/HARS

Nolo's Partnership Maker

Attorney Tony Mancuso & Michael Radtke
Version 1.0
Nolo's Partnership Maker prepares a legal partnership agreement for doing business in any state. The program can be used by anyone who plans to pool energy, efforts, money or property with others to run a business, share property, produce a profit or undertake any other type of mutual endeavor.

You can select and assemble the standard partnership clauses provided or create your own customized agreement. And the agreement can be updated at any time. Includes on-line legal help screens, glossary and tutorial, and a manual that takes you through the process step-by-step.

**IBM PC
(3-1/2 & 5-1/4 disks included)
$129.00/PAGI1**

California Incorporator

Attorney Anthony Mancuso
Version 1.0 (good only in CA)
Answer the questions on the screen and this software program will print out the 35-40 pages of documents you need to make your California corporation legal. Comes with a 200-page manual which explains the incorporation process.

**IBM PC
(3-1/2 & 5-1/4 disks included)
$129.00/INCI**

The California Nonprofit Corporation Handbook

(computer edition)
Attorney Anthony Mancuso
Version 1.0 (good only in CA)
This book/software package shows you step-by-step how to form and operate a nonprofit corporation in California. Included on disk are the forms for the Articles, Bylaws and Minutes.

**IBM PC 5-1/4 $69.95/ NPI
IBM PC 3-1/2 $69.95/ NP3I
MACINTOSH $69.95/ NPM**

How to Form Your Own New York Corporation & How to Form Your Own Texas Corporation

(computer editions)
Attorney Anthony Mancuso
These book/software packages contain the instructions and tax information and forms you need to incorporate a small business and save hundreds of dollars in lawyers' fees. All organizational forms are on disk. Both come with a 250-page manual.

**New York 1st Edition
IBM PC 5-1/4 $69.95/ NYCI
IBM PC 3-1/2 $69.95/ NYC3I
MACINTOSH $69.95/ NYCM**

**Texas 1st Edition
IBM PC 5-1/4 $69.95/ TCI
IBM PC 3-1/2 $69.95/ TC3I
MACINTOSH $69.95/ TCM**

Neighbor Law: Fences, Trees, Boundaries & Noise

Attorney Cora Jordan
National 1st Edition
Neighbor Law answers common questions about the subjects that most often trigger disputes between neighbors: fences, trees, boundaries and noise. It explains how to find the law and resolve disputes without a nasty lawsuit.
$14.95/NEI

Dog Law

Attorney Mary Randolph
National 1st Edition
Dog Law is a practical guide to the laws that affect dog owners and their neighbors. You'll find answers to common questions on such topics as biting, barking, veterinarians and more.
$12.95/DOG

Barbara Kaufman's Consumer Action Guide

Barbara Kaufman
California 1st Edition
This practical handbook is filled with information on hundreds of consumer topics. Barbara Kaufman, the Bay Area's award-winning consumer reporter and producer of KCBS Radio's *Call for Action*, gives consumers access to their legal rights, providing addresses and phone numbers of where to complain when things go wrong, and providing resources if more help is necessary.
$14.95/CAG

Money Troubles: Legal Strategies to Cope With Your Debts

Attorney Robin Leonard
National 1st Edition
Are you behind on your credit card bills or loan payments? If you are, then *Money Troubles* is exactly what you need. It covers everything from knowing what your rights are, and asserting them, to helping you evaluate your individual situation. This practical, straightforward book is for anyone who needs help understanding and dealing with the complex and often scary topic of debts.
$16.95/MT

How to File for Bankruptcy

Attorneys Stephen Elias, Albin Renauer & Robin Leonard
National 3rd Edition
Trying to decide whether or not filing for bankruptcy makes sense? *How to File for Bankruptcy* contains an overview of the process and all the forms plus step-by-step instructions on the procedures to follow.
$24.95/HFB

Simple Contracts for Personal Use

Attorney Stephen Elias & Marcia Stewart
National 2nd Edition
This book contains clearly written legal form contracts to buy and sell property, borrow and lend money, store and lend personal property, release others from personal liability, or pay a contractor to do home repairs. Includes agreements to arrange childcare and other household help.
$16.95/CONT

Divorce & Money

Violet Woodhouse & Victoria Felton-Collins with M.C. Blakeman
National 1st Edition
Divorce & Money explains how to evaluate such major assets as family homes and businesses, investments, pensions, and how to arrive at a division of property that is fair to both sides. Throughout, the book emphasizes the difference between legal reality—how the court evaluates assets, and financial reality—what the assets are really worth.
$19.95/DIMO

The Living Together Kit

Attorneys Toni Ihara & Ralph Warner
National 6th Edition
The Living Together Kit is a detailed guide designed to help the increasing number of unmarried couples living together understand the laws that affect them. Sample agreements and instructions are included.
$17.95/LTK

The Guardianship Book

Lisa Goldoftas & Attorney David Brown
California 1st Edition
The Guardianship Book provides step-by-step instructions and the forms needed to obtain a legal guardianship without a lawyer.
$19.95/GB

A Legal Guide for Lesbian and Gay Couples

Attorneys Hayden Curry & Denis Clifford
National 6th Edition
Laws designed to regulate and protect unmarried couples don't apply to lesbian and gay couples. This book shows you step-by-step how to write a living-together contract, plan for medical emergencies, and plan your estates. Includes forms, sample agreements and lists of both national lesbian and gay legal organizations and AIDS organizations.
$17.95/LG

How to Do Your Own Divorce

Attorney Charles Sherman
(Texas Ed. by Sherman & Simons)
California 17th Edition & Texas 4th Edition
These books contain all the forms and instructions you need to do your own uncontested divorce without a lawyer.
California $18.95/CDIV
Texas $17.95/TDIV

Practical Divorce Solutions

Attorney Charles Sherman
California 2nd Edition
This book is a valuable guide to the emotional aspects of divorce as well as an overview of the legal and financial decisions that must be made.
$12.95/PDS

California Marriage & Divorce Law

Attorneys Ralph Warner, Toni Ihara & Stephen Elias
California 11th Edition
This book explains community property, pre-nuptial contracts, foreign marriages, buying a house, getting a divorce, dividing property, and more.
$19.95/MARR

How to Adopt Your Stepchild in California

Frank Zagone & Attorney Mary Randolph
California 3rd Edition
There are many emotional, financial and legal reasons to adopt a step-child, but among the most pressing legal reasons is the need to avoid confusion over inheritance or guardianship. This book provides sample forms and step-by-step instructions for completing a simple uncontested adoption by a stepparent.
$19.95/ADOP

29 Reasons Not to Go to Law School

Attorneys Ralph Warner & Toni Ihara
National 3rd Edition
Filled with humor and piercing observations, this book can save you three years, $70,000 and your sanity.
$9.95/29R

Devil's Advocates: The Unnatural History of Lawyers

by Andrew & Jonathan Roth
National 1st Edition
This book is a painless and hilarious education, tracing the legal profession. Careful attention is given to the world's worst lawyers, most preposterous cases and most ludicrous courtroom strategies.
$12.95/DA

Poetic Justice: The Funniest, Meanest Things Ever Said About Lawyers

Edited by Jonathan & Andrew Roth
National 1st Edition
A great gift for anyone in the legal profession who has managed to maintain a sense of humor.
$8.95/PJ

Patent It Yourself

Attorney David Pressman
National 3rd Edition
From the patent search to the actual application, this book covers everything including the use and licensing of patents, successful marketing and how to deal with infringement.
$34.95/PAT

The Inventor's Notebook

Fred Grissom & Attorney David Pressman
National 1st Edition
This book helps you document the process of successful independent inventing by providing forms, instructions, references to relevant areas of patent law, a bibliography of legal and non-legal aids and more.
$19.95/INOT

The Copyright Handbook

Attorney Stephen Fishman
National 1st Edition
Writers, editors, publishers, scholars, educators, librarians and others who work with words all need to know about copyright laws. This book provides forms and step-by-step instructions for protecting all types of written expression under U.S. and international copyright law. It contains detailed reference chapters on such major copyright-related topics as copyright infringement, fair use, works for hire and transfers of copyright ownership.
$24.95/COHA

How to Copyright Software

Attorney M.J. Salone
National 3rd Edition
This book tells you how to register your copyright for maximum protection and discusses who owns a copyright on software developed by more than one person.
$39.95/COPY

The Landlord's Law Book, Vol. 1: Rights & Responsibilities

Attorneys David Brown & Ralph Warner
California 3rd Edition
This book contains information on deposits, leases and rental agreements, inspections (tenants' privacy rights), habitability (rent withholding), ending a tenancy, liability and rent control.
$29.95/LBRT

The Landlord's Law Book, Vol. 2: Evictions

Attorney David Brown
California 3rd Edition
Updated for 1992, this book will show you step-by-step how to go to court and get an eviction for a tenant who won't pay rent—and won't leave. Contains all the tear-out forms and necessary instructions.
$29.95/LBEV

Tenants' Rights

Attorneys Myron Moskovitz & Ralph Warner
California 11th Edition
This book explains how to handle your relationship with your landlord and understand your legal rights when you find yourself in disagreement. A special section on rent control cities is included.
$15.95/CTEN

How to Buy a House in California

*Attorney Ralph Warner, Ira Serkes
& George Devine
California 2nd Edition*

This book shows you how to find a house, work with a real estate agent, make an offer and negotiate intelligently. Includes information on all types of mortgages as well as private financing options.
$19.95/BHCA

For Sale By Owner

*George Devine
California 2nd Edition*

For Sale By Owner provides essential information about pricing your house, marketing it, writing a contract and going through escrow.
$24.95/FSBO

The Deeds Book

*Attorney Mary Randolph
California 2nd Edition*

If you own real estate, you'll need to sign a new deed when you transfer the property or put it in trust as part of your estate planning. This book shows you how to find the right kind of deed, complete the tear-out forms and record them in the county recorder's public records.
$15.95/DEED

Homestead Your House

*Attorneys Ralph Warner, Charles Sherman
& Toni Ihara
California 8th Edition*

This book shows you how to file a Declaration of Homestead and includes complete instructions and tear-out forms.
$9.95/HOME

Elder Care: Choosing & Financing Long-Term Care

*Attorney Joseph Matthews
National 1st Edition*

This book will guide you in choosing and paying for long-term care, alerting you to practical concerns and explaining laws that may affect your decisions.
$16.95/ELD

Social Security, Medicare & Pensions

*Attorney Joseph Matthews with
Dorothy Matthews Berman
National 5th Edition*

This book contains invaluable guidance through the current maze of rights and benefits for those 55 and over, including Medicare, Medicaid and Social Security retirement and disability benefits and age discrimination protections.
$15.95/SOA

Legal Research: How To Find and Understand the Law

*Attorneys Stephen Elias & Susan Levinkind
National 3rd Edition*

A valuable tool on its own or as a companion to just about every other Nolo book. This book gives easy-to-use, step-by-step instructions on how to find legal information.
$16.95/LRES

Family Law Dictionary

*Attorneys Robin Leonard & Stephen Elias
National 2nd Edition*

Finally, a legal dictionary that's written in plain English, not "legalese"! *The Family Law Dictionary* is designed to help the nonlawyer who has a question or problem involving family law—marriage, divorce, adoption or living together.
$13.95/FLD

Legal Research Made Easy: A Roadmap Through the Law Library Maze

*2-1/2 hr. videotape and 40-page manual
Nolo Press/Legal Star Communications
National 1st Edition*

If you're a law student, paralegal or librarian—or just want to look up the law for yourself—this video is for you. University of California law professor Bob Berring explains how to use all the basic legal research tools in your local law library with an easy-to-follow six-step research plan and a sense of humor.
$89.95/LRME

NOLO PRESS / 950 PARKER STREET / BERKELEY CA 94710

O R D E R   F O R M

Name

Address (UPS to street address, Priority Mail to P.O. boxes)

Catalog Code	Quantity	Item	Unit price	Total
		Subtotal		
		Sales tax (California residents only)		
		Shipping & handling		
		2nd day UPS		
		TOTAL		

SALES TAX
California residents add your local tax

SHIPPING & HANDLING
$4.00   1 item
$5.00   2-3 items
+$.50   each additional item
Allow 2-3 weeks for delivery

IN A HURRY?
UPS 2nd day delivery is available:
Add $5.00 (contiguous states) or
$8.00 (Alaska & Hawaii) to your regular shipping and handling charges

PRICES SUBJECT TO CHANGE

FOR FASTER SERVICE, USE YOUR CREDIT CARD AND OUR TOLL-FREE NUMBERS:
Monday-Friday, 7 a.m. to 5 p.m. Pacific Time
Order line   1 (800) 992-6656
General Information   1 (510) 549-1976
Fax us your order   1 (800) 645-0895

METHOD OF PAYMENT
☐ Check enclosed   ☐ VISA ☐ Mastercard
☐ Discover Card   ☐ Amer ican Express

Account #   Expiration Date

Signature Authorizing

Phone   HARS

NOLO PRESS / 950 PARKER STREET / BERKELEY CA 94710

When you register, we'll send you our quarterly newspaper, the *Nolo News*, free for two years. (U.S. addresses only.) Here's what you'll get in every issue:

■ INFORMATIVE ARTICLES

Written by Nolo editors, articles provide practical legal information on issues you encounter in everyday life: family law, wills, debts, consumer rights, and much more.

■ UPDATE SERVICE

The *Nolo News* keeps you informed of legal changes that affect any Nolo book and software program.

■ BOOK AND SOFTWARE REVIEWS

We're always looking for good legal and consumer books and software from other publishers. When we find them, we review them and offer them in our mail order catalog.

■ ANSWERS TO YOUR LEGAL QUESTIONS

Our readers are always challenging us with good questions on a variety of legal issues. So in each issue, "Auntie Nolo" gives sage advice and sound information.

■ COMPLETE NOLO PRESS CATALOG

The *Nolo News* contains an up-to-the-minute catalog of all Nolo books and software, which you can order using our "800" toll-free order line. And you can see at a glance if you're using an out-of-date version of a Nolo product.

■ LAWYER JOKES

Nolo's famous lawyer joke column continually gets the goat of the legal establishment. If we print a joke you send in, you'll get a $20 Nolo gift certificate.

We promise *never* to give your name and address to any other organization.

[Nolo books are]…"written in plain language, free of legal mumbo jumbo, and spiced with witty personal observations."

—ASSOCIATED PRESS

"Well-produced and slickly written, the [Nolo] books are designed to take the mystery out of seemingly involved procedures, carefully avoiding legalese and leading the reader step-by-step through such everyday legal problems as filling out forms, making up contracts, and even how to behave in court."

—SAN FRANCISCO EXAMINER

"…Nolo publications…guide people simply through the how, when, where and why of law."

—WASHINGTON POST

"Increasingly, people who are not lawyers are performing tasks usually regarded as legal work… And consumers, using books like Nolo's, do routine legal work themselves."

—NEW YORK TIMES

"…All of [Nolo's] books are easy-to-understand, are updated regularly, provide pull-out forms…and are often quite moving in their sense of compassion for the struggles of the lay reader."

—SAN FRANCISCO CHRONICLE